Advanced Aikido

PRAISE FOR AIKIDO BASICS

I humbly commend Phong Shihan and Dr. Seiser in their ongoing efforts to publish highly valuable insights and truly interesting food for thought for the aikido community and beyond. All serious students of aikido and the martial arts in general would do well to include such publications in his or her library for constant review and source material for discussion, experimentation, and continued growth in aikido and his or her personal missions.

—SHIHAN FRANCIS TAKAHASHI, 6TH DAN, CHIEF INSTRUCTOR AT THE AIKIDO ACADEMY IN TEMPLE CITY, CALIFORNIA, AND AIKIDO ASSOCIATE, WEST COAST

My congratulations to Sensei Phong and Dr. Lynn Seiser. Your book is a clear expression of our beautiful art of aikido and is aptly titled *Aikido Basics*. It addresses the questions and concerns of the beginning student in an intelligent and simple way and is the perfect handbook for advanced students and the established teacher as well. Excellent job well done! Without question I recommend it.

—SENSEI FRANK McGOUIRK, 6TH DAN, AIKIDO-AI DOJO AND WHITTIER DHARMA KAI ZEN CENTER OF WHITTIER, CALIFORNIA.

I have had the chance to read a preview of this book and truly feel it's the best initial offering for aikido beginners and a good foundation to people who are experienced. I thank Lynn Seiser and Phong Sensei for a wonderful book and look forward to the next two. Thank you.

—SHIHAN FRANCIS TAKAHASHI, 6TH DAN, AIKIKAI FOUNDATION, AIKIDO ACADEMY OF TEMPLE CITY, CALIFORNIA

Aikido has been practiced and loved by many people all over the world. Aikido promotes "inner peace" through "circular movement." With the help of the book, I trust the number of followers will increase even more. Aikido is a viable way in this tumultuous world. I believe peace will prevail. I am very delighted about the publishing of this book.

—MASATAKE FUJITA SHIHAN, SECRETARY GENERAL AIKIKAI FOUNDATION

Please note that the publisher and author(s) of this instructional book are NOT RESPONSIBLE in any manner whatsoever for any injury that may result from practicing the techniques and/or following the instructions given within. Martial arts training can be dangerous—both to you and to others—if not practiced safely. If you're in doubt as to how to proceed or whether your practice is safe, consult with a trained martial arts teacher before beginning. Since the physical activities described herein may be too strenuous in nature for some readers, it is also essential that a physician be consulted prior to training.

First published by Tuttle Publishing, an imprint of Periplus Editions (HK) Ltd., with editorial offices at 364 Innovation Drive, North Clarendon, Vermont 05759 U.S.A.

Library of Congress Cataloging-in-Publication Data

Dang, Phong Thong, 1940-
   Advanced aikido / Phong Thong Dang and Lynn Seiser.—1st ed.
     p. cm.
   Includes bibliographical references and index.
   ISBN 0-8048-3785-6 (pbk. : alk. paper)
   1. Aikido. I. Seiser, Lynn, 1950- II. Title.
   GV1114.35.D368 2006
   796.815'4—dc22

                 2005030834

ISBN-10: 0-8048-3785-6
ISBN-13: 978-0-8048-3785-9

Distributed by:

North America, Latin America & Europe
Tuttle Publishing
364 Innovation Drive
North Clarendon, VT 05759-9436 U.S.A.
Tel: 1 (802) 773-8930
Fax: 1 (802) 773-6993
info@tuttlepublishing.com
www.tuttlepublishing.com

Asia Pacific
Berkeley Books Pte. Ltd.
130 Joo Seng Road #06-01
Singapore 368357
Tel: (65) 6280-1330
Fax: (65) 6280-6290
inquiries@periplus.com.sg
www.periplus.com

First edition
10 09 08 07 06   10 9 8 7 6 5 4 3 2
Printed in the United States of America

TUTTLE PUBLISHING® is a registered trademark of Tuttle Publishing, a division of Periplus Editions (HK) Ltd.

Advanced Aikido

SENSEI PHONG THONG DANG

and

LYNN SEISER, PH.D.

TUTTLE PUBLISHING
Tokyo · Rutland, Vermont · Singapore

DEDICATION

I humbly dedicate this book to O' Sensei Morihei Ueshiba, the founder of aikido, the martial art of peace, love, and harmony. That moment in 1967 when, as I was about to return to Vietnam, O' Sensei fondly bestowed upon me the responsibility to propagate aikido training in my own country will forever be ingrained in my memory.

I also humbly dedicate this book to my late and beloved teachers, Grandmaster Vu Ba Oai and Doctor Nguyen Anh Tai, who oriented and coached me along as I hesitantly entered the gate of the Martial Way.

I also wish to dedicate these words to my first aikido teachers, Sensei Dang Thong Tri and Sensei Mutsuro Nakazono, and to the late second aikido Doshu, Kisshomaru Ueshiba.

This book is also dedicated to all of my students, past and present, whose persistence and hard work are the greatest motives for my continuing on my chosen path.

Through this book, I would like to thank the current aikido Doshu, Moriteru Ueshiba; Shihan Masatake Fujita; and the staffs of Hombu Dojo and the Aikikai Foundation for their precious and ongoing support.

My heartfelt appreciation also goes to my devoted student, Dr. Lynn Seiser, Ph.D., and to his wife, Pamela, without whom this book would probably never have come to life.

I sincerely hope that this book will be a useful tool for any reader who is seriously interested in aikido training.

—Sensei Phong Thong Dang, 6th Dan Aikido,
Founder of the International Tenshinkai Aikido Federation
Two-Time Inductee in the World Martial Art Hall of Fame
Chief Instructor, Westminster Aikikai Dojo

I humbly dedicate this volume, the second of three aikido works, with my deepest respect and appreciation to my aikido instructor, Sensei Phong Thong Dang, for his expertise, compassion, and inspiration. It is a humbling honor to train with a legend and to be trusted with his teachings. I hope my simple contributions in some small way help promote, perpetuate, and propagate his teachings, his style, his federation, and the greater good of the world aikido community. *Sensei, domo arigato gozaimashita.*

I respectfully dedicate this work with my deepest appreciation to all my fellow students and training partners (sempai, tohai, and kohai) past, present, and future for their patience, their loving protection, and for sharing the knowledge that is included here. Without them, there is no training.

I lovingly dedicate this book, and my whole life, to my family. They have accepted and supported my life-long passion for the martial arts. They believe in me. They taught me that love is the greatest gift of all and the only one that really matters. They are not just the love of my life, but my life itself.

—Lynn Seiser, Ph.D.
Sandan, 3rd Dan Tenshinkai Aikido
Founder of Aiki-Solutions
Marriage, Family, and Child Counselor
Irvine, California USA

CONTENTS

ACKNOWLEDGMENTS
AND APPRECIATIONS

The authors express their deepest compliments and appreciation to their editor at Tuttle Publishing, Jennifer Brown, whose expertise and patience have guided them brilliantly through three books.

The authors express their deepest respect and appreciation for permission to quote the contributions from several high-ranked and highly regarded aikido instructors and their thoughts in the forward of this book. It is a humbling honor to include their insights from years of training and experience in this book.

The authors express deep appreciation to Stanley Pranin, editor of *Aiki News/Aikido Journal*, producer of Aiki Expo, and aikido historian, for his permission to quote, and reproduce, in its entirety, his interview with Sensei Phong Thong Dang originally published in *Aikido Journal* #101 in 1994 in this work.

The authors also express deep appreciation to Susan Perry and Ronald Rubin, editors of *Aikido Today Magazine*, for their permission to quote and reproduce, in its entirety, their interview with Sensei Phong Thong Dang originally published in *Aikido Today Magazine* (#75; Vol. 15, No. 3; May/June 2001, pages 11–15) in this work.

The illustrations of Waza (techniques) rendered from photographs taken by Shodan John Tran of Tenshinkai Aikido Westminster Aikikai Dojo of members; Sandan Minhhai Nguyen, Sandan Quang Hai Nguyen, Nidan Loc Bui, Nidan Randy Penland, Nidan Rick Neff, Nidan Bryan Tate, Nidan Eric Raye, Shodan Joe Duong Dinh, and Shodan Tu Tu on July 25, 2004. Thank you gentlemen.

The authors express their appreciation to readers from the Tenshinkai Westminster Aikikai Dojo; Tam Do, David Whurlbut, Richmond Neff, John Velardo, and David Marcus.

The authors express their deepest appreciation for the proofreading done by Pamela Seiser, wife of author Lynn Seiser. She proofread, and reread, every word, of every page, of every draft with patience, persistence, and an eye for detail, grammar, and readability. Her support and patience have made this book possible and readable.

PREFACE

In our previous work, *Aikido Basics*, we presented information pertinent to the beginning student. We went from finding a school, to the first day of class, through the basic aikido techniques. This book assumes that the reader already has that basic knowledge, training, and experience in the technical aspects of aikido. This work is about applying advanced concepts to the sophisticated and subtle aspects of aikido training and techniques. Though beginning and intermediate students may find this work a source of inspiration and encouragement, this book primarily focuses on the advanced students who want to broaden their knowledge base to include advanced throws and locks, combinations, counter techniques, and self-defense. Most importantly, the advanced students will gain an understanding of the application of advanced aikido concepts and principles that they can apply to training and the refinement of their basic practice.

Each *waza* (technique) presented in this book will receive a complete and thorough exploration and explanation. This book discusses and describes the waza in reference to its physical technical execution. Each waza will be discussed and described in reference to the sequential process of enter and blend, redirect and unbalance, throw or control, and let go and move on. This book discusses and describes waza in reference to advanced aikido concepts such as *mushin* (calm and empty mind) and *musubi* (connection). This complete and thorough exploration and explanation in description and discussion will lead to an understanding that should provide any student of aikido with the advanced knowledge and insight necessary to improve his or her technique and training in aikido.

However, readers should keep in mind that no one can learn aikido from a book, and no one can teach aikido from a book. One can only learn aikido through direct experience and training with a competent instructor. This, and all aikido books, is only a means of reference and guidance. After reading any portion of any aikido book, the best advice is to get on the dojo mats and train. Listen to your sensei and *sempai* (senior students) and stay open to suggestions and comments from your *tohai* (one of equal rank) and *kohai* (one of lesser rank)—it is only with an open mind that one can get a glimpse of the beauty of the art of aikido.

This book is divided into four parts. The first part offers insight into the inner development of the advanced practitioner; the second part offers insight into theories and concepts for the advanced practitioner; the third part offers insights into advanced techniques; the fourth part offers advanced applications. Finally, this book offers charts on techniques and concepts and two interviews with Sensei Phong Thong Dang.

The techniques and concepts presented in this work reflect the lifelong training and instruction of 6th Dan Sensei Phong Thong Dang, founder of the International Tenshinkai Aikido Federation, and the interpretation, understanding, and expression of those techniques and concepts by his student, 3rd Dan Lynn Seiser, Ph.D.

Tenshinkai means the association, or coming together, of heaven and Earth or heavenly heart and mind. It was the name given by O'Sensei Morihei Ueshiba to the uniquely fluid and powerful style of aikido coming from Vietnam.

SENSEI PHONG THONG DANG

O'Sensei Morihei Ueshiba personally gave the responsibility of spreading this style of aikido throughout Vietnam and the world to Sensei Phong Thong Dang. Tenshinkai aikido is an Aikikai style of aikido that honors and respects its lineage and long association with the Aikikai Hombu Dojo, Aikido World Headquarters, the Aikikai Foundation, the current Doshu Ueshiba Moriteru, and the Ueshiba family.

INTRODUCTION

Aikido is a uniquely beautiful martial art. It is also deceptively powerful, effective, and efficient. In the hands of a master, a smaller person can use the power and momentum of a larger attacker to throw or control that person with little, or no, effort. While aikido may look easy, it is very hard to master; training takes time and discipline. However, as the advanced practitioner finds, aikido benefits all aspects of life—physical and emotional, mental and social, and spiritual.

THE FOUNDER: O'SENSEI MORIHEI UESHIBA (1883–1969)

The art of aikido was developed by O'Sensei Morihei Ueshiba and can be looked at as an expression of his personal life and his struggle with the opposing beliefs and disciplines of the martial way of the warrior and the spiritual pursuit of peace and harmony.

O'SENSEI MORIHEI UESHIBA

Born a sick and weak child on December 14, 1883 in Tanabe, Kishu (Wakayama Prefecture) Japan, young Morihei Ueshiba faced many hardships. He attempted to overcome his physical hardships by studying very hard to develop his intellect and mental capabilities. Besides reading religious classics, he liked physics and mathematics. His mother considered having him enter the priesthood, but his father opposed that idea. His father preferred an education in strength and sumo competition.

Early in O'Sensei Morihei Ueshiba's life, he watched his father receive a severe beating by local thugs who disagreed with his father's political beliefs. At this time, the young Morihei Ueshiba vowed to search for physical strength and martial skills. This vow led to years of severe discipline and training in both martial and spiritual disciplines. His training in these areas led to the development of aikido. This development can be seen through three major areas of O'Sensei Ueshiba's life: his military experience, his martial arts training, and the influence of the Omoto religion.

O'SENSEI IN THE MILITARY

In the late 1800s and early 1900s, Japan competed for influence, trade, and territory with Western countries in China and Korea. After failing in negotiations in 1903 with Russia to get that country to withdraw from Manchuria, Japan severed relationships and sought a solution with its modernized military. The Russo-Japanese War lasted from 1904 to 1905. This conflict grew out of the rivalry of the imperialist ambition of Russia and Japan in Manchuria and Korea. The campaigns of 1904 focused on a series of indecisive naval engagements at Port Charles on the Liaotung peninsula in south Manchuria. Port Charles finally fell in early 1905, allowing the Japanese army to attack northward. Facing its own internal unrest of the Russian Revolution of 1905, Russia elected to negotiate peace. The war ended in mediation by President Theodore Roosevelt of the United States. The defeat of Russia by the Japanese shocked the world. It was the first non-Western victory in a large military conflict. It was inspiring to many noncolonial independence movements. Without this rivalry and with the Western world distracted by World War I, Japan began the efforts to dominate the East. These efforts led to World War II in the Pacific. After World War II, many Japanese historians would look nostalgically on the time of leadership in a sustained effort to liberate the oppressed.

Initially, Morihei Ueshiba did not meet the minimum height requirement for military service. Committed to his decision to serve his country, he embarked on a regime of stretching in an effort to gain the additional height required. After strenuous efforts, Morihei Ueshiba finally met the 5'2" requirements to join the military in late December 1903. He joined the 61st Army Infantry Regiment in Wakayama.

His willingness to take on hard tasks and his skill with the bayonet facilitated rapid promotions. He spent much of his active duty time training others. He spent much of his leave time in ascetic spiritual discipline or strenuous martial training. He originally did not receive orders to fight on the front during the Russo-Japanese war because his superiors considered his ability to train others a higher priority. Finally, he protested enough to receive orders to the Manchurian front in 1905. His intuition and trained reflexes allowed him to see enemy bullets and avoid them.

In 1906, he was discharged from the army and returned to Tanabe. Some say he did not reenlist due to the undisciplined practices of the officers. Others say young Morihei Ueshiba did not reenlist because he was not going to receive orders to go back into combat. Others suggest that it was his deep beliefs in spiritual matters that, after being at war, prevented his further involvement. However, although O'Sensei Morihei Ueshiba did not stay in active duty, his deep connection and commitment to the military, and his patriotism, continued throughout his life. He was active in training and supporting community interests and causes. Aikido is often accepted as both a family and a cultural entity and the property of the Ueshiba family and the people of Japan.

O'SENSEI'S MARTIAL ROOTS: DAITO-RYU AIKI-JUJITSU

O'Sensei Morihei Ueshiba trained in many different martial arts. He began his studies in his mid-teens and studied Tenjin-shin'yo-ryu, Kito-ryu, Yagyu-ryu, and Shimkage-ryu jujitsu styles. He also studied Hozoin-ryu and kendo. Most of these were one-on-one combat styles and did not satisfy the young Morihei Ueshiba. His dedication to martial excellence earned him deep respect and a reputation that he had to defend. Very few people today have the time and energy to devote their entire life to the pursuit of martial excellence. Aikido is more than just a composite of O'Sensei Morihei Ueshiba's past training. In 1908, he received a certificate in Yagyu-ryu jujutsu.

Daito-ryu aiki-jujutsu was perhaps the most influential martial art studied by Morihei Ueshiba. He studied under Sokaku Takeda (1860–1943) in Hokkaido. O'Sensei Morihei Ueshiba received his Kyoju-Dairi teaching assistance certificate from Sokaku Takeda in 1922. Daito-ryu jujutsu is a family martial tradition style that emphasizes jujutsu techniques but also includes swords and other weapons. Sokaku Takeda taught Daito-ryu primarily to military, police personnel, or high-level officials who could afford the lessons. The performance and execution of traditional aiki-jujutsu techniques are with more intent to damage than current aikido techniques.

While O'Sensei Morihei Ueshiba humbly and politely took care of his teacher, he separated from Sokaku Takeda and Daito-ryu and began to call his art aiki-budo.

SPIRITUAL ROOTS: OMOTO RELIGION

O'Sensei Morihei Ueshiba met and became a lifelong follower of Master Onisaburo, of the Omoto religion, in 1920. The Omoto movement with a strong spiritual philosophy on harmony influenced the higher principles of aikido. Some believe that O'Sensei Morihei Ueshiba's spiritual beliefs, influenced by the Omoto religion, caused him to create a softer style of martial art. He wanted an art that would be defensively effective and efficient but that would also protect rather than harm one's training partner, as well as any real-life opponent or enemy. (The philosophies of the Omoto religion are discussed in more detail in Chapter 1.)

TEACHING AIKIDO

There are many stories of O'Sensei Morihei Ueshiba teaching classes to advanced students that represented his lecturing on spiritual and metaphysical aspects of the universe. O'Sensei Morihei Ueshiba saw the universal principles in everything. He would switch from one content area to another in an effort to illustrate the underlying principle. Many students had great difficulty translating these disconnected lectures into direct application to their own personal aikido training and technique. O'Sensei Morihei Ueshiba attempted to bridge the gap but understood that no one can express or explain spiritual truth in words. O'Sensei Morihei Ueshiba relied most heavily on teaching through experience or direct training and practice of the techniques. The techniques would illustrate and demonstrate the principles and concepts that were so difficult to explain or describe. The techniques were concrete examples of concepts that could best be discussed and described through vague metaphors and contradictions. The profound principles of spiritual, theological, and universal truths involved difficult-to-comprehend explanations that were based on O'Sensei Morihei Ueshiba's own long history of austere mental and physical training and discipline. Without a similar historical experience as a frame of reference, few were able to understand O'Sensei Morihei Ueshiba. Throughout history, those who saw beyond what was socially accepted as "normal" received scrutiny and suspicion. Many ideas of yesterday, which were incomprehensible due to their advanced foresight and insight, have become our goals and accepted interpretations or perceptions.

O'Sensei Morihei Ueshiba was a man with foresight, insight, and a vision. O'Sensei Morihei Ueshiba believed that aikido was the medicine for a sick and chaotic world that had seen too much violence.

THE EVOLUTION OF AIKIDO

Morihei Ueshiba married Hatsu Itokawa. She was to have a very stabilizing effect in the Ueshiba family, while O'Sensei Morihei Ueshiba was off on various farming, martial, spiritual, political, or patriotic adventures. Several times, O'Sensei Morihei Ueshiba uprooted his entire family and moved in accordance to what he believed to be his spiritual calling and in the best interest of his country. O'Sensei Morihei Ueshiba was very busy and did not have a great deal of leisure time to spend at home with his family. Ueshiba's first daughter, Matsuko, was born in 1911. The first son, Takemori, born in July 1917, died three years later in August 1920. The second son, Kuniharu, born in April 1920, died five months later in September 1920. The third son, Kisshomaru, born in June 1921, in 1948 went on to become Doshu (keeper of the way).

DOSHU KISSHOMARU UESHIBA

O'Sensei Morihei Ueshiba handed down his vision in 1948 to his son, Kisshomaru Ueshiba, as Doshu. Kisshomaru Ueshiba had been exposed to aikido concepts and training since childhood but did not begin training until he was in middle school. It never occurred to him that he would inherit the art of his father. Most people credit Doshu Kisshomaru Ueshiba (1921–1999) with contributions in the area of administration and the modification, simplification, and standardization of the aikido technical curriculum. Doshu Kisshomaru Ueshiba deemphasized the martial application of aikido. He focused on the discipline and development of technical proficiency, self-improvement, and becoming productive members of society. He believed this emphasis and focus was in keeping with his father's vision of aikido. About the same time, the chief instructor at the Hombu Dojo, 10th Dan Koichi Tohei, separated from the original aikido organization. Tohei Sensei began aikido training under O'Sensei Morihei Ueshiba in 1941 and played a major role in spreading aikido outside of Japan. He wanted to stress the emphasis on ki development based on his spiritual background and orientation.

DOSHU KISSHOMARU UESHIBA

DOSHU MORITERU UESHIBA

In 1986, Doshu Kisshomaru Ueshiba handed the Aikido World Headquarters to his son, Moriteru Ueshiba (b. 1951). As the current Doshu, Moriteru Ueshiba maintains the focus and emphasis on both technical proficiency and the spiritual aspects in his training and instruction. It is with this intent that we see the traditional family style and system of martial arts. While aikido has seen international acceptance and growth, many consider aikido a Japanese cultural entity and the property of the Ueshiba family.

O'Sensei Morihei Ueshiba died April 26, 1969 of liver cancer. O'Sensei Morihei Ueshiba's ashes are buried at Kozanji, a Shingon Buddhist temple erected in 1206 by a priest named Myoe, situated on Mt. Togano in Tanbe, Wakayama Prefecture. Besides being the site of the Ueshiba family grave, Kozanji has the oldest tea garden and is designated as a historical site. Each year most aikido dojos (training hall or school) acknowledge and honor the date of O'Sensei Morihei Ueshiba's passing with a special ceremony.

DOSHU MORITERU UESHIBA

THE FUTURE OF AIKIDO

There is only one aikido. That is the aikido of O'Sensei Morihei Ueshiba. However, there are many branches of aikido that reflect the abilities and preferences of different instructors based on when each personally trained with O'Sensei. Even future generations of students who have never met O'Sensei Morihei Ueshiba will have their interpretations for aikido. Several organizations have become independent in order to pursue their specific vision of aikido.

Aikido is evolving. There is no right or wrong aikido. There are only different perspectives and applications. There is only one aikido, and students of all levels of proficiency should maintain a strong tie to the basic techniques and principles of aikido.

CONCLUSION

In the beginning, a student in basic aikido knows only the physical training and execution of techniques. Eventually, the advanced student knows, and applies, the advanced aikido concepts that make the techniques work.

The concepts are interrelated and interdependent. Any stage, of any technique, is an illustration of each one of the concepts. They all exist simultaneously. Observation, perception, understanding, and application allow all students to see at their personal level of training and experience. In many regards, the techniques of aikido are relatively few and simple. It is the refinement of application that makes them different. As a student progresses from beginning to intermediate to advanced and beyond, he or she will become less dependent on the technical technique or even the concepts presented here. Eventually the goal is simply to spontaneously, creatively, and naturally move in response, not reaction, to any approach or attack. Aikido practitioners move in such a way that they naturally connect and move to avoid damage to either themselves or their opponent, and to take control of the situation and life.

The inner development of the advanced practitioner involves an understanding of the philosophical basis for aikido, developing a training philosophy, training the mind, and understanding and using ki. The theories and concepts for the advanced practitioner are the art of body mechanics, movement, and engagement. The advanced techniques of aikido include strikes, throws and locks, applications, combinations, and counters. Advanced applications include self-defense, demonstrations, competitions, seminars, and teaching.

BUDO

O'Sensei Morihei Ueshiba would say that aikido is by nature essentially different from other martial arts, but Master Sokaku Takeda did open his eyes to the true nature of Budo.

> Budo is a divine path established by the gods that leads to truth, goodness, and beauty; it is a spiritual path reflecting the unlimited absolute nature of the universe and the ultimate grand design of creation. . . . Reform your perception of how the universe actually looks and acts; change the martial techniques into a vehicle of purity, goodness and beauty; and master these things. When the sword of harmonization linking heaven, earth and humankind is manifest, one is liberated, able to purify and forge the self. (UESHIBA, M. 1991, P. 27)

Budo is the martial way, the way of war. Bushido is the Japanese feudal-military code of behavior associated with the samurai. Bushido is the way of the warrior. The original samurai, meaning to serve, were protectors of their superior. The code of bushido developed and died out as the East became more westernized. It was revived and revised during the World War and became a code of nationalism, patriotism, and bravery.

O'Sensei Morihei Ueshiba believed (UESHIBA 2002, PP. 12–13) that true budo was not an aggressive and intimidating demeanor, but rather is calm and gentle. Budo is the way of love and peace. Victory is not in overcoming the enemy, for if you see an enemy you have lost the vision and insight of harmony, unity, love, and

(continued on next page)

peace. True victory is victory over, and loss of, the self. This attitude of budo is possible because of the confidence gained through persistent and consistent training and by using natural movements in a natural state of being, *shizen-tai*.

> *Our enlightened ancestors developed true budo based on humanity, love, and sincerity: its heart consists of sincere bravery, sincere wisdom, sincere loves, and sincere empathy.* (UESHIBA, M. 1991, P. 32)

While Bushido, as the way or code of the warrior, is the way of war, the loss of life should never be over-idealized or romanticized. There is nothing glamorous about the bloody reality of war. At times, there may be a temporary necessity for short-term resolution. It takes courage and honor to live in the spirit of harmony among differences. The greatest enemy is one's own ignorance and fear which makes one feel disconnected and separated from others. Only when this enemy is conquered will we find lasting peace. Each day the warrior must "polish the mirror" and attend to the discipline of facing him- or herself. Aikido is a tool used for "polishing."

> *The true purpose of the methods described herein is to teach a warrior how to perceive and fill his mind and body with a valorous spirit— one must polish one's ki and forge the spirit within the realm of life and death.* (UESHIBA, M. 1991, P. 27)

DEDICATION AND DEBT, RESPECT, AND RESPONSIBILITY

No one makes advanced rank or ability in aikido without the compassionate guidance and instruction from a competent aikido sensei. Eventually, with consistent and persistent training, students openly express their dedication to their Sensei and their style. They acknowledge a great debt that can only be paid or fulfilled by continually showing respect and alliance to their teacher and school and by representing themselves as members of an affiliation in a responsible and ethical manner.

Dedication is not just to one's own training. That would be relatively selfish. Selfishness is not the ultimate goal of aikido. Dedication is what aikido stands for in its concepts, application, and model for human interaction. Eventually, with consistent and persistent training, the students become dedicated to their training and to the training of all those they train with. They are dedicated and proud of their direct lineage traceable back to the founder, O'Sensei Morihei Ueshiba.

Giri is a word that literally means right reason. It is a sense of obligation, duty, and debt. Eventually, with consistent and persistent training, students must always ask themselves if they are doing what they are doing for the right reason. Does it serve the higher good of all and does it honor those who have given their time, patience, and expertise? Is what they are doing or saying, paying back the debt they personally owe for what was given to them? This is a very different concept than the one seen in westernized society. Today, most people take up martial arts as a hobby to fill leisure time. Since they pay their monthly dues, they believe that whatever they are given belongs to them. They can do whatever they want with it. This is very shortsighted and not only goes against aikido's philosophy but also goes against traditional martial arts practice as well. Using the right

(continued on next page)

reasoning in how the gift is honored and perpetuated pays the debt. The sensei was given, and honors, his or her own personal lineage. With consistent and persistent training, students come to know that they are only a temporary point in the passing on of knowledge. Like momentum in the application of aikido techniques, the inertia from the past generates the wisdom of the future.

Respect is another word seldom used in modern westernized society. Most people are more concerned with receiving respect than with giving it. People tend to believe they can demand respect due to their position rather than their merit, genuine knowledge, and by being respectable.

With consistent and persistent training, the student of aikido willingly accepts the responsibility to carry on the tradition of aikido given through his or her sensei and style. Responsibility means accountability to the past and to the future for what one does and teaches today. Responsibility means the acceptance of the consequences of one's behavior. Every behavior has a consequence; some will bring honor and some will bring shame. All behavior and communication has an effect and thus a consequence. The slightest movement in the execution of an aikido technique can add or diminish its effectiveness and efficiency. Likewise, the slightest behavior or communication can show dedication, an honoring of the debt of having been given a great skill and knowledge base, and respect for one's sensei, style, and the lineage of the family of aikido.

Part One
The Inner Development of the Advanced Practitioner

Chapter 1
Omoto Philosophy for Today's Practitioner

While Daito-ryu aiki-jujitsu was the martial root of aikido, the Omoto cult of the Shinto religion was the spiritual root. O'Sensei created aikido based on a fusion of the spiritual and the martial. The Omoto philosophies are deeply ingrained in the study of aikido. Though a practitioner of aikido does not become a convert to a different religious practice, one does encounter and apply universal spiritual truths to strengthen his or her personal philosophies. Above all, aikido emphasizes physical training and practice; in its spirituality, aikido welcomes people of all faiths, allegiances, and denominations in the name of a higher spiritual truth based on inclusion and the loss of judgmental and dualistic thinking.

SHINTO—SPIRITUAL BEGINNINGS

O'Sensei Morihei Ueshiba was originally a follower of the Shinto religion. Shinto, or Shindo, is a native religion of Japan. It is the way of kami, the spirit, deity, or God. Shinto believes that there are invisible superhuman powers in

THE WAY OF PEACE

As any advanced student of aikido knows, the word aikido has many definitions. Literally, it means the way of harmonizing energy or spirit. More often, most know aikido as the way of peace.

O'Sensei Morihei Ueshiba designed aikido as both a martial art and a spiritual art. Aikido is martial in its practical and powerful techniques. Aikido is spiritual in its attitude of application and philosophy of nonresistance and loving protection of even the attacker. Many martial art systems and artists say that the ultimate goal is peace, while their training methods and techniques are extremely violent. Aikido is congruent in training, application, and ultimate goals. All training and application in aikido is practiced in the spirit of harmony, cooperation, peace, and protective love and respect.

Throughout training in aikido, one vacillates between the way of peace and the martial application, the way of war. Eventually, the advanced student trains against realistic honest intention and intensity and applies the techniques of aikido with equally honest intention and intensity. This honest intent and intensity demonstrates and expresses the powerful and effective techniques of aikido, while the practitioner maintains a sense of inner peace and protection of his or her training partner. Honest intent and intensity are very

(continued on next page)

important in aikido training for the advanced practitioner on both a martial and spiritual level. To progress on this journey, one must be honest and genuine in discipline and training. The desire to train and progress must come from deep inside and be something that you are willing to make an honest commitment to and to keep that commitment with honor. Further, you must be very honest about the reason why you are training. Is it your honest and genuine intent that directs your training and your ki? With a genuine committed intent to the discipline and training in aikido, there must be an equally honest and genuine commitment to the physical intensity of that training and discipline. Intent is of the mind. Intensity is of the body. When both share in an honest and genuine commitment toward the same goal or direction, this unity provides the basis of and potential for spiritual awakening and enlightenment.

The way of peace only comes through strength. Peace through weakness is acceptance of defeat and compliance. Strength allows peace to be a choice. Aikido develops and trains one in that choice. Aikido chooses peace through strength. Aikido is not the body of war, but the spirit of loving protection and peace. Most ways of peace have been philosophically strong and physically passive. History suggests that those who challenge peace do not appreciate, respect, or respond to a passive, compliant approach to peace. Those who want control and power often take this passive, compliant position of peace as permission. While fighting to end wars has brought only temporary peace, it has proven to be the only means to stop tyranny. Therefore, a way of fighting had to be developed in which the philosophy of peace and the responsiveness were congruent and did not add directly back into or give perpetuating permission to more aggression. Aikido accepts that there is conflict and aggression in the world. Rather than responding with passivity or fear, aikido enters directly into and blends with the conflict. Aikido can redirect the aggressive energy, utilizing it against itself, without adding more aggression. This blending and redirecting continues until the aggression is subdued. The advanced aikido practitioner responds directly to aggression, requiring honest and genuine strength of character. Using only the aggressive energy offered, without adding to it, requires a relaxed body and mind and a minimum amount of physical strength. This is the beauty of the aikido way of peace.

everything in nature. Spirit and nature become one and emphasis is placed on ancestor worship.

Today in most dojos, Shinto practices are still performed, though more out of respect for the custom than for spiritual conversion. For example, in Shintoism bowing is an expression of worship. The clapping of hands two or three times is also a Shinto practice to summons the kami before offering a prayer. The shomen, meaning head, at the front of the dojo reflects many of these early Shinto practices. A picture of O'Sensei Morihei Ueshiba reflects a respect for ancestors and the gifts they give us, and suggests that our ancestors still watch over us as we train. The frame of the shomen is often a *torri* (gate to a Shinto shrine) that suggests and reminds us that aikido is a spiritual practice.

In part due to these modern reflections of Shintoism, many still hold that the practice of aikido is spiritual by nature and will put one in touch with higher power. O'Sensei Morihei Ueshiba believed that aikido was a gift from the spirit to help heal a violent world. In 1903, O'Sensei Morihei Ueshiba received a certificate of spiritual enlightenment from Reverend Mitsujo Fujimoto at the Jizoji Temple.

AN INTRODUCTION OF THE OMOTO RELIGION

Omoto translates into the great origin or the great source. It is a religious and spiritual movement that came into being based on the insights and experiences of its foundress, Nao Deguchi, in 1892. Its interreligious work of joint worship and exchange with other religions are central to its divine mission. This work continues today.

Nao Deguchi was born December 16, 1836, into a family of a poor carpenter in a mountain village northwest of Kyoto, Japan. It was a time of famine, high taxes, oppression, and social and political turmoil. Her early years were filled with suffering and hardships. Because she was illiterate, her family farmed her out to the Deguchi family as a nursemaid and servant girl.

Eventually the Deguchi family adopted her, and she was given in marriage to another of their adopted children. From that marriage, she produced eleven children, three of whom died at birth. Her husband was a carpenter by trade and overgenerous and a drunkard by nature, leading to a life of extreme poverty. Nao continued to be a model wife even after her husband fell from a roof and broke his pelvis. He died in 1887.

In 1892, at fifty-five years of age, appearing possessed and in a dream state, Nao Deguchi received visions detailing plans for the salvation and reconstruction of the world. She saw a divine palace and figure in her visions. This figure spoke through her. All, including Nao, feared she was insane or possessed by an evil spirit. She questioned the spirit and was tested by fortune-tellers and priest-mediums whose occupations were to verify such entities. It was soon confirmed that she was possessed by or channeling a great deity, Ushitora, who wished to reconstruct the world. Her lifelong suffering was a test and preparation for the task she was about to undertake.

Even though she was totally illiterate, Nao began to produce automatic writing detailing the plan. The content of the *Ofudesaki*, the scripture of Omoto, reached 200,000 pages by her death in 1918. One of the prophecies was the coming of a man from the east.

Onisaburo Deguchi (1871–1948), after meeting Nao, became a follower of Omoto in 1898. He later married the daughter of Nao Deguchi in 1900. Adopting the family name, he became a central figure, spreading the teaching of Omoto. His charisma, humanity, and colorful ways helped spread Omoto beliefs as well as generate controversy. At times, there were disputes about the direction of the Omoto faith and the difference between Nao and Onisaburo. In 1904, at the age of thirty-three, possessed by the spirit of Mizu, he wrote the *Divine Signpost*, a sacred text of the Omoto faith.

The religion gained enough followers to become a significant religious and social force. Due to the movement's growth in popularity, the Japanese government brutally suppressed it in both 1921 and 1935. The Japanese government was concerned about the outspoken Omoto movement, its opposition to many government and cultural practices, and the fact that the Omoto cult had not received official recognition and permission. In both instances, the government destroyed property, and arrested and imprisoned high-level officials of the Omoto religion.

When Onisaburo Deguchi met O'Sensei Morihei Ueshiba in 1919, there was an instant meeting of the minds and recognition of kindred spirits. O'Sensei accompanied him as a bodyguard in several misadventures, including one to Mongolia that resulted in imprisonment. Due to O'Sensei Morihei Ueshiba's long years of martial training and cultivation of a still center, he was able to detect the intent of bandits and avoid bullets during an attack. The ability to detect intention of an assailant encompasses the ability to develop awareness, with minimal body clues, of an attack and the line of that attack; an intuitive awareness of the level of intent to do damage; and the ability to respond by getting out of the line of fire or attack. Onisaburo believed not only that O'Sensei Morihei Ueshiba was a great fighter but also that he was to be a great leader of budo.

Onisaburo influenced, supported, and encouraged O'Sensei Morihei Ueshiba in the development of what was to become aikido—a martial art of peace based on universal spiritual truths. Several of the prayer and meditative practices taught to O'Sensei Morihei Ueshiba by Onisaburo Deguchi sustained and strengthened his intense willpower and unmovable spirit.

Many of the spiritual and metaphysical lectures given by O'Sensei in the teaching of aikido came from this Omoto/Onisaburo influence. Many students did not understand this top-down, universal conceptualization approach to training in what they defined as a very physical martial art. The technical training was the application of the universal spiritual truths.

In a more recent text by Hidemaru Deguchi (Deguchi, H.), successor of the founder, he writes on the creation of meaning. He states that the path of self-cultivation is to know one's true self, to recommend self-examination, to see oneself as part of the whole, and not to be confined by the notion of hell. In the search for human sincerity, one should look for one who can weep and feel anger, shows true merit in times of adversity, lives in freedom, lives devoted to what he or she believes and does his or her very best, practices self-cultivation to the final moment, produces a driving force for advancement, and is not encased in a hard shell. A way of life awakened to love means to not show merit, appreciate action, or be enslaved by ideology and the cultivation of conjugal love. Action cultivates true strength through practice instead of theory, seeking self-knowledge within oneself, spurring on the body, experiencing varied circumstances, and living from the gut. Nature's providence is a world of interest—work in accord with nature's timing, surrounded by innumerable teachers, going with the flow, following the rhythms of heaven and earth, and the world is an interesting place. Living with all one's might means looking above and looking below, seeing between two opposing things or forces, and living appropriately; sometimes fighting is best, overcoming both good and evil with forgiveness and tolerance.

THE OMOTO PHILOSOPHY

The philosophy and practices of the Omoto religion (Deguchi, O. 1904) found practical application through aikido techniques. Musubi, which usually means connecting, also means giving birth to spirit. Musubi is the bringing forth of life by the energy generated when two opposite energies or ki sources come together. The great laws of the universe came from its inherent active energy that demonstrates a will or intent to maintain order. The universe, Mother Nature, and humanity are not separate entities but a single body. Humanity's role is to accept this unity, harmonize, and love all creatures with a sincere heart.

The spiritual truths of Omoto ask everyone, including today's advanced aikido practitioners, to align harmoniously with others, to receive personal understanding and insight, to understand repetitive patterns in all things, and to become more creative.

To align harmoniously with life and the universe requires the advanced aikido practitioner to take responsibility for his or her interaction with others. Resistance is not harmonious; it is discordant. Nonresistance provides the means to enter and blend with others by joining and aligning ourselves. Those of the Omoto belief established, supported, and attended many international interfaith conferences to demonstrate this need to align harmoniously with others. What those of the Omoto belief practice philosophically in coordination and alignment with other faiths and organizations, the advanced aikido practitioner practices in training and discipline with the dojo by aligning harmoniously with their uke, or training partner.

The Omoto teaches us to receive personal understanding, insight, and the revelation of celestial truths and its lessons. This is to make an honest and genuine commitment of intent and intensity to train until one gains and owns the perceptions, concepts, and techniques of the Omoto belief or aikido. Knowledge is the accumulation of knowledge presented by others and still belonging to them because it does not come from one's own experience. To truly know something, not just the knowledge of it, is to pursue the training and discipline necessary until those understandings and insights are the product of the continued validation of one's own personal experience. Knowledge can be gained from others as the reporting of facts as they perceived them. Wisdom is the understanding and insight one can only get from one's self. The Omoto belief and aikido encourage each of us to proceed with our training until we receive personal understanding, insight, and enlightenment.

To understand the repetitive innate patterns of the behavior of man, society, and the cosmos is to accept all things for what they are. Sequentially, the present comes after the past and before the future. Past, present, and future become a repetitive pattern because the present will soon become the past and the future will become the present moment. Each season leads to the next in a repetitive pattern of the year. Day follows night, and vice versa, in a repetitive pattern. The repetitive pattern of life suggests that nothing is permanent, that there is a sequential cause-and-effect relationship in observable and knowable operations, and that we are all creatures of habits with predictable repetitive patterns of thinking and behaving.

Creativity is the basis to respond spontaneously and with an instinctual drive. Creativity provides hope for new thoughts, feelings, and behaviors. Creativity is a means to move beyond our habitual repetitive patterns and to search our own personal experience of understanding and insight to find new ways to align harmoniously with others in peace. Creativity means to accept that many of our old ways of behaving and interacting that have consistently led to fear, hatred, and war need to be abandoned and new ways found. Creativity challenges the established ways and institutions. To be effective and efficient in all aspects of life, we must learn to be creative and resourceful. Training and discipline in aikido basics teaches us the repetitive patterns of entering, connecting, blending, and aligning harmoniously with others. Advanced aikido practitioners will creatively begin to apply the concepts and principles of aikido to their movement and spontaneously execute the appropriate response or technique, takemusu-aiki.

To do this, one follows the four principles. One must train the body and mind for purity and purification. One must maintain optimism by believing in the goodness of the divine will. One must strive progressively for social improvement. Finally, one must unify rather than separate all things by reconciling all dichotomies. These are very wise aspirations for us all, worthy of dedication regardless of where they originated.

This harmonious inclusive philosophy is practiced in the *tenshin-nage waza* (the heaven and Earth throwing technique) in which one hand is held high, representing heaven, and the other hand is held low, representing the Earth. Tenshinkai, meaning the organization of heaven on Earth, is the name given by aikido founder O'Sensei Morihei Ueshiba to a uniquely fluid and powerful style of aikido and the Sensei and federation that oversees it. Overcoming, integrating, and utilizing dualism demonstrates the harmonious congruence in aikido conceptually, philosophically, and in its practical application. These are the basic universal truths represented in aikido application and training. Aikido is the way of harmony and peace in the midst of conflict and aggression.

The concept of divinity, or God, in the Omoto faith is inclusive of all three concepts of monotheism, polytheism, and pantheism. Omoto worships the one ultimate original spirit of God, while acknowledging the same character of spirit of God in many and all things.

SPIRITUAL PRACTICES

For most people, the practicing of spiritual truth is isolated to specific places and times. Aikido encourages its advanced practitioners to maintain these spiritual truths in their hearts and minds because the practice of the techniques is designed to deal with aggression and conflict in a nonresistant, nonviolent, noncompetitive way. It has long been held that the benefits of spiritual truths are apparent when they are practiced and applied in daily life and interaction.

If one wants to go beyond the physical practice of techniques, one can follow some more spiritually based exercises.

Kotodama: Spirit Sounds

Similar to chanting, *Kotodama* is the belief that every sound has some spiritual property and power. Kotodama is a Shinto practice of intoning various sounds to produce mystical or spiritual states. Sounds have a specific vibration or rhythm. They synchronize the brain wave rhythms by repetition. The seventy-five sounds of Kotodama form words that purify the universe and teach the way of aiki as deigned by the universe. The sounds of the kotodama are ka-ko-ku-ke-ki and sa-so-su-se-si. Notice that these consist of the common denominators and most used aspects of even the English language, the vowels a-e-i-o-u. Words in language have a sound, a voice, a rhythm, and a literal, as well as a deeper, meaning. The air and breath give life to these sounds and words. This type of practice is very common in most religious rituals.

O'Sensei Morihei Ueshiba performed Kotodama as part of his daily spiritual and martial practice. He believed that out of stillness comes the resonance of heaven and Earth. This resonance or sound, when chanted, helps one become aligned, harmonized, and at one with the vibratory resonance of the universe. Human beings are a microcosm of the universe. By developing awareness of the connectedness of human nature, one begins to hear Kotodama.

The vibratory resonance of Kotodama makes and moves everything. The Omoto explanation of the origin of the universe suggests that an ever-increasing density and explosion, similar to the Big Bang theory, created the universe. The subsequent birth and movement of Kotodama generated the material and spiritual world. All things first exist in the spirit world before a latent causative predisposition transfers them to the material world, just as all physical behavior comes from thought.

The actual practice of Kotodama may be too esoteric for most aikido students. Further investigation, study, and training should only be done under guidance and supervision.

Chink-Kishin

Chink-kishin refers to the meditative or mind-calming techniques of the Omoto faith. One of the aspects that drew O'Sensei Morihei Ueshiba to the Omoto belief is the methods used to calm the mind. These techniques are referred to as chink-kishin. Very little detailed information is readily available about the specifics of these techniques unique to the Omoto faith. They do tend to follow the generic patterns of mental training and meditation as presented and discussed in Chapter 3: Training the Mind. Calming the mind is very important in any spiritual or psychological progress and evolution. Holding the concept that nature is spiritual, it is often our internal mental consciousness that blocks and prevents a direct experience of understanding, insight, and enlightenment. By learning to calm the learned ego identity of the mind, advanced practitioners will find their training and technique becoming more spontaneous and directed by natural causes. These causes may be attributed to advanced levels of training leading to takemusu-aiki, or a feeling that they are divinely directed, as described by O'Sensei Morihei Ueshiba. It is beyond this book and beyond the expertise of its authors to provide explicit descriptions of or information on the instructions of these techniques. One is encouraged to seek further exposure and experience directly from the Omoto foundation.

Yusai

Yusai refers to prayer. O'Sensei Morihei Ueshiba was known to practice daily rituals and prayers as a part of his spiritual practice and routine. It is sometimes said that prayer is talking to God and meditation is when one listens. The two practices complement and support each other. Many advanced practitioners of aikido, before starting practice and training, bow and offer a prayer to their spiritual godhead asking for guidance and protection. After a training session, another prayer is offered in gratitude to all that was offered, learned, and received.

Misogi: Purification

Misogi usually refers to austere or ritual training practices used for spiritual and physical development. Misogi is a traditional Shinto practice to purify the body and spirit.

The most common image of misogi is standing meditation under an ice-cold waterfall. Other practices include breathing during movement such as the aikido *turifune-no-gyo* (rowing) exercise, hand shaking, chanting long prayers, *kiai* (spirit shout), seated meditation using *mudra* (hand postures) and visualizations, and specific dietetic restrictions, such as fasting. Eventually, with consistent and persistent training, the student practices misogi in more common everyday activities. Regular dojo activities and responsibilities, such as sweating, cleaning, and training can serve the purpose of misogi, a purifying ritual.

Throughout all these activities, there is a focus and emphasis on consciously controlling the breathing. Breathing is essential to life and to the purification of life. Breathing connects the physical and emotional states. Beginning students of aikido will tend to hold their breath as a stress reaction when practicing. Eventually, students will naturally synchronize their breathing with their movement and their training partner's. Breathing creates the connection and joining of the two into one. This process is spiritual and purifying.

Common to the misogi practice is the ability to keep the mind calm and clear, as in mushin, while the body is undergoing severe, often repetitive, experiences. Taking a very cold shower while keeping the mind calm is a common, very private, form of misogi. O'Sensei Morihei Ueshiba was often known to pour cold water over himself to start the day. Another commonly available form of misogi is the use of saunas to provide extreme heat conditions and an opportunity for the mind to be disciplined and to overcome the body's reaction to discomfort.

O'Sensei Morihei Ueshiba believed that the practice of aikido itself was misogi since aikido purified and united all beings in nature and provided a bridge between heaven and Earth. The kami gave O'Sensei Morihei Ueshiba aiki to protect and perfect humanity. Practitioners use misogi as a way to connect with the divine. Misogi is budo, martial arts constantly polishing the spirit of the warrior through rigorous daily practice.

SPIRITUAL TRAINING

In addition to the profound and abstract psychological, philosophical, and spiritual meaning of these spiritual truths, aikido also contains many practical martial applications. Many of the characteristics used to describe peak performances, such as the "flow" and the "zone" states of athletic performance, are similar or identical to those words used to describe a mystical or spiritual experience. One can find and produce these methods and experiences, both athletically and spiritually, through aikido training. In the chapters on training philosophy and training the mind, more specific ideas will be presented and discussed on how to find and produce these methods and experiences. What is required is the honest and genuine intent and intensity in training the body while maintaining a calm and peaceful state of mind.

It is not necessary to acknowledge, endorse, or embrace any of the spiritual concepts and philosophies of aikido in order to gain a high level of technical proficiency and the benefits of training. However, many believe that you will only be limiting yourself from achieving the spiritual benefits of aikido, which are a natural extension of the training.

> *True budo cannot be described in words or letters; the gods will not allow you to make such explanations. Techniques of the Sword cannot be encompassed by words or letters. Do not rely on such things— move on towards enlightenment.* (Ueshiba, M. 1991, p. 28)

The Shinto and Omoto spiritual philosophies that influenced O'Sensei Morihei Ueshiba's thoughts and practice, believed in the spiritual presence in nature. The Shinto practice of having many spirits or gods suggests that all of nature has inherent and innate spirituality. The interfaith practice of harmoniously aligning with others suggests that the same spirit lives in all things natural. Though most of us are acutely aware of distinctions and differences, it is the natural sameness of spirituality that connects us. This is not a byproduct of training or the result training to make it so, but the actual natural state of the universe. O'Sensei Morihei Ueshiba loved the countryside and farming as a means to commune with nature and receive inspiration directly for kami, or spirit. Spirituality, seen as natural and existing in all nature, is not about religious affiliation or denominations but about personal character and having mindful clarity beyond the learned ego identity and duality.

Many aspects of advanced aikido training and discipline can be considered spiritual. These practices have very little martial application but make for a better person and a contributing member of society.

The formal respect given to all and the code of conduct and honor based on natural inherent worth is spiritual. Many of the bowing rituals of aikido are based on Shinto spiritual practices. Bowing formally acknowledges the spirituality in all.

The selfless participation as a training partner offers and sacrifices your time and your body to be of service to another. Placing the interest and advancement of others above one's own personal desires, and even potential safety, demonstrates compassion and spiritual values. It is this attitude of selfless self-sacrifice that makes the training and discipline. If the same participation were practiced purely out of formality with the anticipation of what one will get in return or with resentment, the practice would not be considered spiritual. Learn to practice and give to others freely.

There is the expression of compassion toward and protection of your training partner. The techniques of aikido, especially when applied with honest intensity and intent by an advanced practitioner, can cause great pain and damage. Compassion, restraint, and mercy can only be developed and demonstrated in the presence of potential harm. Overcoming one's own internal drive for power and control over others through violence and aggression leads one to develop a mind, heart, and body based on peace and spirituality.

Facing internal mental fears creates mindful clarity. While it is not always necessary to know the truth, it is necessary to see through illusions if one wants to develop and progress spiritually. Love is spiritual. Some would say that hate is the opposite of love. Hate is produced by fear. Others would say that apathy is the opposite of love. Apathy is also produced by fear. The opposite of love is fear. You must choose a life based on love or a life based on fear. Seeing through and overcoming the internal repetitive negative fantasies that create fear make it possible to face conflict and attack with compassion and love.

There is a deep sense of humility based on personal experience of knowing there is so much more than the individual learned ego identity. Knowing how much one does not know opens one to more learning. True humility is based on acceptance that one has something to be humble about, and accepting that any skills or abilities developed do not make someone any better than anyone else does. Humility is based on the acceptance of the imperfections of being human. The imperfect construct is the learned ego identity and the mental constructs used to define the perceptions of reality. In the midst of severe training (shugyo and misogi) one responds instinctively without the internal reference and analysis of the learned ego identity. There is no longer an "I" that is detecting, assessing, deciding, and responding.

To have a spiritual experience in aikido training, one needs only to train with honest and genuine intent and intensity. Instructors in aikido or spiritual practices can only point the way. They cannot make it happen. One cannot make a spiritual experience happen either. With honest intensity and intent, one must let the spiritual experience happen on its own, at its own time, and in a way that is personally idiosyncratic. The spiritual experience, truths, and benefits of aikido training are simply waiting for one to get out of the way. Truth has always been there waiting and available to all who seek it and are open to letting it come into their life. Aikido provides a means and a place to practice these truths.

AIKIDO PHILOSOPHY BEYOND THE DOJO

Foster and polish the warrior spirit while serving in the world; illuminate the Path in accordance with the divine will. (UESHIBA, M. 1991, P. 28)

Aikido is a powerful and effective means of personal transformation. aikido teaches its philosophical ideation of nonviolence through practical application and training rather than lecturing. Seldom does one hear lengthy lectures on the use of aikido for personal insight, growth, and transformation. Recently, several individuals and books have taken aikido out of the dojo and into the personal and professional lives of its practitioners. Their contributions and insight are worth the investment of time and energy. A higher level of personal transformation becomes the message and messenger of higher social transformation.

Aikido is a means of social transformation only as far as it is a means of personal transformation. Social, and spiritual, transformation means seeing beyond one's self. The social realm extends to one's training community, one's sensei, the school, the style, and the larger aikido world community. It extends to one's family and friends. It extends to the community one lives in. It extends until one sees the common unity in his or her country and the world. It extends until the one includes the all. Society tends to transform one person at a time until it reaches a critical level of acceptance. The more people who express the values and philosophies of aikido in their personal and professional life, the more social choices and responsibility transform. Advanced students of aikido will naturally practice personal and social responsibility because they practice aikido. There should be no distinction or discrimination between the rules of respect inside or outside the dojo's walls.

CONCLUSION

There is much controversy about the spiritual aspects of aikido training. Because of its spiritual emphasis, many people have questioned if a denial of their current faith is required for advancement. Hopefully, this chapter has helped all practitioners understand that the basic spiritual concepts and beliefs of aikido, though based on Shinto and Omoto doctrines, are common to all spiritual faiths as well as social and cultural awareness and responsibility. It is not necessary to undergo any conversion per se, but there is a requirement to accept a nonviolent noncompetitive philosophy of harmonious alignment with others, a quest for personal experience and insight, an acceptance and blending with the repetitive patterns in nature, and the use of creativity to overcome selfishness and work for the mutual benefit of all. Many advanced practitioners of many faiths have found that the training and discipline of aikido complements and strengthens their own individual expression of spirituality.

The inner development of the advanced aikido practitioner incorporates the spiritual concepts in a comprehensive training philosophy.

Chapter 2
Training Philosophy

Practice these methods intently with your entire mind and body, temper yourself ceaselessly, and advance on and on; weld yourself to heaven and earth and unify practice and enlightenment. Realize that your mind and body must be permeated with the soul of a warrior, enlightened wisdom, and deep calm. (UESHIBA, M. 1991, P. 27)

The inner development of the advanced aikido practitioner establishes, incorporates, and utilizes a practical but comprehensive training philosophy.

In the beginning, aikido students simply show up for class and follow the examples of the instructor. Eventually, after consistent and persistent training, the student of aikido understands that the instructor can only teach a limited amount. The student's true success in aikido depends on one's ability to research, understand, and apply the aikido concepts to one's technique and training.

Training in aikido occurs long before you set foot in the dojo. That is the formal training. To get the most out of training, you must develop a good training philosophy. This chapter will present insights into and guidelines for developing an advanced aikido mindset, the hierarchy of training skills, training goals, physical motor training, training psychology, etiquette, dojo training relationships, keiko, shugyo, misogi, takemusu-aiki, and thoughts about the future.

DEVELOP AN ADVANCED AIKIDO TRAINING MINDSET

The appearance of an "enemy" should be thought of as an opportunity to test the sincerity of one's mental and physical training, to see if one is actually responding according to the divine will. When facing the realm of life and death in the form of the enemy's sword, one must be firmly settled in mind and body, and not be at all intimidated; without providing your opponent with the slightest opening, control his mind in a flash and move where you will—straight, diagonally, or in any other appropriate direction. Enter deeply, mentally as well as physically, transform your entire body into a true sword, and vanquish your foe. (UESHIBA, M. 1991, P. 31)

Wherever the head goes, the body follows. To get your body to train, first you must get the right training mindset. There are a few mindsets that can help a student of aikido, or any art in life, progress faster. The idea is not always to simply train more, but to train more effectively and wisely. One of the best training mindsets is to accept that one is learning a martial art, that it will take time to learn, and that you will make mistakes regularly, which give you the opportunity to train and learn.

Train as if your life depends on it. As a martial art, train as if you intend to use aikido someday to protect your life or the life of loved ones. Do not train as if your life is currently threatened, but train as if someday it may be. Take your training seriously with the proper intent and intensity for practical real-world applications.

As a spiritual art, train as if your spiritual life depends on it. No matter what your training partner does, you must uphold your own level of ethics and behavior. One's spiritual development depends on sticking strictly to one's work and progress. No one can do it for anyone else. We can help our training partners, but we cannot do it for them anymore than they can do it for us.

Train as if you enjoy it. O'Sensei Morihei Ueshiba stressed taking training in aikido seriously as a discipline and a dangerous martial art. He also wanted aikido practiced in a joyous manner, celebrating the spiritual nature of the art. Research also suggests that one learns better and maintains training longer if the process is enjoyable.

Train with intense intent. As mentioned, two items that are very important in training are the intent and the intensity with which one trains. Intensity follows intent. If your intention is to spend time socializing with your fellow students, then the intensity of your training will be minimal. If you train with the intent only of achieving physical fitness, you will train with a higher intensity than is the case when the intent is socializing, but not enough to be able to defend yourself. If you train with the intent that you will be able to defend yourself someday if you need to, you will train with a higher level of intensity. Decide what your intent is and train with the appropriate intensity to achieve it.

Train consistently and persistently. Progress does not just come. Acquiring skill requires consistent attendance and persistence in training.

At first, train with a goal in mind. This will help focus your training. Training without a goal in mind is like taking a journey without a destination. You may travel around in circle and get nowhere. Next, train just to train with no specific goal or intent in mind. This is more process oriented, rather than content or intent oriented. Training with no specific goal means that you have a direction set, to progress, but no real destination as in reaching a specific goal or rank. Eventually, the training comes on its own. Training becomes the intent, content, goal, and process all in its own right. The destination and journey become one. Training is not something that you do. Training becomes identity and who you are.

Train to make a statement. Initially train as if your behavior while training is making a statement about who you are. What do you want people viewing your training to think about you? Train in such a way that your behavior communicates that statement.

Train for self-improvement and to improve others. The higher principles of aikido stress the common good and best interests of everyone. Therefore, to train just for self-improvement is still very selfish and does not demonstrate or apply the higher spiritual principles of aikido. One must train the self, but one must also lose the self in order to help improve others.

When practicing as tori (the one executing the technique), stay relaxed, calm the mind, and follow the instructions given. This will lead to self-improvement.

When uke (the one initiating the approach and attack and receiving the technique), give honest intention and intensity to the approach and attack so that the tori can practice and improve. Do not give too little intensity and intent. This makes the practice useless. Do not give too much or you are not training, but fighting for your life. This becomes a contest of muscle and ego, not a training environment for self- and others improvement.

Train slowly and pay attention to details. The best way to progress rapidly is to progress slowly. The best way to make big changes is to pay attention to the little things.

Train in technique and concepts. Train in both the physical techniques that apply the concepts and the concepts that make those techniques effective and efficient.

HIERARCHY OF TRAINING SKILLS

The hierarchy of training skills is similar to the hierarchy of training goals. One can either use the techniques to illustrate and learn the concepts and principles or use the concepts to direct the techniques.

Using the techniques to illustrate the concepts is all too often the usual standard operating procedure. This bottom-up thinking is a way to rationalize and justify what one is doing by finding an overall strategy that will explain the tactic or technique. In most martial arts, the tactical techniques of doing battle by hitting and kicking to overpower another suggests, dictates, or even promises that this route will bring about peace. Some people need to see the little picture before they can see the big picture. Some people will need the concrete before they can grasp the abstract. Some people will learn better by first having some verbal instructions and having an internal frame of reference.

Using the concept to direct the technique is the process of finding the higher belief, concept, or strategy that one sets for oneself in order to find a way, tactic, or technique that is consistent and congruent to it. Aikido is one of the few martial arts to have a belief or strategy of peace and harmony that then dictates taking the strikes and damaging techniques out of the training and application. Some people need the big picture before they can make sense of how the little pieces fit together. Some people will need the abstract before they can grasp the concrete. Some people will learn better by just seeing and imitating the technique, by having an external frame of reference.

The goal in aikido is the loving protection of all people. The strategies for accomplishing this goal are achieved through the concepts, such as *irimi* (entering) and *awase* (blending), redirecting, *kuzushi* (unbalancing), *nage* (throwing), and controlling. The application of these concepts and principles is achieved through the execution of the techniques of aikido. Therefore, the best goals are those that are in the highest and best interests and safety of all people. The best strategies are those principles and concepts that maximize the chances of achieving this goal with the least amount of damage. In other words, do the least to achieve the most. The best techniques are those that follow the concepts to achieve the goal as directly as possible.

In the beginning, the aikido students tend to be bottom up in orientation. Later, the students begin to transition from bottom up to top down. Eventually, the students apply the beliefs in peace and harmony, through the specific aikido concepts, in the actual training and applications of aikido techniques.

TRAINING GOALS

Training in martial arts, like anything in life, is best undertaken when directed toward a specific goal by setting specific objectives, and according to specific schedules. However, one must always take into account motivation and learning plateaus.

Training goals are individual, need to be stated in positive sensory-based terms specific enough to recognize and acknowledge the progress initiated and maintained by the individual student. To obtain advanced status and rank in aikido (goal) the student must show up consistently and persistently to train with the proper intensity and intent to learn what is being taught.

It is important to find your own motivation for practice. What motivates one individual may have no effect on another. Some people move toward a goal, while others move away from fear, shame, or danger. Some people want external public acclaim, while others want an internal satisfaction. Some want money, prestige, or fame, while others want solitude and peace of mind. Some people want to be different, while others want to belong and be the same. Some people train because they feel they have to; others train because they simply want to. There is no right or wrong motivation for studying aikido. Each student must come to understand his or her own motivation and use it to continue training and progressing in aikido.

The training plateau is the understanding and acceptance that there will be times within the training schedule that one is not learning any new skills. There will be times that one does not always have the necessary motivation to maintain a schedule, to do the task to meet the goal. The training plateau can be one of the most exciting and important times in aikido training. The initial learning curve in which one learns a great deal tends to have its own momentum based on the excitement of learning and progressing. The learning eventually, and inevitably, will hit a few plateaus where nothing new appears to be learned and the old techniques may appear and feel boring. Mastery (LEONARD 1992, P. 39) suggests that through the repetitive and realistic rehearsals of training and practice of the known techniques, the skill will go from conscious competence to unconscious competence. The learning curve will then have a new base line from which to learn new skills and concepts. With this goal of unconscious competence in mind, the training plateau is no longer a plateau but a necessary, and welcomed, stage of training and practice.

PHYSICAL MOTOR TRAINING

There are many aspects to physical training. They include nutrition, exercise, and skill.

Nutritional analysis and advice is beyond the scope of this text, but it is important to realize that the fuel the body relies on has direct effects on bodily performance. Eating the wrong foods, drinking alcohol, smoking tobacco, and the use of drugs will eventually take their toll on the body and the mind. Eventually, with consistent and persistent training, the student of aikido will begin to be more nutritionally oriented and healthy.

Strength training is of lesser importance in aikido because the proper execution of an aikido technique does not require physical muscular strength. O'Sensei Morihei Ueshiba specifically stated that training should not be a contest of strength. Nonetheless, everyone can benefit from a toned and conditioned musculature. The only way to strengthen or tone muscles is through weight or resistance training. Visualize the movement to help coordinate and unify the body and mind. Staying completely relaxed and calm, focusing on posture and alignment, and breathing and extending ki from one's center make resistance training a practice in the application of aikido concepts. It is important to put any skill into context, so please remember to lift weights, not people, and to throw people not weights.

Flexibility training incorporates stretching exercises. These exercises increase the range of motion and help prevent injuries in training. Flexibility can help the body respond faster and more efficiently by relaxing antagonistic muscles and improving the full range of motion. Visualize the movement to help coordinate and unify the body and mind. As in strength training, staying relaxed and focused on your center, while breathing and keeping good posture, can help you apply aikido concepts to flexibility training.

One develops cardiovascular fitness through any exercise program that consistently raises and maintains a high heart rate. These exercises include running, cycling, swimming, dancing, or fast-paced *randori* (multiple opponent attack). Aerobic, or cardiovascular, exercise is the only way the body burns fat. Cardiovascular fitness can greatly increase the ability to train harder and longer by increasing stamina and endurance. Visualize the movement to help coordinate and unify your body and mind. Staying relaxed, breathing, focusing on your center, and extending your ki will help you apply aikido concepts to a cardiovascular activity.

Skill training takes into account the technical proficiency needed for powerful execution of techniques. The best way to gain proficiency in a specific skill is through repetitive and realistic training. Specific skill training is best thought of as either gross motor skills or fine motor skills. The gross motor skills are those that the entire body participates in using the larger muscle groups of the body and are often the easiest to practice and gain proficiency in. Under stress, the gross motor skills maintain a higher degree of proficiency and effectiveness. Fine motor skills require the use of the smaller muscle groups and are far more detailed in their action and task. Visualize the movement to help coordinate and unify your body and mind. Staying relaxed, breathing, focusing on your center, and extending your ki can help you apply aikido concepts to skill training and acquisition. Slowing down and paying attention to the persistent and consistent repetitive and realistic training with and against honest intensity and intent will help one build aikido skills. It is hard to tell beginning students to slow down and pay attention to body movement. There appears to be a natural tendency to want to speed up. They need to develop the correct form, alignment, and coordination. It is wisest to pay attention initially to each individual movement and not let momentum, speed, and ego dictate training and condition in sloppy technique execution. Correction to overcome a bad habit is often much harder than learning a technique correctly to begin with.

Block training also tends to help long-term skill retention. Block training refers to the number of repetitions that one does of a task within any execution set. One set may be ten repetitions. Another set may be five repetitions followed by a break followed by another five repetitions. In the beginning, one will practice a single technique repeatedly, as if finding a training groove and staying in it. Eventually, with consistent and persistent training, the student of aikido will practice finding a training groove by doing only as many repetitions as necessary to find that specific feeling. Many know that it is not training more that achieves skill improvement, but training wisely. It is easiest to stay within a training groove or block. It is harder to keep finding that groove. Research suggests that the best long-term retention of a skill comes from repeatedly finding that training groove.

As stated earlier, under stress, the body responds best to the adrenaline pump, rush, and dump, when the advanced student keeps training simple and direct in strength, flexibility, cardiovascular, and skill acquisition.

TRAINING PSYCHOLOGY

The field of sports psychology focuses on providing techniques to facilitate optimal performance. As a field of psychology, its focus is on mental and emotional development and discipline. Initially, sports psychology helps identify those internal mental and emotional blocks to better performance. It then begins to model, install, and imitate a more positive and constructive model of performance. Sports psychologists base these models on elite athletes in the field. Last, the field of sports psychology teaches how to let go and enter the "flow," the "zone," or in aikido, what we call takemusu-aiki.

One sees and experiences aikido mainly through the teaching of physical discipline and practice of the techniques. Most dojos and senseis permit very little, if any, talking while practicing and training. This type of introspection may need to be part of the personal study and journey of the aikido student. Two of the most common obstacles to optimal performance are fear and anger. One creates fear by negative internal fantasies about what might happen. Fear is strong enough to create an avoidance reaction, but usually only brings into one's experience everything that one is afraid of and trying to avoid.

Peak performers in sports and athletics demonstrate an absorption in the activity facilitated by a detachment from conscious awareness of their performance. The athlete feels a sense of ecstasy, a sense of personal power, an altered perception of time, and a sense of unity. "Peak experiences" have a high level of joy or ecstasy, feeling transpersonal and mystical, a sense of passivity, a feeling of unity and fusion, a loss of self, spontaneity, and a feeling of peak power. "Peak performances" demonstrate superior behavior, a high level of performance, a clear absorbed focus, a strong sense of self, and a sense of fulfillment with intended action but spontaneous performance. Most do not necessarily consider it playful.

The optimal arousal level refers to an inverted-u theory in which too little or too much arousal produces a decline in performance. Therefore, for optimal performance, the arousal level must be neither too much nor too little. Too little often leads to a lack of motivation or drive. Too much arousal tends to overwhelm. One need is to know that moderate zone where one is "psyched up" but not "psyched out."

The flow state (Csikszentmihalyi 1990 and Jackson & Csikszentmihalyi 1999) characterizes a challenging activity requiring skill and a merging of action and awareness. The flow state has clear goals and feedback. The athlete concentrates on the task and the possibility of control, and experiences a loss of self-consciousness and a transformation of time. Athletes report the flow as fun, enjoyable, a loss of ego, playful, a feeling of control, a loss of time and space, and an intrinsic motivation. The athletes balance the challenge of the skill to allow themselves to feel neither too much anxiety nor too much relaxation, leading to boredom. Athletes learn to overcome inertia and get moving by facing down failure and by moving beyond their comfort zone by believing in their skill and ability. The flow creates an absorption in the task that transcends normal awareness, allowing the athletes to forget themselves, to let the competitors worry about themselves, to accept the environment as a given, and to focus on the process at hand. This flow of awareness results in a loss of a sense of clock time and any sense of effort. The flow uses winning only as a guidepost from which to set clear and specific goals that will enhance motivation and enjoyment. The flow emphasizes feedback from the kinesthetic (feel) sense of awareness and outcome information from the athletes themselves, the coaching staff, teammates, the opposition, and spectators. The flow focuses awareness in the present since the past is gone and leads nowhere and the future is still under construction. Total immersion in the present requires the ability to refocus, to use task goals, to keep things simple, to plan for the competition, to make backup plans, and to practice concentration that will direct attention. The flow only controls what is controllable by finding the optimal control level, recognizing the controllable, setting the stage, and choosing responses. Above all, the flow is fun.

The zone describes a transcendent experience in sports (MURPHY 1978 AND 1995). The zone has mystical sensations of acute well-being, peace, calm, stillness, detachment, freedom, floating, flying, weightlessness, ecstasy, power and control, being in the present, instinctive action and surrender, mystery and awe, a feeling of immortality, and unity. The zone alters perceptions of size and field, time, extrasensory perceptions, out-of-body experiences, and an awareness of a spiritual other. The zone facilitates extraordinary feats of exceptional energy, overcoming invisible barriers, and fosters an extension of energy, psychokinesis, or mind over matter. Sports and athletic performances evoke this spiritual zone through the physical and mental demands of the activities, the sacredness of time and space, and sustained and focused attention. An athlete in the zone has a sense of detachment from the results and demonstrates a dedication to the creative and integrative powers for the exploration of human limits. The zone has the ability to command long-term commitment to express a perennial philosophy of a fundamental spiritual reality that is a provisional reality of the ordinary world. The zone facilitates the need for discipline, for the knowing and expressing of a deeper perfection, an essential ecstasy, knowledge of and by identity, a rich inner world, and a knowledge and acceptance of the subtle energy body. Elements of a mind/body training program to facilitate the zone would include meditation, biofeedback, visualization and mental practice, inner seeing beyond simple visualization, dreaming, sensory and kinesthetic awareness, and the development of ki, or the energy body.

Athletic programs that facilitate peak performances, the flow, and the zone, all have several things in common. The first is the centering of the athlete's attention and total awareness in the present task. The second is the use of repetitive rhythmic routine and training. The third is to trust one's training to the point where conscious control and thought are removed.

It can easily be seen that training with honest intensity and intent in aikido will produce peak flow and zone performances or what one might call takemusu-aiki, the spontaneous and creative execution of aikido.

ETIQUETTE TRAINING

Everything in aikido begins and ends with etiquette and respect, essential parts of the continuous practice of aikido. Etiquette and respect should find natural expression in all one does. The essence of aikido is to unite *"with the universe's energy (ki) and to follow the dynamic flow of nature."* (UESHIBA, K. 2004, P. 24).

This should be the basic principle in the mind of every practitioner. There are not a lot of formal rules of etiquette in aikido because by following the principles of nature all people will behave respectfully and with the highest good for all in mind. This represents the very positive, even optimistic, point of view of aikido.

HUMBLE CONFIDENCE, RESPECT, AND LOVING PROTECTION FOR OTHERS

In the beginning, students know that they do not know much about aikido. As they progress in training, they will often believe that they know quite a bit. Eventually, with consistent and persistent training, students of aikido come to know that they do not know and enjoy the idea that they will never know most of aikido. The advanced student accepts the lifelong learning process that keeps them actively engaged in training.

In the beginning, students look to the instructor to teach them all the aikido they need to know. Eventually, students of aikido accept that their instructor can only point the way. The path taken by advanced students is completely their own responsibility. The instructor can point the way and teach them the basics, but as for the finer points of the art, the advanced students of any martial art learn to depend more on their own drive to learn and to train.

In the beginning, one will either lack confidence or be overconfident. Aikido is difficult to learn. As one progresses in training, one has some sense of both confidence and humility. Eventually, the student of aikido maintains humility yet has attained a sufficient level of technical and conceptual skill to have something to be humble about.

In the beginning, one can seldom apply the technical skills of aikido in a structured training context. As one progresses in training, one gains technical application within a predetermined routine. Eventually, the student of aikido can apply the technical and conceptual aspects of aikido in spontaneous contexts.

In the beginning, one learns the basic techniques of self-defense. Eventually, the student of aikido is able to apply the concepts of aikido in his or her martial intent as a way of war but also as a way of life, as a way of peace.

In the beginning, one seldom has self-appreciation. As one progresses in training, one begins to appreciate him or herself and all others. Eventually, with consistent and persistent training, the student of aikido develops a deep appreciation and respect both for the self and for all others. The development of compassion implies that the advanced student knows that he or she can do great damage, but chooses to protect his or her training partner.

Eventually, the student of aikido learns to face all of life's opportunities with a humble sense of confidence in his or her ability and training. Such students demonstrate a respect for all of nature, including humanity with all its imperfections. They extend ki toward all in need of assistance, compassion, and loving protection.

Many would say that you can tell an advanced student by the way he or she stands, bows, and pays respect to others. Correct posture, discipline, and the respect of lowering one's head communicate a correct attitude.

A dueling scene in Akira Kurosawa's 1954 film classic, *Seven Samurai*, illustrates this point. Simply by watching the calmness, stillness, and proper alignment and posture of a character in the on-guard position, it is obvious who will and does win.

Eventually, with consistent and persistent training, the student of aikido stands relaxed and erect with the spine straight and eyes forward. When bowing from a standing position, slowly lower your upper body by bending gently at the waist. Your hands should remain at your side.

When moving, glide with a natural step moving from your center.

When seated in *seiza* (kneeling), your spine should be aligned, your body relaxed, your knees placed relatively close together, and your hands placed on your knees or in your lap. When bowing from seiza, slowly sweep your left palm down to the center of the mat in front of you. Follow that by sweeping your right hand around, joining your left in a triangle. As you slowly bow forward, place your elbows on the mat and your forehead on your hands. Try not to raise your buttock as you bow. Return to the upright kneeling position only after your bow has been completed.

Always bow before and after instruction and when taking turns in practice.

Be friendly, but not social on the mat. This is time for training. Keep verbalization to a minimum even if you are making a training point to your partner.

An attitude of respect and gratitude should permeate all you do. That attitude will show.

CODE OF CONDUCT TRAINING

Following a strong tradition of etiquette and respect, and in the same spirit of bushido, the advanced student of aikido will naturally develop and express a code of conduct. This code of conduct is not externally dictated or motivated, but comes from an internally validated sense of knowing.

Eventually, with consistent and persistent training, the student of aikido will recognize and respect the genius of O'Sensei Morihei Ueshiba. He or she will have a deepening faith and commitment to the teaching of aikido and the community that he or she shares practice and training with.

By developing a deep sense of connectedness, the advanced student of aikido will attempt to refrain from all bad or evil acts, to do only those things that are good and in the best and highest interest of all, and to continue to train and practice to unify and purify the body, mind, and spirit.

Pain and suffering in this world come from ignorance. Aikido is a means to offer peace and protective love to the world. Advanced students of aikido refrain from doing harm or killing, from stealing, from sexual inappropriateness, from telling lies, from abusing intoxicants, from misguided speech and slander, from arrogance, and from misusing the lessons and gifts they have received through their aikido training.

Knowing that the best media in which to present a message are modeling and self-expression, the advanced student of aikido expresses, to the best of his or her ability, the qualities of generosity, moral conduct, patience, courage, self-control, and wisdom.

Eventually, the student of aikido trains not only to better his or her self, but also to help and be a model for others in and outside the dojo.

DOJO RELATIONSHIPS AND RESPONSIBILITIES TRAINING

There are many roles, relationships, and responsibilities within a dojo. There are the tori and the uke. There is the status of kohai, tohai, and sempai student. There are the sensei and student relationships. There is also the Shihan and sensei relationship.

The tori/uke relationship is unique in aikido training compared to other martial arts. As mentioned earlier, the tori is the one executing the technique. The uke is the one receiving it. They are the two interdependent partners in training. One cannot train without the other. It is for this reason that the development and expression of the utmost respect, safety, and gratitude is cultivated and facilitated between all training partners. Success in aikido depends on a reciprocal and interdependent relationship between fellow students and training partners. This is the heart of aikido training. Because aikido is noncompetitive, the tori/uke relationship is one of cooperation. The uke must give tori an approach and attack that has honest intensity and intent. Since aikido uses the energy provided by the approach and attack, anything less than honest intensity and intent would not truly allow the training partner to practice. The techniques in which one is training would become ineffective and inefficient in real-life situations. This could lead to harmful consequences. Too much intensity and intent would not allow beginning students to practice and train. Similarly, the technique used by the tori is executed with honest intensity and intent, but not to the extent of harming the uke.

The kohai, tohai, and sempai relationships among students are also unique and special. Few people appreciate the direct interdependent relationships and responsibilities that are at play in these student status relationships. Many times, unconsciously, these roles only have unspoken expectations. Sempai is a senior student. Kohai is a junior student. The kohai will look upon his or her sempai with respect. The sempai will look upon the kohai with compassion, patience, and fond remembrance of what it was like to begin aikido training. Both sempai and kohai benefit from this interdependent relationship. As kohai, your sempai will give you much of his or her time and experience. Your sempai will only ask that once you become a sempai, you too give to your kohai.

Ultimately, there is no sempai, tohai, or kohai. There is only the training. If one thinks too much of rank, one will not be paying attention to the lesson or training and will totally miss the beauty of aikido.

The sensei-student relationship is very important in the training and practice of aikido. The student must learn to trust in the sensei and the sensei must be worthy of that trust. Like all relationships, it takes two to make it work and be productive, but it only takes one to make it fail. Both the sensei and the student make a mutually beneficial and reciprocal agreement that betters not only themselves but also all within the dojo.

Keiko: Everyday Training

The first level of training is *keiko*. Keiko is physical practice and training, but it is more casual. Most practitioners of aikido begin with keiko. They begin training and practicing, but the level of intensity and intent is still rather tentative and restrained. This level of training is necessary in the beginning. Too rigorous, too fast, too soon creates little progress and too many injuries. Accept that as your level of skill and proficiency increase, so will the intensity and intent of your training.

Shugyo: Rigorous Daily Training

The next level of training is *shugyo*, meaning daily practice. Shugyo is the daily struggle of life. Aikido suggests we use our everyday life, inside and outside the dojo, to refine and purify the quality of life for all people. Ultimately, there is only the daily commitment to doing the best possible in everything. Rigorous daily training is a commitment to harmony and peace. It is a commitment to entering, connecting, and blending with others. It is a commitment to redirecting one's own thoughts and behaviors, as a model for others, from anger and separation toward peace and harmony. This is the shugyo aikido inside and outside the dojo.

Misogi: Purification Training

Aikido training is or can be misogi, a means of purification of body, mind, and spirit. It is the honest, genuine intent and intensity of training that provide the opportunity to minimize the learned ego identity interference, and let the unity of body, mind, and spirit occur naturally. Misogi takes the ability to control or reinterpret the signals sent from the body to the mind. What was once thought of as pain, to which the mind would send avoidance signal, now becomes the fire to forge the spirit by accepting it and staying with it or even moving into it. Misogi is the ability to invite, withstand, and even enjoy severe conditions and training.

Takemusu-Aiki: Spontaneous Creative Execution

Takemusu-aiki (spontaneous creative execution) does not just happen. It takes years of realistic repetitive rehearsal, practice, and training, before one's body will respond without effort or thought. It is a goal, but it is not the journey.

Takemusu-aiki uses ki as the natural life force to embrace dynamic and powerful martial techniques. These "divine techniques" come of their own after a lifetime of training. There is no shortcut to takemusu-aiki. There is only the training until the training itself manifests in the spontaneous and creative execution of an aikido response that is beyond, yet embodying, all concepts and techniques.

In the beginning, one will have difficulty practicing the predetermined attack-response patterns taught. The beginning and intermediate students have not learned yet how to respond spontaneously or creatively as they are still too focused on learning the craft of aikido. Eventually, the advanced student will be able to express the art of aikido by responding spontaneously and creatively, without thought.

Like the flow and the zone, takemusu-aiki demonstrates a detached absorption in an activity with a sense of spontaneity and peak power. There are several ways of training toward takemusu-aiki, but the actual experience comes from letting go and trusting that training. This state requires the ability to center solely on the task, the use of persistent and consistent training, and the ability to remove conscious thought and control.

To train toward the goal of takemusu-aiki, the advanced aikido practitioner never forgets to continually train in the basics of aikido. It is only through the honest and genuine training and discipline through realistic repetition that the basics become naturally occurring patterns of behavior and movement. As one gains proficiency in the basics, both the body and the mind relax. The advanced practitioner of aikido begins training against random attacks and allows the development of consciousness and responsiveness. Jiju-waza is the freestyle training against an individual. Randori is the practice against multiple attackers. Both jiju-waza and randori are essential to becoming more effective and efficient in technique and more confident and spontaneous. Takemusu-aiki is the natural product of consistent and persistent training with honest and genuine intent and intensity. At some point, the advanced aikido practitioner simply enjoys the flow of the training. Relaxed and focused, the attack dictates the response. The advanced practitioner follows the natural flow of ki, enters and blends with it, redirects it, and harmoniously resolves the conflict nonviolently.

CONCLUSION: THE FUTURE

Once one understands the past, the present and future are more understandable as well. You know how you got here. If you draw a line from the past through the present, you can get some idea of what the future may hold. Aikido has many possible futures. It can become stronger or it can become weaker. That choice is ours. Each of us plays a part every time we step into the dojo, onto the mats, and train.

Aikido, as a martial art, will only survive if we choose to train with honest intent to apply aikido to a fighting or combat context and scenario. While aikido originally came from a jujitsu fighting system, its current intensity, and intent in training and practice, brings its practical application and effectiveness into question. It is only by ensuring its martial application that aikido can remain a martial art.

The inner development of the advanced aikido practitioner, to make a practical and comprehensive training philosophy a part of life, requires training the mind directly.

TIPS FOR REFINING YOUR TRAINING PHILOSOPHY

1. Decide what you want to accomplish by training in aikido. This may mean a focus on the martial applications or it may mean the development of spiritual expression. Ultimately, what do you want your training to mean to you?

2. What do you have to do in training to accomplish your own personal training goals? If your philosophy tends to be more martial in application, you may want to focus more on the honest and genuine intent and intensity of the attack and responding techniques. Choose partners who want to train with a similar goal and philosophy in mind. If your philosophy of training is to achieve the development and expression of spirituality, then choose a sensei, a school, and training partners with like goals.

3. All training goals are worthless without actual training and discipline. Train with honest and genuine intent and intensity.

4. Be patient. Training is work that takes time. The result is often cumulative.

5. The best way to reach a goal is to enjoy the journey. Approach all training and discipline with a positive attitude and enjoy the process of training itself.

Chapter 3
Training the Mind

Mental training is a very important, but highly neglected, aspect of aikido training. Even very few advanced students actively train the mind with the same intensity and intention they do the body. This is unfortunate since the body does what the mind tells it to do. Current estimations suggest we use, at a maximum, only 10 percent of our mind's capabilities. That would suggest that we also use less than 10 percent of the capabilities of our body.

A common statement in aikido is that wherever the head goes, the body will follow. This is true in psychology too. Training the mind trains and directs the body. All behavior first starts as an internal conscious mental thought. Many times, the mind appears to be on automatic pilot and is engaged in more unconscious mental thoughts or obsessing. It is important to begin to clear the internal unconscious mental obsessing/negative thinking by making it first conscious, then challenging, and correcting the thinking to make it more productive and conducive to harmonious training and living. Internal verbalizations are often slow and filled with criticism and judgment. As one becomes more aware of the internal images and self-talk, one can begin mentally to rehearse behavioral response patterns or aikido techniques. The vivid imagining or mental rehearsing of techniques, as if one were actually doing them, sets up neurological pathways conducive to the actual performance of those behaviors. With practice in mental discipline and training, the mind begins to cooperate and become still and quiet. Meditation can be most helpful for observing and quieting the mind.

There is some debate as to whether the mind should be trained directly. It has only been in recent history that there has been such a divided split between the body and the mind. Many feel that if you train the body, eventually the mind will figure things out. Others suggest that because the mind will eventually need to be dropped, allowing the body to respond naturally and intuitively, the direct training of the mind actually impedes and is incongruent with the training goals. Some do not do teach any mental training because they simply do not know how.

AWARENESS AND INTUITION

Internal conscious mental thoughts first start as external awareness. Minimizing the internal images and verbalization best facilitates conscious external awareness. Awareness is one of the most important capabilities to develop. It is important as a martial artist to focus externally, rather than to be internally absorbed. The more faculties we can use to detect danger sooner, the more we can respond effectively, efficiently, and possibly preventatively. While training in the dojo, one can begin to become more aware of subtle and slight cues that precede and predict attack movement. Such cues include inhalation, eye shifts and pupil dilation, and chambering (pulling back or cocking the arm or leg) before striking. Outside the dojo, one can begin to notice possible avenues and venues of attack, defense, and exit. Awareness is simply the detection of what is and the mental willingness to accept it. There are naturally occurring patterns in nature. When these naturally occurring patterns appear interrupted or something appears out of place, it is critical to detect or to be aware of the discrepancy.

Decision making is part of mental training. One must make decisions as to the intent and intensity of training. Be prepared and forewarned. Accomplish decision making before any actual real-life occurrence necessitating the need for aikido as a martial art. It is too late to try to decide what to do once someone is already in a bad situation. One must decide to train with honest intent. One must decide to repetitively and realistically rehearse a response until it is automatic. One must decide to follow through. These decisions should be forethoughts, not afterthoughts. It may be too late to decide what to do once you are in a position to utilize your martial arts skills.

Intuition is trainable. It starts with quieting the mind and body. We are all equipped with subtle senses of awareness that can be cultivated. Intuition knows that we already know. Intuition is more a "let" process than a "make" process. You cannot "make" yourself be more intuitive, you can, however, "let" yourself. Through years of consistent and persistent training with honest intensity and intent, the body becomes used to detecting subtle cues of approach and attack. The hours of sweat and repetition will produce an automatic response. One must learn to trust oneself and the training. Learn to trust your instincts and intuition.

Another generalized statistic is that 80 percent of the work is done in 20 percent of the time, and 80 percent of the benefits come from 20 percent of the workout. Learn to train more wisely, not just more.

SHOSHIN: BEGINNER'S MIND

Sho (beginner's) *shin* (mind) is about being open to learning. Shoshin (beginner's mind) is the mind of a child. It is not immature, but in awe of learning and open to new experiences. Shoshin, paradoxically, is more the mindset of the advanced student than of the beginner because only the most advanced practitioners of any art realize that there is always more to know.

Often the beginner in aikido will try to fit aikido into a preexisting idea or concept. Perhaps he previously studied another martial art. He will usually attempt to practice aikido "as if" the previous art provided a means to formulate or make sense of aikido. This is not shoshin. Shoshin is simply being open. New learning and experience is new learning and experience. Shoshin is being open and enthusiastic to learn more and cultivate great humility in accepting what knowledge or skills are obtained. Shoshin is an attitude, a state of mind, and a perception that there is always so much more to learn. Many people mistakenly think of shoshin as a state of not-knowing in the sense of deepest ignorance and even stupidity. Learning does not mean that you are "less than" in the sense of ego identity or status. Shoshin, as not-knowing, is more a statement of letting go or suspending past learning and looking forward with excited anticipation to learning more.

Think of an experience in life where you truly looked forward to learning something new. Remember what your body felt like. Remember what you said to yourself internally. Remember what you visually showed yourself in your mind as you prepared for this new learning. As you remember what beginner's mind was, remember that every time you experienced it, you grew. Learning was easy and uncomplicated. Take a deep breath and relax knowing that you can do it again. If you make it a point to leave your ego and past learning at the dojo door, you will find that you will naturally develop shoshin and improve your training as an advanced aikidoka.

MUSHIN: CALM AND EMPTY MIND

Mushin means having a calm and empty mind. *Mu* means empty and *shin* means mind. Empty usually means containing nothing and void of all content. It is vacant and meaningless. Why would someone consciously and purposely cultivate such a state of mind, or no-mind?

The old metaphor would say that the mind is best when it is open and empty. When it is empty the mind is receptive to new ideas and has the ability to be filled. A mind already full can learn nothing new. Once something is learned, we must let that new learning go in order to learn more. The interesting point is that, in learning, even if you empty your mind, you retain the lesson. We never actually forget anything. One records, recognizes, retrieves, and remembers everything one experiences. It is only our attachment to old learning that is released so that new learning and information can come in. That is why a mind held open and empty can best learn and respond to any situation, because it is not attached to old ways of thinking and old patterns of responding.

There is an old story of a scholar who had prepared for an interview with a great master. On entry, the master first offered the scholar some tea. Politely the master begins to pour. The master continues to pour the tea into the cup until it is overflowing onto the table and floor. The scholar tells him to stop because his cup is already full. The master smiles and says he knows, and asks him to come back when his cup is empty.

Mushin is a mind free of thought. An empty mind is free to be externally aware and adaptive in its responsiveness. Empty does not mean dormant or vacant, it means "no-thing." The mind fills with "no-thing-ness," not "nothing-ness." It is not fixated or preoccupied with anything in particular. This allows the mind to detect, assess, decide, respond, and move without becoming stuck. Mushin is a goal as well as a process.

Before one studies aikido, movement is just movement. These movements often manifest without much thought. As a beginning and intermediate student, the movements of aikido become a science. Each movement, well thought-out, follows the prescribed steps. Eventually, the advanced student just moves without much thought. This time the movement is very different from the original untrained movement.

A mind that is empty allows the advanced student to maintain external awareness and responsiveness. Since thoughts create feelings, without thoughts the advanced student remains calm and has peace of mind.

Psychologically, the mind creates our difficulties. It is not the outside world, but the inside world of our own creation, that hurts us. Fear is an internal negative fantasy. Anger is hurt created by taking things personally. When you are happy and you are most creative, your mind is quiet. When one focuses on and attaches to negative feelings, one's mind creates negativity and is overactive. Since the body follows the mind, mental training and discipline are the best way to control both the emotional and physical states of mind.

To cultivate mushin one must first accept that we create our own thoughts. We create our own mind. We can choose to change the content of our minds. We can choose to think positively rather than negatively. We can choose to be love-based rather than fear-based. We can choose to change the pace at which we think. Allowing our minds to function slowly, we gain more clarity. As we gain control of our mind, we can become a spectator or observer of its workings. Soon we can calm the mind and feel comfortable in its quiet stillness. Learn to sit with a quiet mind. Learn to walk with a quiet mind. Learn to act with a quiet mind. Learn to let go and be empty.

HEIJOSHIN: EVERYDAY MIND

The natural extension and evolution of shoshin and mushin is *heijoshin*. Heijoshin is normal or everyday mind. The development of shoshin and mushin, at least initially, remains only an aspect that is consciously established and maintained as a separate or somewhat altered state of consciousness and perceptions. In aikido training, you will leave your ego identity and past learning at the dojo door to establish shoshin, beginner's mind. As an advanced practitioner, you will allow the energy and movement to flow without conscious thought or predetermination into mushin and takemusu-aiki. For most people, this state of consciousness and perception stops when the training is over. They bow in, open and empty. They bow out, closed, and full. Most people go back to their normal way of socially indoctrinated and reinforced ways of thinking, feeling, and behaving.

Heijoshin encourages you to extend and evolve by taking the concepts and philosophy of aikido into your everyday life. At this point, everything you do becomes aikido practice and expression. Aikido has a unique model of conflict prevention, intervention, management, minimization, and resolution. What you practice on the dojo mat works outside the dojo as well. Begin to think of problems, conflicts, and situations within an aikido context and realize that there are alternative ways of resolving them besides the resistance or compliance models. As you begin mentally to practice aikido off the mat and outside the dojo, you will begin to cultivate heijoshin, everyday mind.

MEDITATION

No discussion on training the mind would be complete without some mention of meditation. Even Western psychology is beginning to address, support, integrate, and encourage the use of meditative practices.

For beginners, meditation requires the establishment of a peaceful and quiet space and time away from the distraction of the everyday world. This may be a corner of your room or a special place you can go consistently. It is helpful to establish a routine of short practice periods every day at the same time. Some people use music to help mask outside sounds.

The first step in mediation is learning to relax. There are some progressive relaxation exercises that encourage you to tense muscles, hold them, and then to let go. This exercise teaches you the difference between a tense muscle and a relaxed muscle, a distinction very few people know well. Many people accept tension and stress as normal and have held it in their bodies so long that they no longer sense it as anything but normal despite the discomfort and illness it produces. Another means of learning relaxation is visualization. Think of a very safe, peaceful, and relaxing place. See all that is around you as if you were actually there. Notice as you visualize, the mind-body connection helping you automatically relax. Some find that just by inhaling and then exhaling while saying the word relax gives a direct command or suggestion to the body to relax.

The next step in meditation is concentration. Many techniques for meditation use concentration as a preparatory step. The purpose of concentration is to begin to train the mind to narrow its focus to one point. One technique uses an external picture, a mandala, to fix the visual focus of the eyes and mind. Another technique uses a sound or phrase, a mantra, to repeat over and over again. *Mundra* are hand positions that are used as point of focus or concentration. The purpose of concentration is to provide a focus to bring consciousness back to. The mind will wander in training. When the mind does wander, simply bring it back to the point of concentration. Notice that the implication in any concentration exercise is that there is an objective observer or witness to the mind who can detect and direct. This goes contrary to many people's popular belief, which is that, identifying the mind, they think that it is their root or source. Actually, the mind is a very useful tool. Especially after you learn to focus it through training.

Meditation begins when you begin to let go of technique and learn to sit with the quietness and emptiness of the mind. Notice that when you are the happiest and most creative, the mind is relatively quiet. Notice too that when you are angry, hurt, scared, stressed, anxious, depressed, or experiencing anything that can be thought of as a negative emotion, the mind is very active. This suggests that we do not have to do anything to be happy, but we have to do a lot to be miserable. We create our own negativity. Meditation is not a state that you can make or force. Meditation is a state that you *let* yourself have. Sitting everyday in meditation assists the body, mind, and spirit in finding its own natural homeostasis, or place of balance and equilibrium. After you can sit quietly in meditation, you can begin to walk around slowly and learn to hold the same state of peaceful consciousness. Eventually, you might even learn to do aikido while meditating actively.

INTENT

A lot has been made of the idea of intent. Intent is the mental capacity to focus the mind and direct your behavior and actions. Intent is the substance that provides the map and the directives for reaching a goal or accomplishing a task. Genuine and honest intent is the decision to commit all of oneself and one's resources to accomplishing a goal or task. Intent is not indecisive. You intend to train and learn aikido, or you do not. The advanced aikido practitioner has made a decision to train, for a time with no perceivable results, for as long as he or she can train, for the pure joy of training.

CONCLUSION

In the beginning, one pays very little attention to mental discipline or conditioning. The goal of the beginning student is to first get off automatic pilot and consciously train the body to move differently and the mind to think differently. Eventually, advanced students know that the body follows the direction of the mind. They no longer have to think about what they are doing. Their movements happen in accordance with the attacker's movement. As you develop your awareness and intuition as an advanced aikidoka, you will develop beginners mind, empty mind, and your everyday mind.

The inner development of the advanced aikido practitioner trains the mind to understand the use of ki.

TIPS FOR REFINING MENTAL TRAINING

1. The first step in training is to become aware that the mind is filled with visual images and talk that directs how you feel and behave. If you have peaceful thoughts, you will probably feel and behave peacefully. If you have angry thoughts, you will probably feel and behave with anger. Become aware of the thoughts you have that create problems. Become aware of the thoughts you have that solve problems by creating solutions. Notice that these thoughts are different. Many of the problems and obstacles we face in life are more a product of these internal factors than external circumstances.

2. Decide how you want to feel or behave. What thoughts would you have to hold in your mind in order for that to happen? The ability to learn is more a factor of the belief that something can be learned than any intellectual capacity. If you believe that you can learn advanced skills and concepts of aikido, you will. If you believe you cannot, you will not. Decide to train and live peacefully but with genuine intent and intensity.

3. Mentally rehearse the feeling or skill you want to achieve. Mental rehearsal is a valuable tool in training the mind. Mental rehearsal is accomplished by creating a vivid imaginary context or situation in which you want to perform well. Mentally step into the fantasy as if it were actually happening. See, feel, and hear everything from the internal subjective frame of reference. The more vivid the association, the more likely your body will accept it as real and develop neural pathways that will assist in the automation of the response the next time you are in that situation. Mental rehearsal is a skill used by top athletes and taught by sport and performance psychology consultants.

4. Meditation practiced on a regular basis will help minimize stress and promote a sense of well-being. Ultimately, meditation, like training in aikido, will be an undertaking for the simple process of just sitting there.

Chapter 4
Understanding and Using Ki

Underlying the forms, or physical techniques, are the spiritual principles of aikido, which are based on the notion of ki, or life force. Ki is the fundamental element of understanding aikido. (UESHIBA 2002. INSIDE JACKET COVER.)

Ki is energy. Everything is energy. Everything is ki. The inner development of the advanced aikido practitioner requires one to understand and use ki.

The techniques of aikido harmonize the human body and the ki of heaven and Earth. By definition, aikido is the way in which to harmonize ki. This harmonizing occurs by harmonizing your energy with the energy of the attacker. Ki is one of the major foundations, if not the major foundation, of aikido. This chapter will focus on ki training, kokyu training, and exercises. It is very important to demystify ki and see it as a natural extension and combined product of training in technical proficiency, structural alignment, applied physics, visualization, timing, and breath.

KI

Ki is energy, the basic life force that exists in everyone and in all things. It is as mysterious and illusive, yet as practical and accessible, as air or electricity. One does not see the air, but one knows it is there because one can breathe it and one is alive. One does not see electricity, but one knows the energy is there by the effects it has in application.

The first step to even theoretically developing ki is to accept, even hypothetically, and be aware of its existence. The student of aikido then learns that ki can be projected thought physical momentum and inertia, that one can project ki mentally by seeing and extending through an obstacle or situation, and that attitude and belief can also develop, direct, and extend ki.

KOKYU

Closely related to ki is the concept of kokyu, or breath power. Kokyu is more than just lung capacity; it uses the entire body to unify and concentrate the power of body and mind with ki. Breathing is what connects the conscious body processes with the unconscious. Usually one does not have direct control over one's metabolism or heart rate, but both can be directly influenced by conscious control of the breath. Breath too is usually on automatic and something one does not think about. One can learn to consciously become aware and take control of one's breathing, thus directly influencing and controlling all bodily systems and responses.

Controlling the breath also has a direct impact and influence on the emotional system. Under stress, one usually holds one's breath or hyperventilates. These breathing patterns actually contribute to and perpetuate that emotional state. Slow, deep breathing is a way of centering the mind, controlling the oxygenation process of the body, and calming one's emotional state. Controlling the breath develops and controls ki.

Tohei Sensei, founder of the Ki Society, stressed the development and extension of ki in all aspects of aikido training and practice.

KI AND KOKYU TRAINING

All training in aikido is ki training. In most aspects, ki and kokyu form the foundation of aikido and life. Both are essential in all aspects. The Aikikai style of aikido places greater emphasis on technical proficiency and practical application of aikido techniques, but the ki and kokyu aspects and foundations should never be minimized or overlooked. Many of the movements presented below as ki exercises are part of the warm-up exercises of most aikido training halls. It is the conscious and direct application of ki concepts, or rules, that make these exercises an expression of ki development and extension. Sensei Koichi Tohei places larger emphasis on these exercises.

> *Ki development is the bridge between psychology, which concerns itself exclusively with the mind, and physical education, which deals only with the body. Ultimately, mind and body are one—no borders exist between them. The mind is refined body, the body refined mind. It is foolish to consider them two separate things.* (TOHEI, K. 1976, P. 10)

Tohei Sensei developed four basic rules (TOHEI, K. 1973, PP. 2–4) that are practiced and applied at all times during the execution of aikido techniques:

1. The first is to keep the one point, or the center, located in the hip area, as the center of the body's gravity.
2. The second is to relax completely, body and mind.
3. The third is to keep the weight of your body on the underside in compliance with the laws of gravity.
4. The fourth is always to extend ki. Always maintain metsuki (soft eye focus) and mushin (a calm and empty mind).

Keep the one point. The one point is the exact center of the body. To locate the one point, think of that point in your hip region that is the middle between top and bottom, left and right, front and back. This center, as known as the *hara* or *tan tein*, becomes the focus of consciousness and movement. Often we hear the expressions of "having guts" or "a gut feeling." It is said that our feeling is actually generated from this one point. Standing, the one point is the natural and perfect point of balance. When movement originates from this one point, it allows full body weight, momentum, inertia, and power to be placed into it.

Relax completely. Ki energy flows best through a pathway that is unimpeded by tension. In Chapter 3, we offered suggestions on progressive relaxation, visualization, and other techniques to learn relaxation to aid meditative practices. Those same exercises and techniques are useful in maintaining that relaxation to develop awareness of ki.

Keep your weight on the underside. The natural laws of gravity state that the weight of an object will naturally fall to its underside. It is easier to support something from underneath than to hold it from above. Therefore, keeping your weight on the underside can facilitate greater ki development. When extending your arm, keep your elbow down and slightly bent, following the natural curve of your relaxed arm. Visualize a bar of metal on the underside of your arm, giving it support and strength. In visualization, the arm is a relaxed hose that is filling with water. As the hose fills the arm straightens and becomes hard. The water will first run along the bottom of the hose before the entire hose is filled. This is feeling the support and strength of ki. In many of the ki exercises and testing that follows, it is this supportive element of ki that is manifest and validated.

Extend ki. Ki is energy. Ki is universally external and physically internal. Everything is energy. Some view the development and extension of ki in very mystical terms, unfortunately making ki very esoteric and hard to understand or practice with. When ki is demystified, it is simply seen as energy, which cannot be created or destroyed, but can be focused and extended. Relaxing the body allows energy to flow without obstruction. Breathe in and focus on accumulating energy in your one point or center. As you exhale, visualize the energy extending out beyond the physical limitations of the body. Just like the breeze created by motion, ki extends naturally. Just as when you throw a ball, the ball continues on a path after it leaves the hand, ki may not need to be extended, but thought of as already extended naturally. It is the awareness of the already existing extension of ki that needs development.

KI EXERCISES

Ki exercises are actually tests of one's ability to focus and direct ki. The exercises are used as a part of everyday warm-ups or workouts without the necessity to test for the stability and strength extended. These exercises done on a consistent and persistent basis with honest and genuine intent and intensity will result in the advanced practitioner of aikido being able to naturally produce, focus, and utilize ki.

Ki Exercise 1

Seated meditation can be the beginning of ki training and development. Cross your legs or sit in a half- or full-lotus position. Stretch your spine upward, keeping your nose and navel and your shoulders and ears in line. Sit still and do not wobble. Let your mind center on the one point in your lower abdomen. Relax completely. Let your weight settle naturally to the underside. Extend your ki. Breathe naturally through your nose. Your body should not be able to be pushed, pulled, or lifted off-balance.

Ki Exercise 2

Assuming a natural stance, let your mind center on the one point in the lower abdomen. Relax. Let your weight settle to the underside. Extend ki. Raise your arm. Visualize your arm being strong with ki as if it is being held up from the underside by a metal bar or as if a strong stream of water is running through it. Your arm should not be moveable or bendable.

Ki Exercise 3

To test ki, assume a natural stance with your arms hanging at your sides. Have someone grab your wrist and push upward. Shake your wrist and keep your mind centered on your one point, relax, and let your weight rest to the underside of your arm, and extend your ki. Your arms will become immovable. Ki development exercises include wrist bending palm down (*nikyo-undo*) and palm up (*kote-gaeshi-undo*) followed by wrist shaking or vibration (*tekubishindo-undo*).

Ki Exercise 4: Tekubi-Dosa-Undo (Crossing Hands Exercise)

Assume a relaxed natural stance with your mind centered on the one point in your lower abdomen. Let your weight settle to the underside, and extend your ki. Let your hands swing forward naturally, meeting in front of your center. Visualize and feel the continuous flow of ki extending from one hand into the other. If tested, your hands should not be able to be pulled apart or pushed together, and you should not be able to be pulled, pushed, or lifted off-balance.

Ki Exercise 5: Ude-Furi-Undo (Arm Swinging Exercise)

Assume a relaxed natural stance, keeping your mind centered on the one point in your lower abdomen. Let your weight settle to the underside, and extend your ki. Smoothly pivot or turn your hip on a horizontal plane to one side and then the other. Coordinate your breathing with the movement. This exercise may also be done with *tenkan* (pivoting turning step) as *udefri-choyaku-undo* (swing and leap exercise). At no time should you be able to be pulled, pushed, or lifted off-balance.

Ki Exercise 6: Rolling Exercises

You can also test ki before and after the rolling exercises, such as *kohotento-undo* (back roll exercise) and *zenpo-kaiten-undo* (forward roll exercise). Keep your mind centered on the one point in the lower abdomen; relaxing, let your weight settle to the underside, and extend your ki. Keep the image of a circle in your mind and exhale as you roll. From an initial standing or seated position, your body should be unmovable if attempts are made to push, pull, or lift you off-balance.

Ki Exercise 7: Funekogi-Undo (Rowing Exercise)

Assume a *hanmi* stance (relaxed ready stance with body aligned forward). Keep your mind centered on your one point in your lower abdomen. Relax and allow your weight to settle to the underside, and extend your ki. Exhale as your hips move forward. Extend your arms at waist height and roll your wrist, pointing your fingers toward the floor at the last second. Inhale as you pull your arms back to your hips. Keep your fingers extended in *te-gatana* (hand blade) and your arms with a natural curve. Visualize and feel ki coming from the earth through the one point and flowing through your arms and hands as if a steady flow of water were rushing out through them. You should be unmovable if pushed or pulled from behind or in front.

Ki Exercise 8: Shomenuchi-Ikkyo-Undo

This is a forward rising protecting block of the head against an overhead strike exercise. From a hanmi stance, keep your mind centered on the one point in the lower abdomen. Relax and let your weight settle to the underside and extend your ki. Exhale as you raise your arms, with your hands held in *te-gatana* in a natural arch upward as if protecting your head by blocking an imagined overhead strike to it, and push your hips forward. Inhale as you bring your hips back and your hands to the side. Visualize and feel ki coming from the earth through the one point. Extend your ki energy out through your arms and hands as if a steady flow of water were rushing out through them. You should be unmovable if pushed, pulled, or lifted. Shomenuchi-ikkyo-undo can be performed in *zenpo-undo* (two-directions exercise) by turning or pivoting your hips horizontally 180 degrees as you retract your arms and then raising them in the opposite direction.

Ki Exercise 9: Sayu-Undo and Kokyu-Nage (Breath and Timing Throw)

Assume a natural stance with your mind centered on the one point in the lower abdomen. Relax with your weight settled on the underside and your ki extended. As you inhale, raise your arms along a natural arch to one side, keeping your palms up. When your arm reaches shoulder height, exhale and slightly turn your hips to the rear. Inhale and swing your arms to the other side. Visualize and feel ki coming from the Earth through the one point and flowing out your arms and hands as if a steady flow of water were rushing through them. Your body should be unmovable if pushed, pulled, or lifted.

Ki Exercise 10

Another interesting ki exercise is to rest your hands on your training partner's shoulder. Focus on your hands and push. Your partner will be able easily to resist you. Now, let your mind center on your one point in your lower abdomen. Relax completely and let your weight settle to the underside and extend your ki. Allow your eyes to focus through your training partner. Exhale softly and reach or walk toward a distant point as if your training partner were not there. Do not attempt to push them. To *push* implies resistance and force. To *reach* implies only the path. Do not let your mind create and focus on what it does not want. Visualize and feel ki coming from the Earth through the one point. Extend the ki energy out your arms and hands as if a steady flow of water were rushing out through them. You will find that your training partner cannot resist your effortless power.

KOKYU-NAGE

Kokyu-nage are breath or timing throws. They look simple but are the product of consistent and persistent training with honest and genuine intent and intensity to advanced stages of aikido training and discipline. They are the essence of advanced aikido skills and proficiency. Kokyu looks as natural as breathing. Kokyu enters and blends with the attacker's momentum, inertia, and rhythm so that the defender appears hardly to move to evade, unbalance, and throw the attacker. In kokyu one inhales, inviting the attacker in as one enters and blends. In kokyu one exhales as the ki is extended and the attacker is thrown or secured.

Focus the Mind

Simplistically, ki flows at the direction of the mind. Learning to focus on the mind has a direct influence and impact on the ki flow. A mindset that indicates the successful completion of a task will be the most successful. A winning attitude will provide a better potential for and possibility of winning. Looking at your training partner and thinking that he is too big or too advanced will interrupt the ki flow. He may be bigger or have trained longer, but this is not an excuse to get the technique wrong. When you think you can do something, you can do it. Ki follows the dictates and direction of your beliefs and expectations. It is your choice to keep ki from flowing in a negative fearful direction or to extend and embrace a positive, powerful, and peaceful state of mind and body.

Kiai: Spirit Yell

One does not hear the kiai (spirit yell), so very common in most martial arts, much around the aikido dojo. The use of kiai is most associated with the concentrated focus and energy in striking. Since striking an opponent is not the usual course of study in aikido, congruent with its nonviolent philosophical position, the use of kiai is not universally practiced. Some would consider it an unnecessary component for the old jutsu or fighting roots. However, O'Sensei Morihei Ueshiba could time his kiai at a time of transition and imbalance so powerfully that his attackers would fall.

Kiai forces the air out of one's lungs and projects ki forward. The forcefulness of the sound itself will demonstrate the intensity and intent of the person yelling. Even if one wishes not to make a sound, a silent "kiai" will add to the focus and should be a part of one's regular training and technique execution and application.

CONCLUSION

Ki can be understood as a mystical universal energy or spirit. This esoteric approach often leaves ki misunderstood and underdeveloped by many beginning and advanced aikido practitioners. Understanding ki as the already existing, already extended, naturally occurring energy that is the product of consistent and persistent training with honest and genuine intent and intensity allows ki to be used at all levels of training and discipline. Aikido is the way of harmonizing and aligning this energy between an attacker and oneself, and with the universe. Without ki, there is no aikido.

The inner development of the advanced aikido practitioner incorporates a spiritual perspective, a comprehensive and practical training philosophy, direct training of the mind, and understanding and using ki. Next, the advanced aikido practitioner must understand and apply the theories, concepts, and art of body mechanics, movements, and engagement.

TIPS FOR REFINING KI

1. Practice Tohei Sensei's four rules: relax completely, let your attention focus on your one point at your center, let the weight settle naturally to the underside, develop awareness of the already extended ki or energy.
2. Breathe in as you gather and concentrate ki in your center. Breathe out as you extend it.
3. Breathe in as you enter and blend with the momentum, inertia, and timing of an attack. Breathe out as you execute a throw or immobilization technique.
4. Visualize the energy extending past the physical limitations of the body.
5. Maintain a positive attitude.
6. Consistently and persistently practice with honest and genuine intent and intensity.
7. Let yourself become aware of the subtle flow of ki.

Part Two

Theories and Concepts for the Advanced Practitioner

Chapter 5
The Art of Body Mechanics

The theories and concepts the advanced aikido practitioner applies in the art of body mechanics, movement, and engagement make aikido effective and efficient as a spiritual and martial art.

There are many aspects and subjects contained within the art of body mechanics. At the beginning of all workouts should be warm-up exercises, and there should be cool-down exercises at the end. The art of body mechanics is to always establish, maintain, move from, and become the center of the technique. Body mechanics include maintaining correct posture and a relaxed body, keeping structural alignment with one's own body and in relationship to the attackers, maintaining a soft eye focus, and increased environmental awareness and sensitivity.

WARM-UPS AND COOL-DOWNS

With consistent and persistent training, the student of aikido must take responsibility for his or her warm-up and cool-down. The exact exercises and sequence may change based on instructors, schools, and affiliations. In many seminars very little time is spent warming up, because those in charge figure it is the responsibility of the attending students to be ready when the guest instructor begins to teach.

Make sure to warm up your body and get ready to train. General and gentle stretching should begin any workout. Remember to keep your body relaxed and breathe during warm-ups. Remember to stretch your muscles and get a full range of motion into the joints. The student of aikido readies all parts of the body for practice and training because aikido is a full body workout and one wants to be ready and prevent injuries as much as possible. Warms-ups are a great opportunity to incorporate ki exercises if they are not already a formal part of one's regular warm-up routine.

Warm-up exercises include rotation of the neck, shoulders, hips, knees, and ankles in both directions. Stretching exercises include the neck, the back, the legs, and especially the wrists. For full body warm-ups, try rolling forward and backward as well as performing break falls. A series of tenkan, circular step and turn movements, while maintaining alignment, will help warm up the body.

Cool-downs at the end of the workout are very useful. Making a moment slowly to stretch the muscle helps the transition from being active to being more passive. Using a partner to stretch out your back is especially helpful. Some people enjoy a few rounds of *kokyu-dosa* (two-person seated *ryote-tori* [both hand grab] ki exercises). Spending a few minutes in *seiza* (kneeling) and quietly men-tally reviewing the training is helpful for retention of the skills practiced. Many people enjoy a moment of quiet meditation to let the mind become calm. The ritual bowing at the end of a training session shows respect, and appreciation for what one has done and toward those one trains with.

It is important for all students to take both warm-ups and cool-down exer-cises seriously. Too many do not pay attention to form and concept while exer-cising. For training to progress from conscious competence to unconscious competence, one must train seriously and consciously. The attitude of serious stu-dents of aikido shows in everything they do. Keep your body structurally aligned and balanced. Always maintain me-tsuke (soft eye focus) and musubi (connec-tion). Always maintain the center. Inhale as the movement contracts, and exhale as it expands. Keep your body completely relaxed, your mind focused on the one point, keep your weight settled on the underside, and extend your ki. Practice hard in *keiko* (training) and *shugyo* (rigorous daily training) in a manner to achieve *mis-ogi* (purification of body and mind), *sumikiri* (total clarity of body and mind), and *tashinaramu* (training for its own sake without recognition or promotion).

Always remember to clean the training area before leaving the dojo.

CENTER: MAINTAIN IT, MOVE FROM IT, AND BECOME IT.

All performance and execution of aikido techniques focus and center on the con-cepts of maintaining your center, moving from your center, and becoming the center.

We all know the center as the point within a circle or sphere that is of equal distance from all points on the circumference. In aikido, it is the point from which one pivots, rotates, or revolves. The center is the source of influence, action, or power and is the focus of interest and concern.

Maintaining your center means to find that part of your body that is at your exact center. Think of the centerline as that line that divides the body directly in half running from head to toe. Then run a second line that equally divides the top from the bottom. Now draw a third line that equally divides the front from the back. The point where all three lines intersect is the center. It is usually a point just below your navel and inside between your hipbones. By maintaining your center, you maintain your balance.

Maintaining your center also suggests maintaining your mental and emotional center. It is important not to be caught up in the other person's plans and action but to stay centered on who you are and how you want to handle the situation.

Physiologically, moving from the center means that the action initiates and is generated from the hip area. Your body moves as one with your hip, or your cen-ter, leading the way. If your head leads, you will be off-balance in the forward direc-tion. If your feet lead, your body will become off-balance backward. By moving from the center, your head can be aligned over your feet and your balance main-tained. When turning, turn your body as one from your center. With your hands aligned on the centerline, simply move your hips to turn. Your body, moving from the center, moves as a single unit. This allows the utilization of the strength and the momentum of your whole body rather than the isolated muscles of the arms. This puts great power into a technique with very little effort on your part.

Becoming the center means to connect and blend with your training partner as if you were one. There is your center within yourself. There is the center within your training partner. The shared center determines the combative distance between both people. In the beginning, when the student enters and blends into a technique, the orbital spinning is oblong, demonstrating a lack of a stable center, causing a wobble. Eventually, with consistent and persistent training, the student enters and blends. The motion is a circle in which the two members become and move as one.

The center becomes the pivot point from which all movements originate. Eventually, the student becomes and controls the center of the technique. One needs very little movement from the center of a circle to generate great speed and power on the outside circumference of that circle. This spinning motion of centripetal and centrifugal forces combines into a powerful and fluid execution of an aikido technique. Think of a spinning top. If the center stays straight, the top spins quickly and effortlessly. If the center constantly changes and the alignment is not straight, the top wobbles and soon topples over due to its own motion.

In the beginning, the student incorrectly circles around his or her training partner on the circumference of the circle. The advanced student becomes the center of the technique, and the training partner rotates around him or her.

Tohei Sensei stressed keeping your mind settled on the one point in the lower abdomen throughout all aspects of aikido training and practice.

POSTURE AND THE RELAXED BODY

Posture is very important in aikido. It is important to keep the spine erect and the body relaxed. Keeping the spine straight allows the central nervous system to function at its optimal level. This posture provides space between the vertebras and the nerves to go optimally from the spinal column to the part of the body they attach to and activate.

Relaxation also allows the body to function at its optimal level. Tension cuts off needed circulation. Relaxation increases circulation and conserves energy. Tension provides antagonistic resistance to slow movement and prevents a flowing motion. Most beginning students do not even know that they are tense. As they progress and become advanced students, their ability to relax increases, allowing them to move faster, freer, with more fluidity and responsiveness.

You can often tell a more advanced student by the tension in his or her body. When beginning students grab, they use their whole arm. Often the initiation is jerky. An advanced student will grab with the hand muscles, but leave his or her arms and shoulders relaxed. The grip slides onto and melts into the body. The grip establishes a connection without undue telegraphing or disruption. This applies to offense and defense. Once grabbed, if the defender tenses too much the attacker can sense movement and offer counterresistance. A relaxed body is the sign of an advanced student.

One way to increase relaxation is to breathe at a normal rate no matter what movement or technique one is doing. Under stress, one tends to hyperventilate or forget to breathe. Normal breathing signals a loss of stress. Beginning students breathe either too much or too little. Intermediate students coordinate their breathing consciously with the execution of the techniques. Advanced students simply relax and breathe.

Tohei Sensei stressed keeping the body completely relaxed during all aspects of aikido training and practice.

STRUCTURAL ALIGNMENT

Structural alignment refers to how students hold their body and how they align and connect with their training partner's body. Structure is the manner in which something is constructed, composed, and organized according to its natural organic interrelatedness. Alignment is the adjustment or arrangement along a line, creating a state of agreement and cooperation and increasing responsiveness. Structural alignment applies to how one holds one's body posture and the way one aligns with the body of one's training partner.

Structural alignment of one's own body means holding the body vertically in a way that allows the skeletal system naturally to support itself. The legs are aligned directly over the feet, and over them the neck and shoulders, over the spine, supported by the hips, support the head. A good way to think of structural alignment is correct posture. If you take an imaginary string from the middle of the top of your head and pull upward, all the bones of the body would naturally align along the "plumb line." This also allows the body musculature to support the body much more easily. Structural alignment also maintains the center and the centerline.

Structural alignment also refers to the way one connects and blends with one's training partner. Rather than opposing the partner's force by directly resisting it or opposing it at a direct angle, advanced students align their skeletal system with that of their training partner. This alignment makes a very strong connection and allows the advanced students to directly transmit their movements and take control of their training partner's skeletal system. This is especially powerful when the training partner's skeletal system aligns in such a way as to create a locking of the joints. This alignment simulates a chain manipulated until the links lock into a solid alignment. Then one movement moves the entire skeletal system. This can be seen in the way the entire body moves in relationship to the wrist manipulation of *kote-gaeshi* (wrist turnout) or the body's response to controlling the elbow in *shiho-nage* (four-direction throw).

Control of the elbow becomes extremely important in defenses against strikes. Failure to control the elbow, by intercepting it between the elbow and wrist, allows the elbow to bend and blend into an elbow strike.

In the beginning, one will practice *irimi-nage* (entering throw) by simply pulling the arm away. As one progress in training one will enter and blend with the motion. Eventually, the student will align the skeletal system of the arm with his or her training partner's arm until it is pointing in the exact same direction.

METSUKE: SOFT EYE FOCUS AND ENVIRONMENTAL AWARENESS

Eye contact is one of the best and easiest ways to establish contact and connection to another person. You can often feel when someone is looking at you. You can often tell something about how another person thinks or feels. People express and betray themselves by their eyes. Look deeply into someone's eyes and you will become connected to them and they to you.

Metsuke develops naturally by not really looking at anything. It is looking through the individual as if looking at some nonexistent distant horizon. Do not mistake this as gazing at the distance because that diminishes the capacity to see closeby. Think of it as observing whatever comes into your field of vision without attaching to any of it. This soft focus allows a greater use of the peripheral vision that detects movement faster than the usual focused vision.

Metsuke allows the advanced student to be more environmentally aware. Environmental awareness means being able to pay attention to the outside world as opposed to being internally absorbed in thought. The advanced student of aikido does not focus on any one particular thing; thus, he or she sees all things. In most environments, some elements fit the context and situation. In addition, some elements do not fit. Soft eye focus and environmental awareness allow the advanced student to detect the difference and to respond accordingly. In all situations, especially self-defense, the training and ability to be aware of one's surrounding before, during, and after an approach or attack is critical.

According to some sources, there is a physiological and neurological connection between pupils dilation and emotional states. The more emotional one feels the larger one's pupils dilate. The advanced student may be able to discern his training partner's intention through his or her eyes. One way to control the neurology of the eye is to control the point of focus. Maintaining a soft eye focus on the distance results in the pupils remaining at a set dilation and one's maintaining a steady emotional state. Since the soft eye focus does not stop to focus on details, but moves around to maintain environmental surveillance, the mind does not fixate on external details or internal cognition. This contributes to a calm mind and body.

To cultivate metsuke, first sit back and relax. Let yourself look around. Do not let your eyes rest too long in any one direction or on any one thing. Do not let the mind rest too long or on anything. Relaxing the eyes relaxes the mind, which in turn relaxes the body. When doing aikido, relax and look through your training partner. Do not let your eyes rest on your partner's hands or look into his or her eyes. This is an easy way to be deceived. Look at the wall behind your training partner. This allows your eyes to detect subtle clues of approach, attack, or change. Let your eyes focus on the distance and your centerline align with your shoulders and hips as you move through your technique. Do not gaze at any one point. Attempt to take in your training partner's entire form.

In the beginning, students tend to watch their opponent's hands while performing a technique. With more training and experience, they watch the eyes. Eventually, the advanced student just watches.

CONCLUSION

Advanced practitioners of aikido know the benefits of the warm-up exercises. They will establish, maintain, move from, and become the center. They will maintain correct posture, a relaxed body, and structural alignment. By establishing and maintaining a soft eye focus, the advanced practitioner will increase internal calm and external environmental awareness and sensitivity. At the end of a training session, bow, cool down, clean the dojo, and look forward to the next time.

The theories and concepts used by the advanced aikido practitioner take the art of body mechanics into the art of movement.

TIPS FOR REFINING THE ART OF BODY MECHANICS

1. Always warm up.
2. Establish, maintain, and move from your center.
3. Keep a correct posture and a relaxed body.
4. Keep structural alignment.
5. Maintain metsuke, soft eye focus.
6. Always cool down.

Chapter 6
The Art of Movement

The theories and concepts used by the advanced aikido practitioner include the art of body mechanics, movement, and engagement.

One of the characteristics of an advanced practitioner of aikido is the way they move. Ultimately, their movement alone becomes the technique itself. Their movement enters and blends with an attack. Their movement redirects and unbalances the attacker. Their movement throws or immobilizes the attacker. Their movement releases the connect with the attacker and moves on to the next attacker. Their movement is fluid and effortless.

There are many concepts that aid in achieving this type of movement. These concepts include following the contour of the body, utilizing power from behind or beneath, using circular motion and forces, following the momentum and inertia of the movement, minimizing movement, the wave movement, and dropping weight.

Ultimately, footwork and body turning initiate all movement.

CONTOUR: FOLLOW IT
Following the contours of the body makes all movement efficient and effective. When intercepting an arm, first connect, block, and control the elbow, then follow the body contour by sliding down the forearm to the wrist. On *irimi-nage* (entering throw), allow the hand to follow the arm or body contour up into the jaw line. On *sayu-undo* (a kokyu-nage, or breath/timing throw) let the hand, held palm up, follow the body's contour up into the jaw line. When blending, hug the body and allow your body to follow the contour of your training partner's body. Strikes can also follow the body contour to their destination.

Once initial interception, contact, and connection have been established, it must be maintained in the most natural and least detectable manner possible. The easiest way to accomplish this is to allow all movement to follow the natural contour of the body. When entering, allow the attacker's body to tell you where the openings are by following the contour of the arm into the body, making your own movement virtually invisible or keeping it hidden within the bodylines. When blending, align yourself with the contour of the attacker's body, making your bodies move as one body. Movement that gently follows the contour of the body also sends a subtle message to the attacker's body, controlling and utilizing the response. As will be presented in the wave motion section, to suggest an upward movement will naturally bring about a resistant downward response, which can then be used to blend with, unbalance, throw, or immobilize the attacker. A subtle movement backward along the body's contour will elicit a response in which your opponent's weight is thrown forward. This forward reaction can be utilized to facilitate the successful resolution of the technique.

POWER FROM BEHIND OR BENEATH

From where do you generate your power and in what direction is it most powerful? For example, how should one attempt to move a car? A beginning student may stand in front of the car and try to pull it. An intermediate student may align with the car and move it from the side. Eventually, the advanced student knows that it is easiest to push a car from behind. Equally, one can lift more weight by getting underneath it and pushing with the large muscles of the legs than by bending over and lifting from above with the smaller muscles of the back and legs. While this concept is hard to explain in words, it is easy to experience and validate simply by trying it.

The advanced aikido practitioner will move his or her center and centerline back behind the attacker's. This movement allows the alignment of the muscular and skeletal structural system forward and into the center. Techniques that are executed with the body positioned in front of the attacker place the body structurally at a disadvantage. The alignment is not structurally supported and is vulnerable to loss of balance.

One way to generate greater power from behind is to move from the rear hip and leg when doing a pivot or tenkan. Initially when turning, it will feel natural to move off your front foot and step. Next, it will feel more natural to pivot or rotate around your own center or the center of the technique. Later, the front will begin to become the center and the rear hip and leg will rotate, creating power. Keep your forward hand and leg in place, and rotate your rear leg to perform tenkan (circular turning step).

Likewise, it is easier to move an object by getting beneath it and pushing with your legs than to stand over it and pull with your arms from above. Dropping your elbow underneath allows your body alignment to move upward. When power is transmitted upward from beneath, one uproots one's training partner and he or she loses balance. To push downward would only help your partner stabilize and ground him- or herself.

Gravity will naturally place the weight on the underside. Rather than hanging on from above, it is easier to support something from underneath. Therefore, let the weight of your arm settle on the underside, beneath. Picture a metal rod running under the arm holding it up. Let the mental metal bar hold the arm rather than using any muscular strength. Movement originating from the center in the hips region comes from underneath in relationship to the upper body weight of the attacker. Movement from underneath uproots and unbalances the attacker, making it easier to blend with, redirect, unbalance, throw, or immobilize him or her.

CIRCULAR MOTION AND FORCES

The two most common circular forces are the centrifugal and centripetal forces. Centrifugal, outward from the center, force is the tendency of those things held on the outside circumference of a circle to move farther and farther outward. Centripetal force means force directed toward the center, pulling those objects held closest to the center of a rotating circle inward. An object pulled toward the center moves inward while an object pushed away from the center will move outward on a circular path.

Circular movement avoids colliding with opposing, approaching, and attacking forces. Circular movement facilitates harmony and aids in taking away your training partner's balance. Circular movement explodes with power when it has a stable center.

Eventually, with persistent and consistent training, students take and become the center of the technique. They bring their training partner's head in toward the center. This causes the training partner's legs to travel outward on the circumference of the circular rotating path. His or her legs will not be able to keep pace and the training partner will easily lose balance. As with the spinning top mentioned earlier, the circular motion, momentum, and force stays constant, while the center is stable and aligned. If the center moves, or if the alignment is not straight, the top loses its smooth circular path, wobbles around, and eventually falls over. Similarly, a figure skater spins, pulling his or her hands and arms into a tight center to increase the speed of the spin. When the skater expands out from the tight center, the spinning slows and stops.

Another aspect of circular motion and force pertains to the circle of power of an approach or attack. When an attack reaches its maximum extension, it has its maximum power. Anything beyond that range and the circle of power will have a diminished ability to resist. Your training partner's power is contained within his or her circle. Extended beyond the power boundaries of the circle, your partner is powerless. Eventually, advanced students of aikido will always remain within their circle of power, while extending their training partners beyond theirs.

In watching and performing all aikido techniques, it is possible to follow the circular path. There may be a subtle rotation of the wrist at the moment and point of contact. There may be a horizontal circular pattern in the footwork and movement. There may be a vertical circular path moving up and down. All motion is circular motion.

Eventually, the student of aikido initiates and generates all basic aikido movement by *tai-sabaki* (body turning) that draws the training partner in, and then blends with the partner's approach or attack in a circular path. In judo and jujitsu, when pulled you push and when pushed you pull. O'Sensei Morihei Ueshiba added that when pulled, push in a circular direction and when pushed, pull and turn in a circular direction.

In the beginning, one will struggle with moving one's body in a circular path because most people are used to moving linearly. As one progresses in training, one will move one's body in a circle while maintaining somewhat of a linear mind. Eventually, the advanced student thinks and moves in a circular pattern, while understanding and applying the concepts of circular forces.

MOVEMENT, MOMENTUM, AND INERTIA

Aikido is a dynamic art. At advanced levels, the movement itself becomes the technique. The movement is to enter and blend with, then redirect and unbalance, then throw or control. Movement is the process of getting from one point to another. Momentum is the concept that even after the initial force that set something in motion ends, the force will continue the motion in that direction. Like the extension of ki, momentum continues beyond the body. Inertia is the concept that something at rest will stay at rest unless acted upon, and something in motion will stay in motion unless acted upon. The advanced practitioner of aikido knows that to block or stop the forward momentum and inertia of an attacker or strike takes more force than to intercept and utilizes its energy. Aikido is based on the principles of nonresistance by aligning or harmonizing with the energy and force of an attack. The greater the momentum intertia, energy, of an attack, the easier and greater the responding technique.

In the beginning, one waits for contact to occur. It is very difficult, if not impossible, to move a training partner's body while he or she is standing still. The timing is incorrect to take full advantage of momentum, and inertia of the initial attack or approach. In the beginning, one moves step by step. As one progresses in training, one begins to move just before one's training partner reaches to grab or strike one. Eventually, the advanced student moves with his or her training partner. There is no break in connection or movement. The advanced student's movement takes full advantage of momentum and inertia by continuously adjusting the *ma-ai* (distance) to maintain *musubi* (connection) that keeps the inertia and momentum of the waza. He or she moves in one continuous motion.

MINIMIZE: BIG AIKIDO TO SMALL AIKIDO

Aikido comes in all sizes. As one matures in aikido, one often sees that by applying the concepts, the technique actually becomes smaller and smaller. Big aikido becomes small aikido.

As mentioned earlier, in the beginning one tends to move in linear patterns and directions. The patterns begin to become circular, but those circles are rather large. As one progresses in training, one becomes more fluid and the circles become smaller.

The advanced student who moves minimally becomes the center of the circle. The circle, at the center, becomes a dot. Advanced students suggest to their training partner that he or she move. Advanced students rotate their wrists in circular directions. This subtle rotation changes the alignment of their training partner's skeletal system, reducing or eliminating the effectiveness of his or her muscular system. The more advanced the student, the more he or she will begin to move his or her weight internally rather than externally. There will be very little noticeable movement as the weight and momentum move from the center in a circular motion that is so small (yet powerful) that it is unperceived. Only years of conscious practice will facilitate this type of action.

Likewise, to minimize movement and motion, move only that part of the body necessary for the effective and efficient execution of the technique. Many students will move their entire body when the actual movement is simply twisting or a turning of the center. A circling of the arm may be required, but the student will twist his or her body. While entering, the student may feel more protected by a bob-and-weave movement when it adds nothing to the overall effectiveness, and compromises the efficiency of the technique. Many people will watch other's head and shoulders for signs, cues, or clues of an impending approach or attack.

Eventually, more advanced students will not telegraph their intentions, by entering and executing without moving, or by keeping movement of the head and shoulders to a minimum. Minimize your movements, and use only those movements that contribute directly to the effective and efficient execution of the technique.

LEVERAGE AND PIVOT POINTS

Aikido uses the physics law of leverage to overpower a larger training partner. The use of leverage allows a small initial investment of power or ability to act effectively and gain relatively high returns.

A pivot point is that point around which everything else turns. A deceptive part of aikido is that often the point of contact is not the point of movement. The leverage or pivot point remains stable while the aikido practitioner moves around it. Rather than force the point of contact or resistance, use it as a pivot or leverage point and move something else. That something else may be to move your rear hip in a *tenkan* (circular pivot step) to get your body behind your training partner. It may be to drop your elbow below the grabbed wrist to get the leverage from underneath.

Tenbin-nage, the elbow-locking throw, illustrates the use of pivot and leverage point. As the lower hand is held securely into the center, it becomes the pivot point from which the technique rotates. The elbow then is raised up as a leverage point, taking the body off-balance by forcing it to compensate for its position to minimize the potential damage to the joint. The shoulder is rotated up and forward, steering the technique toward a *kuzushi*, balance-breaking point. As you step forward, your arm rotates at the leverage point from palm up to palm down, placing full body power behind and beneath the technique.

WAVE

The wave motion is a rolling movement. It is continuous. In many advanced aikido movements, one can observe the rolling motion of the wave. The motion of the vertical wave movement is up-down, down–up, down-up-down, or up-down-up. One can also use the wave movement horizontally in an in-out, out-in, in-out-in, or out-in-out pattern. The initial move may meet with some resistance. Rather than resist your training partner's force, let up on the pressure slightly. Done smoothly, the wave motion overrides the neurology of your training partner. He or she will resist the first motion, but will accept and let go of resistance for the second. The wave motion somewhat overloads or confuses the neurological system, which is used to responding and resisting. Immediate sequential reapplication of the movement will usually meet with little or no resistance. Your training partner will be temporarily tactilely disoriented and receptive.

DROPPING YOUR WEIGHT

In the beginning of aikido training, the student will attempt to force a technique by using muscular strength. While this does work, the techniques will only benefit the stronger opponent. However, this is not the way of aikido. It is hard for students to realize that strength is actually working against the effectiveness of their technique.

As one progresses in training, one begins to depend more on technical proficiency than strength, but will still have a tendency to try to muscle through the technique. One will be more relaxed. Eventually, the student of aikido will become technically proficient but will gain the ability to use body weight to make his or her application much more effective and powerful. Rather than force a technique, the advanced student will set up the mechanics of the application and then drop his or her body weight into it. The strength of the entire body is stronger than just the arms. Bring the weight of your entire body, as relaxed dead weight, to bear in the direction of your training partner's kuzushi, or balance point, and it will make throwing your partner an easy task.

Bending at the waist or using the muscular force of the upper body does not drop one's body weight. Rather, drop your weight by subtly bending or buckling your knees. Accomplish all vertical movement in aikido by naturally bending your knees to lower your body. You can use your body weight by leaning or resting against your training partner, letting your natural dead weight extend toward his or her balance point. A subtle movement or dropping of weight when your training partner is off-balance will facilitate an effective and efficient technique.

Sensei Tohei stressed that the weight held on the underside follows the natural laws of gravity and should be applied in all aspects of aikido training and practice.

FOOTWORK

Footwork is the basis of all movement. To move vertically simply bend your knees, keeping the spin erect and aligned and maintaining good posture. To move horizontally, move your feet. The basic footwork patterns, or ashi-sabaki, in aikido are the natural step forward, the shuffle, the cross-step, and the tenkan, a circular step and turn.

The natural step forward, or *ayumi-ashi*, is a walk forward step. Like most movement in aikido, the natural stride is respected and maintained in order to keep correct posture, structural alignment, and balance. Simply place one foot in front of the other as if walking down the street. Try to maintain your head and center on the same horizontal plane with no bobbing up and down. A variation is the C-shaped step in which the rear foot is brought in to the other foot and then back out forward in a semicircle or C shape. This step is commonly used when delivering a strike, or *atemi*. The C-shaped semicircular step can move your body slightly off the attack line without interrupting or intercepting the momentum of the attack.

The shuffle step, or *tsugi-ashi*, is like a fencer's lunge, but not so overextended. Two ways to execute the shuffle step are to first move the forward foot and then bring the rear foot up or to first move the rear foot up to the front and then move the front foot forward. Like the C-shaped semicircular step, the shuffle can take you slightly off the attack line as you enter into the approach and attack.

The cross-step is less common in aikido. To advance forward, keep the front foot in place and step forward with the rear foot crossing over in front or behind the front foot. To retreat, maintain the rear foot and step back, with the front foot crossing over in front of or behind the rear foot. During all movement, maintain an erect and aligned posture without movement up or down, and maintain a steady, stable forward momentum.

The circular step and turn, or tenkan, is the most characteristic footwork pattern of aikido. While it is a simple step and turn, it can generate great power. From a neutral ready stance, take a walking step forward and then turn your body, swinging the leg in a half-circle, turning the body 180 degrees. Use your front leg as the pivot point, and turn using the rear hip. This movement can be done to the front, *omote*, or the rear, *ura*. It can also be combined with an entering move and become *irimi-tenkan*.

A good practice exercise for improving footwork is to alternate 90-degree tenkan and 180-degree tenkan. For additional skill building for timing and flow, try doing this alternating pattern to the beat of music. Rhythm training can greatly improve coordination. Start with relatively slow music that has a steady beat and slowly, over time, increase the speed or tempo and the duration.

BODY TURNING

Closely associated with the movement of the feet is the movement or turning of the body. As mentioned earlier, an old jujitsu saying encourages one to pull when pushed and push when pulled. This is the concept of aligning, harmonizing, or going with the direction of energy. O'Sensei Morihei Ueshiba added the circular body turning by saying when pushed, pull and turn, when pulled, push and turn.

CONCLUSION

One of the most unique characteristics of aikido is the way that the advanced practitioner moves. Many say that it looks a lot like dancing. There is something very graceful and rhythmic about aikido. The full body movement and momentum of aikido follows the contour of the body, generating its power from behind and beneath in circular movement, momentum, and inertia. Aikido generates the most power by minimizing its movement, using pivot and leverage points, overcoming resistance with wave movements, and dropping one's weight. To move vertically, the advanced practitioner bends his or her knees. To move horizontally, the advanced practitioner uses footwork and body turning.

TIPS FOR REFINING THE ART OF MOVEMENT

1. Keep your body relaxed, your mind calm, and your posture structurally aligned.
2. Breathe slowly and deeply.
3. Move in one constant consistent rhythm or speed throughout the movement.
4. Move so that power is generated from behind or beneath.
5. Practice footwork and body turning.
6. Keep a positive attitude.
7. Consistently and persistently train with honest and genuine intent and intensity.
8. Be patient.

Chapter 7
The Art of Engagement

After advanced aikido practitioners apply and practice the theories and concepts of the art of body mechanics and movement, they must learn the art of engagement.

Within any conflict, there are rules of engagement. These rules dictate the directives, structure, and means by which contact will be made and the conflicts fought. There are supposed to be rules for fighting. Seldom are these rules of engagement adhered to because they are often idealistic and impractical, and they do not always contribute to the survival of the combatants. Some would say that if you actually have to use aikido in a fight, then you have not learned the highest levels of aikido. Aikido is a martial art that supports love, peace, and harmony and is to be employed only in loving protection and as a last resort.

It is not the rules, but the art of engagement that makes aikido unique as a martial art in which a practitioner directly enters and blends with conflict but upholds nonviolence and nonresistance as its truths. It is the concepts that direct the tactical techniques used when an opponent or enemy approaches or attacks. These concepts include the symbols of the triangle, circle, and square. These concepts address the distance, contact, connection, blending, balance breaking, lines of attacks and centerlines, timing, and the lingering spirit connection that leaves a lasting impression after the conflict is successfully and peacefully concluded.

THE SANGEN: THE TRIANGLE, CIRCLE, AND SQUARE

O'Sensei Morihei Ueshiba often attempted to communicate the essence of aikido by drawing three geometrical shapes or symbols. The first is a triangle. The second is a circle. The third is a square. The number three, representing a trilogy, is important in mythology and mysticism.

The triangle represents the aikido triangular ready stance, used for stability, and the musubi, or triangulation point, for breaking one's opponent's balance. The triangle represents entering by the forward point of the triangle and stepping off the attack line from the triangle's rear points. The triangle represents the interdependency of body, mind, and spirit. Substitute ki for universal energy or spirit, and you have the unity of body, mind, and ki.

The circle represents the circular path that all aikido movements follow. There are vertical and horizontal circles. There are large and small circles. There are circles that are so small and subtle that motion is beyond observation, but is felt when received. Philosophically, the circle represents eternity since there is no beginning and no end. Likewise, the training and discipline in the subtleties of aikido will keep building on themselves. There is no beginning or end to aikido. There is just the training.

The square represents stability. As two triangles placed side by side, the square does not lose balance. The square contains two equilateral triangles.

Another interpretation (DOBSON AND MILLER 1993, P. 153) is that of the fight, flight, freeze, and flow response patterns. The two triangles facing each other represent a fight. The next, facing the same direction, is flight. The square is a freeze response. All responses (attack, fight, flight, and freeze) are fear-based responses. Only the circle represents the flow response and a means to avoid and neutralize the power of an attack.

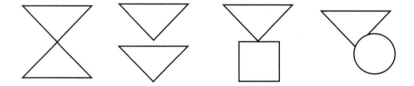

The sequential process of aikido can be illustrated and seen in these three geometrical shapes. Two individuals connect and enter, moving forward as two triangles, both entering slightly off the line of attack. They connect, blend, and become one square. As one turns, so does the other, and they become a circle redirecting the energy of both attack and defense. The circle becomes a triangle used to balance. The throw is secured as a square, eventually separating into two triangles again. Masatake Fujita Shihan is the secretary general of the Aikikai World Headquarters and Aikikai Foundation. He would say "to enter as the sharp point of the triangle, move as a circle, and suppress with the firmness of the square." (FUJITA 1997, P. 24).

The footwork of aikido is also represented in these shapes. As one steps forward, one steps off the line of attack (1), tenkan 180-degrees (2), and steps forward (3) creating a triangle. Done omote and ura, the two triangles become a square. The blending step of tenkan becomes the circle and this is the basic movement of aikido.

MA-AI: COMBATIVE DISTANCE

One of the most important concepts for advanced aikido training is *ma-ai*, or combative distance. Ma-ai refers to assuming the proper distance in the initial stance as well as maintaining an effective and efficient distance from an opponent for the execution and safety of performing a technique.

Too close and the technique is too small and cramped. This renders it ineffective and is easy to resist. If one executes a technique too closely, it is easy for one's training partner to strike you. It is important to maintain the appropriate ma-ai from the time you make visual and mental contact, through the execution, and to the moving away with lingering spirit.

If you are too far away, the technique will fail to connect or will pull the wrong person off-balance. Being too far away from your training partner leads to poor form and injury.

One can learn and develop only a basic sense of ma-ai intellectually. Like so many advanced concepts of aikido, one must experience it through consistent and persistent training.

The cultivation of a sense of ma-ai takes patience and practice. First, relax and let your training partner slowly approach you. Try to pay close attention to your sense of distance. Begin to feel your training partner as he or she gets just within your reach. Just as you feel your partner's presence, but before he or she actually makes physical contact, begin to move. To practice, move when your training partner is too close and too far away and evaluate what happens. You will begin to develop a sense of distance.

In the beginning, one will define ma-ai as when one's training partner is too far away to strike or so close that he or she already has. As one progresses in training one will define ma-ai only in terms of appropriate but adequate physical execution of the technique. Eventually, the advanced student will naturally connect, enter, bridge the appropriate ma-ai, and move, maintaining the appropriate distance necessary to be effective and efficient.

NONRESISTANCE

Fundamental to aikido is the concept of nonresistance. Rather than resistance, or meeting force with force, in aikido one learns to use one's training partner's momentum, effort, and intent against that person.

Accomplish nonresistance by getting off the line of attack and allowing the momentum and inertia of your training partner to become overextended and carry him or her safely out of range and off-balance. Likewise, if grabbed, accomplish nonresistance by following and redirecting the force or energy of the initial attack. It is easiest to accomplish this by following the circular movement on the radius or circumference of the arm's range of motion rather than pushing into its muscle and strength.

Lines: Attack Lines and Centerlines

The advanced student of aikido pays close attention to two lines. The first is the attack line. The second is the centerline.

The attack line is the line that denotes the direction of the attack. It is as if a line were drawn directly out from the body toward you. Many beginning students will remain in the path of the attack, on the line. Eventually, advanced students will always get out of the way or off the attack line.

The centerline is an imaginary line that runs from the top of your head straight down, like a plum line, to a place between your feet. The centerline divides the body into a left and right side. Advanced students will keep their hands on this centerline and will align their centerline with their attacker's centerline, while getting off the attack line. When a defender holds his hands on his centerline, everything the attacker does is on the outside and away for the vital targets on the torso or trunk of the body. The centerline when defended provides safety; when violated or exploited, the centerline is a direct line to defeat, pain, and injury. Therefore, when involved in an engagement or altercation, one's hands are held in front on the centerline, and all movement is initiated through footwork and body turning. When contact and connection are made into the opponent's center and centerline, it is easy to control and direct his or her structural alignments and initiate a loss of balance.

The cultivation of awareness and the ability to use these lines takes patience and practice. First, as your training partner approaches to attack, begin to align and connect mentally your centerline. Just before making physical contact, smoothly step off the attack line.

CONTACT: INITIATING, INTERCEPTING, AND INTENT

By taking the initiative to establish the first contact in a fight, you take control of the situation and have a decided advantage. Whoever initiates contact and connects has some advantage in the execution of a technique.

Interception means to take possession during an attempt to reach a goal. Two nonparallel lines intercept at their point of contact. Generally, because aikido is primarily a defensive martial art, your training partner will attempt to strike or grab you. As this happens, before your partner achieves his or her intended goal, your movement should intercept them.

As mentioned earlier, intent is to firmly and steadfastly follow through on a goal. When you move with honest intent, you move in a meaningful goal-directed way with full motivation and momentum. When your training partner approaches and attacks you, your intent should be that you have invited them in, and it is you, not they, who are in full control.

In the beginning, students will wait until their training partner grabs them before making any movement. This often turns the technique into a standing static technique rather than a fluid dynamic one.

As one progresses in training, one will begin to move as one's training partner approaches. This makes the technique much more fluid and uses the momentum of the attack. Eventually, advanced students actually move slightly into their training partner's approach and initiate the contact and connection. They will offer their hand in such a way that the hand position dictates the grab and sets up the responding technique.

To begin practicing initiating contact, have a training partner slowly strike at you. At first, just stand as a target and establish that your partner will in fact make contact and hit you. It is important in training to have partners who will not "give" you the technique but make you actually work for it. Next, as the strike gets close, simply raise your hand on your centerline, intercepting and initiating contact with the striking arm. You gain the best control by intercepting and initiating contact at the elbow, since from the elbow it is easy to control the arm and the body of the attacker. The interception and initiating of contact does not need a lot of force or power to be effective. In fact, the least amount of force or power allows the strike to be blended with and redirected in true "aiki" fashion. Intercepting and redirecting are effective and efficient ways to utilize the momentum and inertia of the strike. The advanced practitioner of aikido learns patience and confidence by waiting until the very last, least expected, moment to get off the attack line, intercept, and redirect the attack.

MUSUBI: CONNECTING

Connecting with your training partner is crucial for the execution of effective techniques. If you do not connect, it does not matter what you do. The connection starts when you first sense your training partner. This may be a vague feeling as if someone is looking at you or an actual visual sighting that reveals a person is headed toward you with intent to do damage. This preliminary connection sets up the aikido technique. Your training partner usually telegraphs the attack. Eventually, the advanced student pays attention to subtle clues and cues as to where the partner's hands and shoulders are and what is the line of attack. The advanced student aligns himself or herself and connects with the intention and momentum of the attacker even before making any physical contact or connection.

Once physical contact is established, the connection is a tactile or kinesthetic feeling. Usually the person is too close to depend effectively on visual contact, and the sense of feeling replaces it. Beginning students of aikido will still attempt to keep their eyes on the technique. They often watch their hands. Advanced students simply trust their sense of touch and momentum to communicate to them. They stay connected to their training partner and stay informed about what he or she is doing. This connected sensitivity builds up after many years of practice and experience.

TIMING: RHYTHM

Timing is crucial for the effective and efficient execution of aikido techniques. Timing means that the movement of the uke and the tori synchronize as one. Timing is finding the tempo that will produce results. It is the control of speed to impact for maximum power. Timing is everything.

Timing is the ability to sense the pace and tempo of an attack. Aikido blending is the art of matching and flowing with that rhythm. It is like two dancers on a dance floor who are dancing together to the same beat. As one moves with the music, the other will unconsciously respond. Two dancers dancing to different beats have trouble connecting with each other. They often collide. There is no harmony or unity between them. Two dancers, two people, in rhythm with each other, form a close bond.

Timing is more important than speed. There is a minimal amount of effectiveness or power in speed if you do not hit a target or accomplish a goal. Many martial artists train in speed but forget accuracy. Timing is the ability to move at the speed appropriate to combine power and accuracy.

In the beginning, one has no rhythm and is unaware of the rhythm of the approaching training partner. One will wait until actually seeing an attack or feeling a grab. One waits until the rhythm stops.

As one progresses in training, one will detect and respond earlier by watching for signs of the approaching rhythm. Students begin to move, or dance well, with each other. They begin to hear the same musical beat, but have some difficulty moving in synchronization with their training partner. In the beginning, one is concerned with speed. This concern actually interferes with effective and efficient execution and slows training progress.

Eventually, the advanced student will detect minimal cues that reveal intent and rhythm. Advanced students hear and respond to the rhythm before their attacker can even touch them. They enter and blend into their partner's rhythm. They become one with the rhythm and join the dance in perfect harmony. They become the center beat and gently lead the attacker into their rhythm and influence. They also know when to break the rhythm to interrupt and unbalance their training partner. Advanced students train slowly and focus on form and accuracy. They forget about speed because they know that speed comes on its own with consistent and persistent training with conscious intent and intensity.

AWASE: BLENDING

Blending is the act and art of intimately and unobtrusively combining various elements into an integrated whole to produce a harmonious effect. Blending implies making an honest and genuine connection to one's training partner by developing sensitivity and responsiveness. Blending means to "go with" or "flow" with the power, force, momentum, and inertia of an attack. Blending follows the rule, mentioned earlier, that states when pushed, pull, and when pulled, push. Rather than resisting an attack, blend with it. By blending with the movements of one's opponent, one learns to be effective and efficient with the minimal amount of effort.

The ability to blend with an attack is one of the most important aspects of aikido. The "aiki" way of nonresistance is to never confront force with more force, and never to meet resistance with more resistance. In many aiki movements, O'Sensei Morihei Ueshiba added circular movement to blending. When pushed, pull and simultaneously turn from the center. When pulled, push and simultaneously turn from the center. The simultaneously turning from the center assists you in getting off the attack line and becoming the center of the technique. This way you join with the power, momentum, and inertia of your training partner's approach or attack. Blending allows you to get maximum results with little or no effort.

Think of blending as being like one of those rotating doors. First, when you get to the door, thinking that it is locked, you expect to be met with some resistance. You may even put some added force into opening it. To your surprise, the door is not only unlocked, but also unlatched, and flies open easily. You can feel your body propelled forward off-balance. You try to hold on to the door to maintain some sense of balance. The door not only continues to open and fails to offer stability, but it also rotates at the center, spinning you out of control. The door behind you rotates too, and you are not only pulled from the front but now also pushed from the rear in a tight circular motion until you let go and fall flat on your face. This is blending. When attacked, rather than forcibly resisting, the advanced aikido practitioner intercepts, moves off the attack line, and turns his or her body, redirecting the attack until the attacker is off-balance.

KUZUSHI: BALANCE BREAKING AND TRIANGULATION

Triangulation is the theory of balance based on using three points. Think of your balance as a three-legged stool. If you take one of those legs away, you topple easily in that direction. The actual point of triangulation is the distance of a shin in an equal-sided triangle. There is a point out in front of your feet and one behind. Take a natural ready stance. Picture an imaginary line extending from foot to foot. From the center of this imaginary line, directly beneath the center of your body, measure out one shin's length to the front and the back. The point at the end of this line, to the front or the rear, is the triangulation point. This is the position of the third leg of the stool. When falling, your opponent will naturally attempt to fill this space, at this point, to maintain stability and balance. If your opponent uses you for that support and then you step away, your opponent will naturally fall into the emptiness created.

Aiming at *kuzushi* (balance-breaking) points makes it easier to unbalance anyone. Extending the body beyond this distance, in any direction, will take away power and balance. Extended off-balance and beyond the circle of power, one loses the priority of striking and movement and tends only to focus one's concern on falling.

In the beginning, students know very little about breaking balance. They simply follow the technique as demonstrated and, if lucky, throw or take their training partner safely down to the ground or mat. As one progresses in training one becomes more aware of the concept of triangulation and begins to aim the throw. The advanced student knows and uses triangulation.

When intercepting and initiating contact, move and blend off the attack line so that the attacker moves or bends toward the kuzushi balance point, making that person unstable and unbalanced from the first move. Keeping an opponent or attacker constantly looking for the kuzushi balance point makes that person easy to control. His or her priority is on gaining balance to keep from falling and not on attacking you. Very few practitioners of martial arts teach or train in the ability to continually strike even when off-balance or falling. Due to a lack of a secure foundation, if an opponent or attacker does strike while off-balance, there is minimal power in the strike.

When practicing to find and develop sensitivity for the kuzushi balance-breaking point, move into any technique slowly. At the point of balance, pause. Move around, relaxed and slowly, until you can feel the balance being broken. In the case of shiho-nage, aim the back of your wrist directly toward the rear (ura) kuzushi balance point; a slight rolling of the wrist will accomplish the removing of your opponent's balance. In *shayu-undo kokyu-nage*, your forearm is placed alongside the opponent's jaw line from chin to ear. Raise your arm slightly to suggest lift, and then let the weight of your elbow drop toward the rear (ura) kuzushi balance point, bending your opponent's head backward and removing your opponent's balance. In kote-gaeshi, the wrist is turned out and down toward the front (omote) or rear (ura) kuzushi balance point. Tenbin-nage uses a slight rotation of the elbow and shoulder upward and then down in a wave motion toward the front (omote) kuzushi balance point. All throws can be facilitated by using the triangulation of the kuzushi balance point.

ZANSHIN: LINGERING CONNECTION

Once you throw a training partner, there remains a connection or link through focus and concentration. Think of the musubi with a training partner as making the statement, "I have you now." Hold on to that statement after you have thrown your training partner, as if to say, "I still have you." That lingering connection or statement of intent is *zanshin*.

CONCLUSION

The art of engagement goes far beyond the rules of engagement. The advanced practitioner of aikido develops sensitivity and skill in mastering the concept of nonresistance, attack lines and centerlines, timing and rhythm, and the intercepting and initiating of contact. Further, the advanced aikido practitioner understands and applies sangen, ma-ai, musubi, awase, kuzushi, and zanshin.

The advanced aikido practitioner understands and applies the theories, concepts, and art of body mechanics, movement, and engagement. They also learn the advanced techniques, refining the fundamentals of strikes and feints, throws and locks, applications, combinations, and reversals.

TIPS FOR REFINING THE ART OF ENGAGEMENT

1. Relax and breathe.
2. Maintain a calm mind.
3. Practice awareness of distance.
4. Blend with an attack by intercepting, initiating contact, and subtle redirection.
5. Aim all techniques through the center and toward the kuzushi balance point.
6. Allow your spirit and energy to remain connected and lingering.

Part Three

Advanced Techniques:
Refining the Fundamentals

Chapter 8
Throws and Locks

The advanced aikido practitioner applies advanced techniques by continually refining the fundamentals of throws and locks.

The beginning student in basic aikido learns the basic stances, grabs, strikes, and defensive techniques. There is much more for the advanced student—many throws and locks are more advanced. There are infinite variations and refinements of basic techniques created by applying advanced aikido concepts. Eventually, all students of aikido must learn all techniques from all attacks and approaches, using the right and left hands, and going to the front (omote) or rear (ura).

The level of smoothness and effectiveness illustrates and demonstrates proficiency from the elementary through intermediate and advanced stages of training and experience. In the beginning, one will think aikido looks easy. Eventually, the student of aikido will make it look easy.

ADVANCED UKEMI

To be able to practice advanced techniques and variations, the advanced student needs an advanced training partner. Being able to execute a proper ukemi (break fall) protects your body while you are being thrown or pinned. Being on the receiving end of techniques also enhances your understanding of their dynamics.

Ukemi are accompanied by striking or slapping the mat in order to absorb the shock of the fall. Uke can also reduce the amount of shock by keeping the body relaxed in the form of a ball, and continuing movement and momentum as soon as one regains a solid and stable footing.

When blending before executing a throwing or locking technique, one's training partner must give full intent and momentum to the attack and be able to follow or flow along with the movement. This training to blend and flow with another movement is excellent training both offensively and defensively.

Rather than taking a back fall, the advanced training partner will execute ukemi by rolling backward into a standing position.

Eventually, students of aikido use ukemi for the purpose of pins or locks, while either flat on their face or on their back. The training partner will bend his knees and help break the fall by placing a hand and arm down on the mat toward the kuzushi point. Some students of aikido do not take the ukemi as a roll; doing so may twist the arm to the point of injury.

One performs a basic break fall on an elementary level simply by lying out after a roll. Eventually with persistent and consistent training and conditioning, the student of aikido performs ukemi by executing the break fall more from an aerial flip.

REFINING BASIC THROWS

There are several basic throws in aikido. These will be reviewed here briefly before presenting the more advanced throws. There are many ways to execute every technique in aikido. These throws, along with their subtle variations, keep the possibilities for aikido infinite. A variation may be the type of attack, the approach of an attack, the incorporation of the right or the left hand, or the execution of the attack from omote or ura. The subtlest turn of the hand becomes a variation.

These basic throws are presented here with variations and ways to further refine each technique.

The basics throws are *irimi-nage* (entering throw), *kaiten-nage* (rotary throw), *kote-gaeshi* (wrist turned out throw), *shiho-nage* (four-direction throw), *tenbin-nage* (elbow lock throw), *tenshin-nage* (heaven and Earth throw), and *sayu-undo*. These throws are learned at a basic level and refined even at very advanced stages of aikido practice. Advanced practice only means the continual refinement of the basics. After one learns the basic technical moves, these throws illustrate and demonstrate the advanced theories and concepts of aikido. Variations help one understand and apply these theories and concepts in a more generalized approach and application. The common denominators in movement and concepts become mutually reinforcing. Training in variations also helps one gain confidence in the application of a basic or advanced aikido technique without the rigidity of its being prearranged. The variations presented here are generic and suggest the training and discipline required when studying variations of a technique. They are not meant to be all-inclusive.

Before every throw, establish and maintain *mushin* (empty mind), *me-tsuki* (soft eye focus), *musubi* (connection), and *ma-ai* (distance). Establish the aikido ready stance by remaining centered and balanced. Make sure that your spine is straight, not rigid. Make sure that your breathing is natural. Let your mind center on the one point in the lower abdomen, relax, let your weight settle to the underside, and extend your ki. Mentally invite your training partner to approach and attack.

To finish each throw, let go and move away by maintaining zanshin (lingering spirit), mushin (empty mind), me-tsuki (soft eye focus), musubi (connection), and a safe ma-ai (distance), while maintaining environmental awareness as if anticipating and being ready for the next approach or attack.

BASIC IRIMI-NAGE (ENTERING THROW)

Irimi-nage, in its basic execution, is accomplished by allowing the lower portion of your body to proceed as the top part is stopped. Step forward, just off the attack line, intercepting your training partner's approach and attack. Allow the lower portion of your training partner's body to keep its forward momentum and inertia. Step behind and push forward with one hand on your partner's lower back, while cutting or rotating your other hand backward along your partner's jaw line from chin to ear toward the rear balance point. The movement should be very smooth and clean, and you should keep a relaxed structural alignment. Your top hand should follow the contour of his body up the front and then down the back of his body; this facilitates a sense of connectedness and energy direction. The movement is suggestive. A slight touch to his lower back and his hips will want to move forward. Sliding up the front of his body and slightly touch-

IRIMI-NAGE BASIC

ing the jaw line suggests a movement of his upper body and head in the opposite, or backward, direction. Your hands should move in a coordinated circle as if on a steering wheel. Slightly dropping your weight through your body toward the balance point completes the throw. You can either drop your training partner on the spot into a back break fall or extend beyond the balance point and circle of power to allow him to roll out of the technique.

IRIMI-NAGE VARIATION

As your training partner approaches and attacks mune-tsuki, a punch to the midsection, enter by stepping forward and slightly off the attack line to the blind side or ura. Hold your partner's elbow down to prevent your training partner from slipping and swinging the strike, while intercepting, not interrupting, the strike. Take control of the elbow of his striking arm. Overextend his arm in order to unbalance your training partner. Swing his striking arm on an upward circular path, while stepping around with a tenkan pivot step omote. This redirection will pull your training partner into an irimi-nage. Complete the throw by stepping forward, while turning your head over to the rear kuzushi point and pushing in the opposite direction, like turning a wheel on the lower back.

HENKA-NAGE-WAZA (VARIATION THROW TECHNIQUE) IRIMI-NAGE

BASIC KAITEN-NAGE (ROTARY THROW)

Execute and practice kaiten-nage, the rotary throw, by lowering and pulling in your head, while pushing your arm diagonally across your partner's back. The approach or attack hand is intercepted, following its natural momentum or circular path, and is used as a pivot point and for leverage to extend and bring your training partner down. It is important to lower your head and to allow your body to extend forward enough to begin to lose balance. Your arm is further extended on its path diagonally across your partner's back. The defensive hand is used to bring your head into the center and to secure the downward position. Use the web between your fingers and thumb to secure your partner's neck and stop any slippage and loss of control. Continue your motion forward. Hold your hands at your neck and arm and step forward bringing into play the motion of your entire body for power.

KAITEN-NAGE BASIC

KAITEN-NAGE VARIATION

To perform or execute one of many variations of kaiten-nage, your training partner approaches and attacks with a *gyaku-hanmi* (standing or grabbing with the opposite side) grab. Your partner's inertia and momentum should be intercepted, not interrupted, by allowing your training partner to grab you while initiating contact, by moving into the grab. Step forward, slightly off the attack line, to the front of your training partner. Allow him to maintain his grip. Redirect his attacking hand in an upward vertically circular path. This will take your training partner by surprise. Redirect his energy and body in the direction from which he initially came. Your defensive hand should be held on the centerline and slightly forward to protect you from his other hand and to keep the focus on a possible atemi. The circular path pulls your training partner forward toward his front kuzushi point. Your defensive hand stays between you to maintain effective combative, but protected, ma-ai (distance). The circular path brings your training partner down. Maintaining the vertically circular path, bring your arm up diagonally across his back, while securing his head down and into the center. Maintaining hand position, while rotating slightly as if a wheel, step forward

HENKA-NAGE-WAZA (VARIATION THROW TECHNIQUE) KAITEN-NAGE

REFINING KAITEN-NAGE

1.   Maintain erect posture and structural alignment.
2.   Rotate your arm slightly forward and down to break your partner's balance on the initial move.
3.   Bring his head down, into the center, in front of his body. Secure his (uke's) neck.
4.   Bring your rotating arm on a circular path slightly backward, continually breaking your opponent's balance.
5.   Bring your rotating arm up, while keeping your head down, and angle your arm across your body.
6.   Keep your arms straight in front of your body on the centerline.
7.   Step forward into the throw to produce full body power.

from the center with your inside leg. Extend your momentum, inertia, and ki forward, releasing your grip to allow your training partner to roll away safely.

BASIC KOTE-GAESHI (WRIST TURNED OUT THROW)

Kote-gaeshi, the wrist turned out throw, is executed by entering and intercepting the approaching or attacking hand. If a block is used, control your partner's elbow and then slide your blocking hand down the contour of his arm until you grasp his wrist. Continue a slight pulling motion, following the natural momentum and inertia of your training partner to help facilitate an initial loss of balance. Follow a slightly circular path and begin to turn your hand over, turning the wrist out. The defensive hand then is placed on top of the secured hand and adds to the circular motion. Continue turning from the center, adding the power and torque of your entire body. Aim the fingers of the secured hand toward the kuzushi (balance) point and continue to turn your partner's wrist in a circular, downward direction until your training partner completely loses balance and falls.

KOTE-GAESHI BASIC

KOTE-GAESHI VARIATIONS

To perform this kote-gaeshi variation, have your training partner approach and attack with an *ai-hanmi* (standing or grabbing with the same side) grab. Initiate contact and connection by stepping forward slightly off the attack line and intercepting, not interrupting, the momentum and inertia of the attack. Align your

HENKA-NAGE-WAZA (VARIATION THROW TECHNIQUE) KOTE-GAESHI

centerline with your partner's. Redirect his arm in a small vertical circular path. Shift your weight off your hip to get behind the movement. Continue to follow the vertical circular path upward and over, while twisting or pivoting from the center to add full body power into the turning out of the wrist. Your training partner's skeletal alignment will facilitate his entire body following the vertical circular path and his losing his balance. The only other option for your training partner would be to risk serious injury to his wrist, elbow, and shoulder. Pulling up slightly on his arm and following through on the vertical circular path will facilitate a safe break fall.

HENKA-NAGE-WAZA (VARIATION THROW TECHNIQUE) KOTE-GAESHI

To perform another kote-gaeshi variation, your training partner should approach and attack with a gyaku-hanmi grab. Initiate movement and connect by turning in the same direction as the inertia and momentum of the grab. A slight twisting of your center will assist in the redirection of the attack line, causing your training partner to begin to lose his balance. Follow a vertically circular path with your hands, rotate or pivot from the center, and secure the back of your partner's hand with your defensive hand. Your training partner, in an effort to regain some balance, will have already shifted some weight in the opposite direction, adding to the ease of this motion. Continue the vertically circular path of your hand and pivot at the center, turn his wrist over, aligning your training partner's skeletal system and causing the loss of balance toward the forward kuzushi point. Continue in one fluid motion to facilitate a high throw. Holding on will assist you in the rotation of his body and assist in achieving a safe break fall.

REFINING KOTE-GAESHI

1. Maintain erect posture and structural alignment.
2. Enter and blend, keeping your attacking hand on the same horizontal plane as the initial contact.
3. Pull your attacking hand slightly forward to unbalance your attacker.
4. Keep the circular rotational turning of the wrist low, do not raise your hand.
5. Lay the palm of your hand on the back of your opponent's attacking hand.
6. Exhale and rotate your hand and your opponent's hand, pointing your first finger toward the kuzushi balance point.
7. Step through or pivot at the center to provide full body power.

BASIC SHIHO-NAGE (FOUR-DIRECTION THROW)

Execute shiho-nage, the four-direction throw, by initiating and intercepting your opponent's approaching or attacking hand. Allow your opponent's hand to overextend slightly, following its natural forward momentum and inertia to help facilitate an initial loss of balance. Initially control should be relaxed and you should bend while securing your partner's elbow before sliding down to his wrist. As the defensive hand is added to secure your partner's wrist, align your forearms to prevent a loss of elbow control. If you are performing the technique omote (to the front), redirect your arm on a horizontal circular path to your training partner's front while lifting his elbow and arm, causing your training partner's body to turn. Step under his arm; do not raise it. Do not raise his arm too high or he can regain his balance and counter the technique. Step through to the front under both your own and your opponent's arm, and turn so that your centerline aligns with your partner's. If you are performing shiho-nage ura, keep your partner's secured hand on the attack line and begin to redirect it on a vertical, circular path and tenkan to the outside, following and staying close to your partner's body contour. This is further facilitated by using your elbow under your training partner's forearm and elbow and lifting up. Your securing hand should be tucked behind your partner's neck with his wrist pointing straight down toward the rear kuzushi point. A slight dropping of your body weight or a slight step forward will facilitate the fall. Either let go, allowing your training partner to fall, or bend your knees and follow him, at his pace, as he falls to the mat, for a secured pin.

SHIHO-NAGE BASIC

SHIHO-NAGE VARIATION

Shiho-nage can be performed 180 degrees or 90 degrees off omote (to the front) or ura (to the rear).

SHIHO-NAGE OMOTE 180 DEGREES

180 Degrees off Omoto

Your training partner should approach and attack with an ai-hanmi (same-hand grab). The inertia and momentum are intercepted, not interrupted, by stepping forward slightly off the attack line while turning your wrist upward on a vertical circular path omote. Turning or pivoting from your center adds full body power to enter, blend with, and redirect the action. Your defensive hand comes underneath to help secure his wrist and to control his elbow. Continuing the forward momentum and inertia of the upward vertical circular path, step underneath your training partner's arm, facilitated by raising his elbow. Be sure not to raise your training partner's elbow above his shoulder line, since that will help him regain his balance at your expense. Continuing the vertical circular path of his arm, turn your body from the center and pull his arm straight down his back toward the rear kuzushi point. The throw is a complete 180-degree movement.

90 Degrees from Omote

Your training partner should approach and attack with an ai-hanmi grab. You should connect with and redirect your partner's forward momentum and inertia

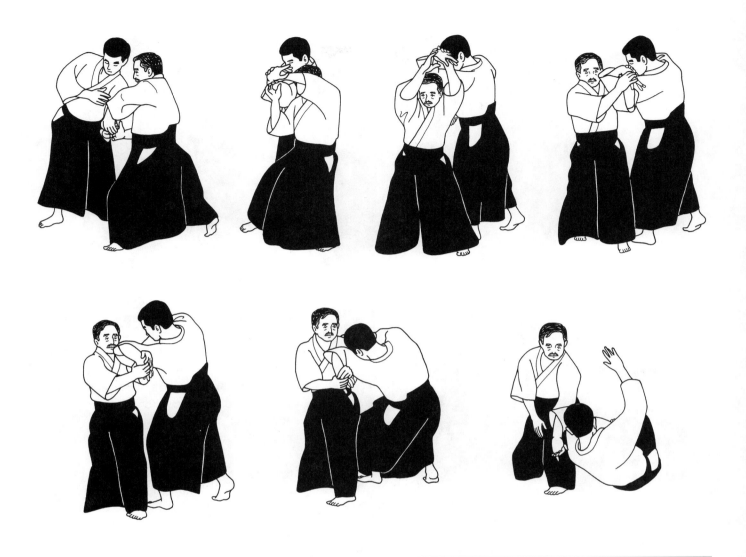

SHIHO-NAGE OMOTE 90 DEGREES

by entering and blending omote of your training partner. Grab and secure the wrist of his attacking arm. Keeping your center aligned and stepping forward adds full body power to the technique. Keeping your training partner's elbow below his shoulder line, continue to step through under his arm, while turning your body from the center. Step deeper than in the 180 degrees shiho-nage to completely clear your training partner's body, while keeping the momentum of his arm forward and in front of the center. Turn his wrist and aim it toward the kuzushi point at a 90-degree angle, while aiming at and aligning with the center. Continuing the downward motion of the arm toward the kuzushi point and stepping forward from the center achieves the total loss of balance and the throw. Allow your training partner to fall safely to the ground.

90 Degrees from Ura

Your training partner should approach and attack by grabbing ai-hanmi (same hand). Enter and intercept your partner's inertia and momentum by stepping slightly off the attack line ura. Simultaneously, redirect the attack by twisting his wrist in an upward vertical circular path. Slide your defensive hand from his

SHIHO-NAGE URA 90 DEGREES

elbow, check for control, and assist the turning motion to secure your wrist. Align your forearm with your partner's, with your elbow under your training partner's elbow. The twisting will prevent your training partner from reaching across your body and striking. Continue the vertical circular path of your arm, while stepping under his arm. Do not raise his elbow higher than the shoulder line or your training partner will regain his balance and your balance will be compromised for a possible counter. Take a very short step ura that does not move you past your training partner. Quickly pivot or turn your body from the center underneath his arm. Continue the forward vertical circular motion up, over, and down toward the rear kuzushi point. Align your center in the direction of the throw. Continue to move the center forward by shifting your weight and pulling downward until your training partner has completely lost balance and is safely falling to the mat.

180 Degrees from Ura

Your training partner approaches and attacks by grabbing ai-hanmi (with the same hand). Initiate contact, connect, and intercept the attacking hand, while slightly stepping or sliding forward ura. Simultaneously, begin turning his wrist in an upward vertical circular path, maintaining the inertia and momentum of the initial attack. The slight forward momentum and lack of resistance will help induce an initial loss of balance. Your defensive hand should come in and align with the attack arm to secure his wrist and control his elbow. Continue the vertical circular path upward while tenkan ura of your training partner. Do not raise his elbow above the shoulder

SHIHO-NAGE URA 180 DEGREES

REFINING SHIHO-NAGE

1. Maintain erect posture and structural alignment.
2. Grasp attacking hand firmly.
3. Enter and blend by getting off the attack line and moving with the momentum of the attack.
4. Swing your attacking hand slightly outward and overextended to initially break balance.
5. Stay close enough to attacker's body to facilitate the attacker's elbow to bend.
6. Control the attacker's elbow; lifting it upward to raise the attacker on his or her toes.
7. Stay low by bending your knees while going under the attacker's arm. Do not raise his or her arm above the shoulder line or let your hands move behind your head and out of your field of vision.
8. Step through and turn your body so that your centerline is aligned with attacker's rear kuzushi balance point.
9. Rotate attacker's wrist until the back of his or her wrist is aimed directly down the spine toward the rear kuzushi balance point.
10. Exhale while stepping forward, rotating your wrist, and dropping your weight.

line or your training partner will regain his balance and be able to counter. His hand should always be in your sight. Completely pivot your body, turning from the center, 180 degrees. Bring his hand down toward the rear kuzushi point while stepping forward from the center for full body power to facilitate a fluid throw.

BASIC TENBIN-NAGE (ELBOW LOCK THROW)

Tenbin-nage is an elbow lock throw. As your training partner approaches and attacks, initiate and intercept his hand. Blend with the momentum and inertia of the attack by moving slightly off the attack line. Redirect the attack by securing your training partner's wrist low at the center, while raising him up on his toes by placing pressure upward on his elbow with the arm held palm up. To perform tenbin-nage omote, blend your attacking hand on a horizontal circular path to the front while stepping in from the center to redirect your training partner's body. To perform tenbin-nage ura, allow your attacking arm to continue forward and step tenkan behind your training partner. Holding his hand low, step forward while turning his arm under his elbow, palm down, moving from the center and aiming toward your training partner's kuzushi (balance) point.

TENBIN-NAGE BASIC

REFINING TENBIN-NAGE

1. Maintain erect posture and structural alignment.
2. Relax and breathe.
3. Position your body behind the opponent's body.
4. Anchor your lower hand to your center and use it as the pivot point.
5. With your other arm, align the forearm at elbow (or just above) with the palm up. Lift and subtly rotate your opponent's shoulder forward toward the front kuzushi balance point.
6. Step forward, rotate your opponent's arm at the elbow, curved over, and palm down, in a subtle wave motion toward the front kuzushi balance point.
7. Follow through and maintain zanshin.

HENKA-NAGE-WAZA (VARIATION THROW TECHNIQUE) TENBIN-NAGE

TENBIN-NAGE VARIATION

As your training partner approaches and attacks with an ai-hanmi grab, initiate contact and connection by intercepting, not interrupting, the inertia and momentum by twisting your center in the direction of the attack and redirecting it slightly off the attack line. As his arm comes across your body, slide your defensive arm, palm up, forward on the centerline intercepting his arm at the elbow. A slight pull forward on a horizontal circular path toward the front kuzushi point will assist you in gaining and maintaining control and compliance. Stepping forward, holding his hand at the center, and raising his arm at the elbow will further turn your training partner in a new direction. While raising his arm, maintain forward momentum and place him on his toes with no balance or support except that which you provide. Stepping forward with your inside leg from the center, keep his hands in front of his body centerline, turn his arm over at his elbow, rotating it on a slightly vertical circular path. The rounding of his arm will assist you in rolling your training partner forward.

BASIC TENSHIN-NAGE (HEAVEN AND EARTH THROW)

As your training partner approaches and attacks, grabbing with both hands ryote-dori, enter and intercept your partner's forward momentum and inertia. Direct his lower hand toward the Earth kuzushi point, while directing his upper hand (heaven) over his shoulder backward. Getting off the attack line allows the lower portion of your body to continue forward while redirecting your upper body backward. Continue to break balance with the lower hand, redirecting with the upper hand, and step forward from the center to finish the throw.

TENSHIN-NAGE BASIC

TENSHIN-NAGE VARIATION

Your training partner approaches and attacks by grabbing both of your wrists ryote-dori. Enter by immediately lowering your elbows and pushing slightly upward to redirect the grab. This begins to unbalance your training partner. Take a backward tenkan pivoting step while maintaining contact, connecting, and aligning your centerline. Allow one hand to drop lower, toward the center, while your other hand continues to rise upward. Complete the 180-degree tenkan pivoting step. Continuing the circular momentum and inertia, step omote of your

---

REFINING TENSHIN-NAGE

1. Maintain erect posture and structural alignment.
2. Relax and breathe.
3. Allow the forward momentum of the lower body to continue by getting off the attack line slightly to the side.
4. Slightly overextend and gently swing your opponent's lower arm out to the side and back toward the rear kuzushi balance point.
5. Simultaneously, te-gatana (hand edge or knife blade) to the inside of the opponent's other wrist. Follow a circular path upward toward his head.
6. Step through and follow through.
7. Maintain zanshin.

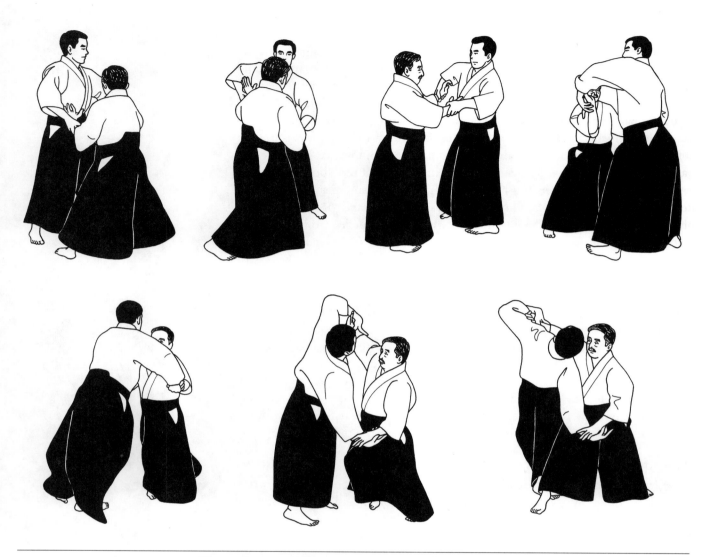

HENKA-NAGE-WAZA (VARIATION THROW TECHNIQUE) TENSHIN-NAGE

SAYU-UNDO BASIC

training partner, still maintaining the contact, connection, alignment, and hand position. As your training partner's inertia and momentum spin him around, using tori for support, intersect or cut the circular motion by stepping forward while simultaneously lifting one hand up and over on a circular path and bringing your other hand down and into the center on a circular path. Shift all of your weight forward from the center, and step forward while continuing the rotations of the arms as your training partner loses total balance in the direction of the rear kuzushi point.

BASIC SAYU-UNDO

As your training partner approaches and attacks, enter by stepping slightly off the attack line to his rear. As his momentum and inertia continue, intercept his upper body by raising his arms and catching his jaw line from the chin to the ear. Your arms may follow a vertical circular path leading forward then back, taking his head toward the rear kuzushi point. Otherwise, your arms may simply follow the contour of the attacking arm to the jaw line. Allow the momentum to carry and turn your head toward the rear kuzushi point. Stepping forward from the center completes the throw.

SAYU-UNDO VARIATION

As your training partner approaches and attacks by grabbing morote-dori, initiate contact and connection, and intercept his forward inertia and momentum by redirecting his arms upward on a vertical circular path, keeping his elbow low. Turn your body and the center adds full body power to the redirection. Continue the vertical circular path along the centerline, while stepping ura of your training partner. Keep your training partner's elbows down and control his elbow for further control and to prevent any counter or reversal techniques. Following the circular path downward to the rear kuzushi point, add additional push from the elbow.

These illustrations show the details from a different angle. Your training partner approaches and attacks by grabbing both wrists in morote-dori. Enter and blend by turning diagonally across the front of the body centerlines, redirect the grab, and begin an upward vertical circular path. The shifting of your body weight,

---

REFINING SAYU-UNDO

1. Maintain erect posture and structural alignment.

2. Relax and breathe.

3. Move slightly off the attack line and behind your opponent.

4. Swing your front arm upward, palm up, making contact with the opponent's jaw line from chin to ear. Do not let the arm come forward in front of your body. Keep the arm aligned with your shoulders. Begin to allow the opponent's body to lean backward toward the rear kuzushi balance point.

5. Push your secondary hand into the center of the opponent's centerline, toward the same rear kuzushi balance point.

6. Holding your arms steady, turn to the rear by rotating at the waist toward the back.

7. Lean into your opponent making rib-to-rib contact and pressure.

8. Follow through and maintain zanshin.

HENKA-NAGE-WAZA (VARIATION THROW TECHNIQUE) SAYU-UNDO

ANOTHER VIEW OF MOROTE-DORI SAYU-UNDO

turning at the center, adds full body power and momentum. Continue the upward vertical circular path directly along your training partner's centerline. Your training partner will begin to turn in an attempt to reposition himself to gain some sense of balance and will begin to rely more on tori for support. Continuing with the inertia and momentum of the vertical circular path, your training partner continues to turn and lose more balance. Step into the throw and continue, now downward, on the vertical circular path toward your training partner's rear kuzushi point. Continue to push his elbow for additional power, but also to protect against any counter or reversal attempts. Follow your training partner down at his rate of falling. Once his balance is taken away, there is no real need to continue pushing. The additional strain may begin to take tori's balance too.

ADVANCED THROWS

Several throws are considered rather advanced. They are *koshi-nage* (hip throw), *juji-nage* (propeller or cross-armed throw), *kokyu-nage* (breathing/timing throw), *aiki-nage* (emptying throw), *otoshi-nage* (leg pickup or sweep throw), *uke-waza* (lateral dash sacrifice technique), and *ude-garami* (arm hook takedown).

Koshi-Nage (Hip Throw)

Shown is the koshi-nage from an ai-hanmi position. As your training partner approaches and attacks by grabbing ai-hanmi, initiate contact, connect with, and intercept his inertia and momentum by turning your wrist over in a small, relaxed, circular motion, turning him around, while stepping in from the center. Continue to control and redirect your training partner by placing your other hand on his elbow and pushing in an upward circular motion, aiming the elbow toward his ear until he is turned. Step in front of your training partner's center, lifting his elbow up and dropping your own hips down beneath his center of gravity, and align your body with his. A slight tension or pulling motion forward will assist you in keeping him continually off-balance and under control. As his full weight comes over your body, continue to lift and pull forward in a circular motion. Raise his hips to allow him to fall forward to his kuzushi. Pulling up on his arm as he comes over your hips will help your training partner execute a safe break fall.

Koshi-Nage Variation

As your training partner approaches and attacks by grabbing gyaku-hanmi morote-dori (two hands grabbing one wrist), enter by stepping slightly off the attack line while blending with the momentum and inertia of the attack. Redirect the attack by turning your wrist over the top of his arms, suggesting the rotation while initiating a forward vertical circular motion. Your defensive hand should move to his hip. Align your center with his. The momentum and inertia of the attack is interrupted and redirected back toward the direction from which your training partner was coming. Your training partner's rapid turn causes an initial loss of balance and a dependency on you for support. Stepping into the forward momentum, you should intersect the centers, dropping your hip below your training partner's center, while further extending his arms forward to keep the forward motion and getting your training partner's weight over the center or leverage point. Lifting your hips slightly facilitates the weight coming farther forward and requiring your training partner to fall over your hip. The arm in the small of your training partner's back helps facilitate both control and safety. Letting go assists your training partner in performing a safe break fall.

KOSHI-NAGE (CONTINUED ON NEXT PAGE)

Koshi-nage (continued)

Henka-nage-waza (variation throw technique) koshi-nage

REFINING KOSHI-NAGE

1. Maintain erect posture and structural alignment.
2. Relax and breathe.
3. Get slightly off the attack line to the front.
4. Extend the forward hand and arm.
5. Step in and under the opponent's center of gravity by bending the knees, not the waist.
6. Allow the weight of the opponent to settle forward past the hips and lower back.
7. Keep the momentum flowing, raise your hips, let the opponent's body weight carry them over you.
8. Allow your opponent's free hand to grasp the gi (traditional Japanese training uniform) to help guide and stabilize the throw.
9. Maintain control of the throw.
10. As your opponent lands, pull up on his arm to protect your head.
11. Follow through and maintain zanshin.

JUJI-NAGE (CROSS-ARM THROW)

Juji-nage is the cross-armed throw. To execute or perform juji-nage, initiate contact and connect, and intercept your training partner's approach and attack. Grab his opposite wrist while maintaining your own forward momentum and inertia. Keep his hands in front, cross his arms so the back arm applies pressure to the forward arm. Your forward momentum will begin to upset his balance and allow you to control your training partner. Step through with the center while rotating his arms in a circular motion, pulling the lower hand in and the upper hand out and forward. Continue to rotate his arms toward the kuzushi point. Letting go will allow your training partner to roll out of the throw. A tighter circular motion of the arms will direct your training partner to take the throw as a break fall. To add to the power of inertia and momentum, drop to your front knee. This motion empties the space and support that your training partner has been using.

JUJI-NAGE VARIATION

Your training partner should approach and attack ai-hanmi morote-dori (grabbing one wrist with both hands). Immediately initiate contact, intercept, and blend with the approach, and attack by stepping backward slightly off the attack line with the inertia and momentum. Bring your defensive hand over the top of his first arm and in between them both. His arms begin a vertical circular path, starting with maintaining the initial horizontal plane of attack. Shift your weight and posture slightly backward, adding to the blending effect. Keep his arms separate by continuing to reach between and under his arm. The initial loss of balance, from being pulled toward a front kuzushi point, facilitates the loss of focus on his arm and makes the separation and arm control easier. Change the direction of the vertical circular path upward and forward and shift your weight from the center, adding full body power, pushing his arms into and through his center, forcing him to turn to avoid the momentum. Cross and pull his arms, and begin to rotate him in a coordinated wheel action; his upper arms are over and

JUJI-NAGE

out while his lower hand is under and in. Stepping forward with the inside leg adds full body power. Continue to impose forward momentum and arm rotation toward the front kuzushi point. If you release him at this point, your training partner can roll safely away. If you hold the grip and pull up slightly, your training partner can take a safe break fall.

REFINING JUJI-NAGE

1. Maintain erect posture and structural alignment.
2. Relax and breathe.
3. Tenkan to the rear, aligning behind your opponent.
4. Holding both wrists, keep both your arms and your opponent's arms extended in front of the centerline.
5. Cross your opponent's arms so they intersect directly behind the elbow. Hold them tightly.
6. Simultaneously step forward with full body power, while rotating both arms as if turning a wheel.
7. Follow through and maintain zanshin.

HENKA-NAGE-WAZA (VARIATION THROW TECHNIQUE) JUJI-NAGE

KOKYU-NAGE (TIMING AND BREATH THROWS)

All throws are in essence kokyu-nage. Kokyu-nage relies almost entirely on the ability to apply advanced aikido concepts and take a high level of technical proficiency.

Kokyu-nage are breath and timing throws. These throws require precise timing to unbalance an opponent by taking their balance in very subtle means, allowing the opponent to flow or blend into the throw. The opponents appear almost to throw themselves. The gentle subtleties of kokyu-nage emphasize the breathing in as one enters and blends with the attack, while redirecting it and beginning to break the opponent's balance. Then one breathes out as the opponent is thrown easily. It appears almost as if the very breath of the defender throws him or her.

There are an infinite number of these throws. Unless a throw is otherwise specified and named, it is probably a kokyu-nage. The essence of aikido is in these breath and timing throws, since they require the proper execution of technical, mechanical, and conceptual factors facilitating the throwing of the training partner.

KOKYU-NAGE

HENKA-NAGE-WAZA (VARIATION THROW TECHNIQUE) KOKYU-NAGE

As your training partner approaches and attacks, initiate contact and connect, and intercept the attack (in the shown example, the attack is a yokomen-uchi, or a strike to the side of the head). Step in from the center, slightly off the attack line. One hand should softly block the strike, while your other hand goes toward his face. Do not block too hard to stop forward momentum and inertia, or strike too close to his face since this will cause your training partner to pull his weight backward, and that would be a different kokyu-nage. Control and redirect the inertia and momentum by entering and blending with the movement. Begin to control and redirect him by overextending the path of attack, pivoting or turning from the center while dropping down on one knee to direct the circular path of the throw toward the kuzushi point. Projecting the throw outward and letting go will facilitate a roll out. Holding on and projecting a tighter circular path will facilitate a break fall.

KOKYU-NAGE VARIATION

Your training partner should approach and attack with a forward thrust or grab. Interrupt his inertia and momentum abruptly by entering and initiating contact directly with his wrist and his attacking forearm. The abruptness of the interception and interruption early on the attack line will cause your training partner to abruptly turn his body, change direction, and lose balance. Dropping your weight to one knee, while following a vertical circular path with his arm toward the center, facilitates his total loss of balance and throws your training partner. Keeping control of his arm on a vertical circular path allows your training partner to land safely with a break fall.

REFINING KOKYU-NAGE

1. Maintain erect posture and structural alignment.
2. Relax and breathe.
3. Enter and blend by getting off the attack line and matching or mirroring the opponent's timing, rhythm, and pace.
4. Let the opponent's natural momentum and inertia overextend him.
5. Use footwork and body turning to redirect your opponent's body.
6. Use one continuous motion to keep your opponent off-balance and moving in an attempt to regain stability.
7. Interrupt the flow and direct him toward a kuzushi balance point.
8. Follow through and maintain zanshin.

AIKI-NAGE (DROP)

As your training partner approaches and attacks with a shomen-uchi (downward head strike), enter and intercept his forward momentum. As you come into range, simply drop down in front of your training partner, interrupting the anticipated contact, connection, and resistance. By dropping down, you block the momentum and inertia of the lower part of your body, while letting the upper part continue forward. The circular path creates an empty space and facilitates your opponent's falling in the direction of the front kuzushi point. Sweeping your hand upward supports the forward throw.

REFINING AIKI-NAGE

1. Maintain erect posture and structural alignment.
2. Relax and breathe.
3. Maintain a defensive posture but do not attempt to interrupt or intercept the attack.
4. Timing is everything. Just before impact, drop down directly on the attack line.
5. Allow your opponent's body weight and momentum to follow a vertical circular path, throwing himself by his own action.
6. Immediately pivot on your knee and assume a defensive posture.
7. Maintain zanshin.

AIKI-OTOSHI-NAGE (LEG-SWEEP/PICKUP THROW)

As your training partner approaches and attacks, enter slightly off the attack line—to the rear. Rather than intercept the attacking arm, duck low and grasp his legs. This action will catch your training partner off-guard and will trap him between the scissor effects of your body position. The angle naturally created will begin to break your training partner's balance as he leans backward. His legs are blocked to prevent any regaining of his balance by repositioning his feet by stepping backward. Bend your knee to get a low center of gravity and to position his body below his center. Begin to lift his legs in a slightly circular path upward and back. Shift your body weight to facilitate his further loss of balance to execute the throw.

REFINING AIKI-OTOSHI-NAGE

1. Maintain erect posture and structural alignment.
2. Relax and breathe.
3. Enter and blend by sliding slightly off the attack line behind your opponent.
4. Without allowing your opponent to grab you, bend your knees to drop below his center.
5. Reach in front across his body and grab both his legs separately by the outside of the knee.
6. Straighten your back and legs to create a lifting motion, while pulling his knees up and back toward the rear kuzushi balance point.
7. Let your opponent's body weight create an imbalance and facilitate the throw.
8. Allow your opponent to fall; do not force it.
9. Follow through and maintain zanshin.

AIKI-OTOSHI-NAGE

UKE-WAZA (LATERAL DASH SACRIFICE)

As your training partner approaches and attacks, in this case with a yokomen-uchi, or diagonal head strike, enter and intercept the momentum and inertia of the attack. Do not interrupt his forward momentum, but get off the attack line and begin to redirect the power of the attack into an outward and downward circular path. Control his body and arm by grabbing his arm and his gi near the shoulder or under the armpit. Trap or block his forward leg with your foot. Blend and redirect the forward inertia and momentum by leaning backward toward the front kuzushi point. Keep the centerlines aligned and your bodies connected. Allow yourself to fall backward while pulling your training partner with you. Since the forward momentum has not been stopped, it is easy to throw because

REFINING UKE-WAZA

1. Maintain erect posture and structural alignment.
2. Relax and breathe.
3. Establish a strong connection.
4. Do nothing to interrupt or intercept the opponent's forward momentum or inertia.
5. Timing is everything. At the last moment, grab and attach yourself to opponent's body.
6. Block the opponent's front foot with your own.
7. Use the opponent's forward momentum and the weight of your own dropping body to pull opponent over you in a vertical circular path toward the front kuzushi balance point.
8. Let your opponent's body fall at its own pace. Do not force it.
9. Let go and your opponent will roll away. Hang on, and he will break fall.
10. Follow through and maintain zanshin.

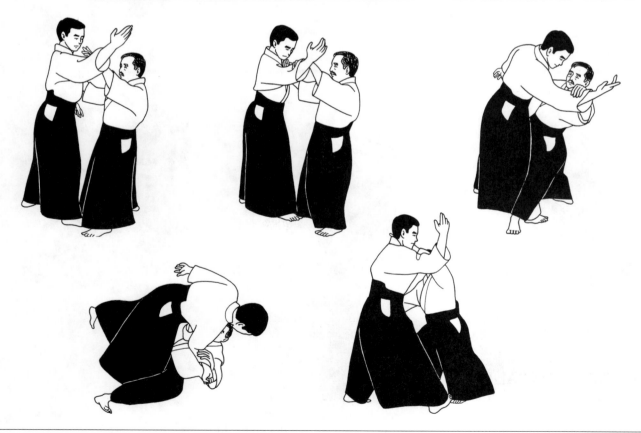

UKE-WAZA

you have utilized his energy, blocked his leg from repositioning or regaining balance, and redirected him on a downward circular path. Let go and allow your training partner safely to roll.

UDE-GARAMI (HOOK ARM TAKEDOWN)

To perform ude-garami (the hook arm takedown) initiate contact and connect, and intercept your training partner's approach and attack. This example illustrates a yokomen-uchi (diagonal head strike). Blend with the path of attack by stepping slightly off the attack line to your training partner's front. Without necessarily blocking his striking arm, gain access and take control of his nonattacking arm. Keep your centerlines aligned. Reach under and then over his nonattacking hand, while entering and blending with a forward tenkan. The blending and redirecting begin to unbalance your training partner. Continue the circular downward path as a spiral until your training partner is face down on the mat.

REFINING UDE-GARAMI

1. Maintain erect posture and structural alignment.
2. Relax and breathe.
3. Enter and blend by moving slightly off the attack line.
4. Empty the front kuzushi balance point.
5. Intertwine both your arms and your opponent's arms at the elbow, coming up behind the elbow.
6. Lift your opponent's elbow up, rotating the shoulder down toward the front kuzushi balance point.
7. Step tenkan 180 degrees to the rear.
8. Bend your knees, directing your opponent face down on the mat.
9. Follow through and maintain zanshin.

UDE-GARAMI (CONTINUED ON NEXT PAGE)

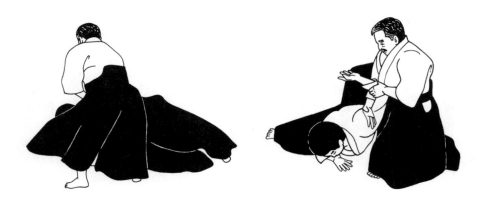

UDE-GARAMI (CONTINUED)

THROWS AS LOCKS

To advance your throwing techniques further, you can sometimes modify or apply them as locking techniques. This is yet another way to add to the infinite possibilities of aikido.

Shiho-Nage Lock

SHIHO-LOCK

Perform the initial basic shiho-nage technique. Rather than follow the inertia and momentum of the vertical circular path over the shoulder and directly down the rear centerline toward the rear kuzushi point, stop the motion when your training partner has lost his balance and lock his arm. Your training partner will be totally dependent on you for support. His forearm will be locked between his upper arm and wrist. Held tightly, his wrist will turn out, and you can apply pain compliance until your training partner taps out. Your defensive hand should be brought in to secure his forearm and also to protect yourself from a strike with his other hand, or to atemi (strike) to your training partner's face. Once your training partner signals submission, simply letting go will facilitate the remainder of the throw.

Irimi-Nage Lock

IRIMI-LOCK/CHOKE

Perform the initial basic irimi-nage technique. At the height of the vertical circular path, abruptly stop the momentum and inertia aimed at the rear kuzushi point, and secure his head. Your training partner's body will be dependent on you for support because of his loss of balance. Holding his back and stepping underneath on the kuzushi point will provide a stable base from which to apply pressure to his jaw line. This pressure will lock out his motion. If your upper arm or bicep is held slightly over the throat, this same movement becomes a choke. Slowly apply pressure until your training partner taps out, signaling the successful execution of the technique and submission. Removing the support of your body and letting go allows your training partner to fall safely onto his back.

Sayu-Undo Lock

Perform the initial basic sayu-undo throw. At the top of the vertical circular path, abruptly stop the momentum and inertia toward the rear kuzushi point. Turn your partner's arm over and wrap his arm around his head. Stepping underneath,

SAYU-UNDO LOCK/CHOKE

on the rear kuzushi point, support the weight of your training partner. He is totally dependent on you for support, since he has already lost his balance. Your arm can slip down over his throat and become a chokehold. Your defensive hand holds his wrist across the front of his body and secured to the opposite hip; this creates an arm bar for further pressure and compliance. Once your training partner has tapped out, signaling successful execution of the technique and submission, let go and remove your supporting leg to allow your training partner to fall safety to the ground.

TURNOVERS
It is unsafe to allow a training partner to remain face up on the mat after a throw is completed. The best, and safest, approach is to turn your training partner over to a face down position. There are several ways to accomplish this.

Turnover 1
After a throw is completed, remain connected to and in control of your training partner. Holding his wrist securely, stretch out his arm and apply downward pressure to his elbow. Pressing down on his elbow while lifting slightly on his wrist produces enough pain to gain compliance and submission at this point. Maintaining pressure, tenkan to the opposite side of your training partner's body. Pull his body with the center and full body momentum to roll him over.

Turnover 2
After a throw is completed, remain connected and in control of your training partner. Secure his wrist and begin bending his arm while sliding one hand to his elbow. Stepping tenkan, maintain his elbow as the pivot point; holding his arm at a 90-degree bend, crack your training partner's arm to turn him over. Straighten his arm and bend his wrist directly down his arm and into his shoulder for a compliance submission lock.

MAWASHI: GROUND ARM BAR
Once your opponent is thrown and turned over, it is wisest, and safest, to secure the completion of a technique with a compliance submission lock, such as the kneeling mawashi.

TURNOVER 1

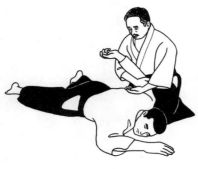

MAWASHI 1

Mawashi 1

After your training partner has been thrown and turned over, kneel and secure his shoulder between your knees. Your training partner's arm should be secured up the centerline and secured between your arms and body. Your kneeling body should be held relaxed and erect; do not lean forward. One hand should be held higher than the other, with both palms up. A slight twisting and leaning action will send pressure directly into his shoulder joint as the pivot point. Submission and compliance is signaled by tapping twice on the mat. Release his arm, place your hand in the middle of his lower back, and exit by *shikko* (knee walking) in the direction of his head, away from any possible hand or leg attack.

TURNOVER 2

Mawashi 2

After your training partner has been thrown and turned over, kneel and secure his shoulder between your knees. Your body should be relaxed and your spine erect. Place pressure on your partner's arm by securing his lower hand and utilizing his upper arm at the wrist to apply leverage into his shoulder joint as the pivot point. Slowly keep applying downward and forward pressure until your training partner taps out to signal successful execution of the technique and submission. Release and place his hand in the small of his back. Shikko away toward his head to avoid attacks from his hands or legs.

MAWASHI 2

MAWASHI 3

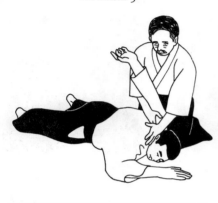

MAWASHI 4

MAWASHI 5

IKKYO

Mawashi 3

After your training partner has been thrown and turned over, kneel and secure his shoulder between your knees. Your body should be relaxed and your spine erect. Secure your training partner's arm up the centerline and between his arms and his body. Securing his elbow with one arm, fold his fingers over with the other, while slowly applying pressure to the fingers and elbow as leverage into the pivot point of the shoulder joint. Once your training partner taps out, signifying the successful execution of the technique and submission, release his hand, placing it in the small of his back. Shikko toward his head to avoid possible attacks from his hands and legs.

Mawashi 4

After your training partner has been thrown and turned over, kneel and secure his shoulder between your knees. Your body should be relaxed and your spine erect. Secure your training partner's arm up the centerline and between his other arm and his body. Leverage your training partner's arm straight between his body and the securing arm. Use his shoulder joint as the pivot point, and slowly apply pressure forward and across his back. Also, apply pressure to his neck with the edge of your hand. Once your training partner taps out, signifying successful execution of the technique and submission, release your hand, placing it in the small of his back. Shikko toward his head, avoiding possible attacks from his hands and legs.

Mawashi 5

After your training partner has been thrown and turned over, kneel and secure his shoulder between your knees. Your body should be relaxed and your spine erect. Secure your training partner's arm up the centerline and between his other arm and his body. Securing his elbow with one arm, fold the first or the first two fingers over with your other hand. Slowly apply pressure to his fingers and elbow as leverage into the pivot point of the shoulder joint. Once your training partner taps out, signifying successful execution of the technique and submission, release your hand, placing it in the small of his back. Shikko toward his head, avoiding possible attacks from his hands and legs.

REFINING BASIC LOCKS (KATAME-WAZA)

There are only a few basic locks, but there are infinite variations possible. The basic locks are numbered; *ikkyo* for the first immobilization technique, *nikyo* for the second, *sankyo* for the third, *yonkyo* for the fourth, and *gokyo* for the fifth. *Hiji-gime* is an additional arm-bar type of lock. The basic locks of aikido are refined at advanced levels. Locks provide means to immobilize an opponent or to gain compliance and cooperation. The student improves through consistent and persistent training and discipline with honest and genuine intent and intensity against a variety of approaches and attacks in many different contextual and situational applications.

Ikkyo: The First Teaching or Lock Pinning Technique

To perform ikkyo, the first teaching or lock pinning technique, rotate your training partner's wrist, elbow, and shoulder forward. This will force him off-balance to his front kuzushi point. Usually your training partner is taken to the ground face first. With his arm outstretched beyond his shoulder line, additional pressure and rotation can be applied to his wrist and elbow to facilitate a tap-out.

Nikyo: The Second Teaching or Lock Pinning Technique

Your training partner approaches and attacks gyaku-hanmi. Enter by sliding forward slightly off the attack line ura of your training partner. Secure his hand into his shoulder socket. Create an S-shaped curve in his arm with his wrist and elbow bent at 90 degrees. Apply pressure by rotating his elbow downward into the center while maintaining the position of his wrist. Slowly apply pressure until your training partner taps out to signify successful execution of the technique and submission.

NIKYO BASIC

Nikyo Variation 1

Nikyo is applied gyaku-hanmi, but instead of securing your training partner's hand in his shoulder socket, hold his hand away from his body, with your second hand securing his wrist instead of his elbow. Rotate his wrist upward and into his body and center, while simultaneously rotating his other wrist downward and into your center. By twisting in opposite directions you use his wrist as the pivot point with opposing leverage. Slowly apply pressure until your training partner taps out to signify successful execution of the technique and submission.

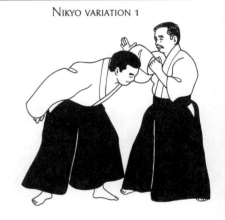

NIKYO VARIATION 1

Nikyo Variation 2

Nikyo is applied gyaku-hanmi. Secure your training partner's hand in his shoulder socket. Fold his arm into an S-shape. Apply pressure directly behind his elbow, driving it into the secured wrist. Slowly apply pressure until your training partner taps out to signify successful execution of the technique and submission.

Sankyo: Third Teaching or Lock Pinning Technique

Your training partner approaches and attacks gyaku-hanmi. Secure his fingers with one hand by squeezing them together while securing his wrist with your

NIKYO VARIATION 2

SANKYO BASIC

SANKYO VARIATION 1

other hand. Slowly twist his hand so that his palm is forward on the centerline. Lift his elbow up so that they are even with his shoulder line. The lift and twist will force your training partner to compensate by rising on his toes and will initiate a loss of balance and a dependency for support. Slowly apply pressure until your training partner taps out to signify successful execution of the technique and submission.

Sankyo Variation

From the basic ikkyo position, rotate your training partner's elbow forward on a vertical circular path toward the forward kuzushi point. Interrupt the forward rotating motion by sliding your hand at his elbow down to his wrist and hand. Initiate a horizontal rotation motion while maintaining a tight grip on his fingers. Step back, pulling his hand with the momentum and full body power from the center. This motion causes your training partner to follow, rising up on his toes in an effort to compensate for the pressure and for losing balance. You provide your training partner's only stability. Slowly apply pressure until your training partner taps out to signify successful execution of the technique and submission.

Yonkyo: The Fourth Teaching or Lock Pinning Technique

From a gyaku-hanmi position, secure your training partner's hand, palm up. Place his other hand, palm down, on the inside of his wrist. Hold his wrist between your thumbs and last three fingers. Extend your first finger so that your inner knuckle protrudes against the pulse or pressure point on his forearm just above your thumb. Align his hands with the centerline at waist level. A slight

YONKYO

inward rotation of his hand pushes your protruding knuckle into the pulse or pressure point, eliciting pain. Slide your foot forward and turn his wrist toward the front kuzushi point. Continue the downward motion. Slowly continue pressure until your training partner taps out, signifying successful execution of the technique and submission.

Gokyo: Fifth Teaching or Lock Pinning Technique

After throwing and turning your training partner over face down on the mat, assume a kneeling position to the side. Secure his arm at his wrist and elbow. Lifting up on his elbow, slide his wrist, palm up, directly toward his shoulder until his wrist is directly below his elbow at a 90-degree angle. Apply slight pressure downward on his elbow, directly into his wrist to produce pain compliance and submission. Slightly turning his wrist while pressing will add torque to the technique and make it even more effective. Slowly apply pressure until your training partner taps out, signifying successful execution and submission. Let go of his arm and shikko away from his body, avoiding any possible attack.

Hiji-Gime Lock: Arm Bar

Your training partner should approach and attack with an ai-hanmi grip. Initiate contact and intercept his attacking arm by entering directly in, but slightly off to the rear of, the attack line. Take control of the attack hand by pointing his fingers upward and rotating his elbow over downward. The rotating motion bends your training partner over and initiates a loss of balance. Continue the rotation of his elbow into the center, while lifting his hand. As you lift his hand, apply leverage and pressure directly into his shoulder joint. The pressure on his elbow locks it out in a direction it does not want to go. Once your training partner taps out, signifying successful execution of the technique and submission, release his hand and arm or continue into another technique.

GOKYO BASIC   HIJI-GIME

LOCKS AS THROWS

Katame-waza (locking techniques) can also be used as *nage-waza* (throwing techniques).

Ikkyo-Nage Throw

After securing the wrist and elbow of your training partner in a basic ikkyo, move his arm in a vertical circular path forward. Hold his hand steady and rotate his

IKKYO-NAGE

NIKYO-NAGE

NIKYO-NAGE (CONTINUED)

elbow over. Step forward from the center to add full body power and momentum. Bring his arm down and forward, keeping his wrist and elbow aligned on the centerline. Extend his elbow forward toward the front kuzushi point. Let go and allow your training partner to roll safely away.

Nikyo-Nage Throw

After securing the arm of your training partner in a basic nikyo, slide your hands along the contour of his arm down to his wrist. Rotating his fingers upward and his wrist downward and into the center, push into your training partner's center to create pain compliance and break his balance. Stepping forward slightly off the attack line, use nikyo to aim his elbow to the rear kuzushi point. Let go, allowing your training partner to safely fall backward.

Sankyo-Nage Throw

After securing the arm of your training partner in a basic sankyo, lift his arm up and forward in a vertical circular path. Step forward from the center to add full body power. Maintain the pressure on his finger and the twist to his wrist. Leading with his wrist, continue to cast his arm and body forward on the center-line toward the front kuzushi point. Letting go will facilitate your training partner's ability to roll safely away. Holding and continuing to pull the vertical circular path back toward the center along the centerline will facilitate a safe break fall. Maintain your hands on the centerline toward your training partner.

CONCLUSION

Advanced techniques in aikido are most often the refinement of fundamental techniques through training that is more detailed and disciplined. Besides strikes, throws, and locks, advanced aikido practitioners must train in varied applications, combinations, counters, and reversals.

SANKYO-NAGE

TIPS FOR REFINING LOCKS

1. Maintain erect posture and structural alignment.

2. Relax and breathe.

3. Move slowly. Never move rapidly or jerk a movement. The risk of injury is very high. Apply only enough pressure to gain compliance.

4. As uke, learn to tap out, signaling enough pressure and compliance. Do not endure pain.

5. Watch the angles of the wrist, elbow, and shoulder.

6. Learn to flow from one lock to another or to use locks as a feint to interrupt resistance before going into a throw combination.

7. Maintain zanshin.

Chapter 9
Application Techniques

In the beginning, students learn to apply the physical techniques of aikido to a standing training partner while attacking with a single technique. As one advances in aikido, the student learns to apply the concepts of aikido to techniques from a variety of situations and against numerous training partners.

There are many different contextual and situational applications other than the traditional and usual standing (*tachi-waza*) one-on-one training environments and exercises. These advanced applications include *kokyu-dosa* or *seiza ryote-dori* (two-hand grab) exercises; *suwari-waza*, where both attacker and defender are kneeling; *hanmi-handachi*, in which the attacker is standing but the defender is kneeling; *ushiro-waza*, or attacks from the rear; applications in which you are grabbed by two people, or three people; and randori, being attacked by multiple opponents.

Kokyu-Dosa: Seiza Ki Extension Techniques
Kokyu-dosa is an excellent exercise to practice at the beginning and end of class. It provides a great opportunity to work on technique and conceptual application. It also develops and extends ki.

Kokyu-Dosa: Starting Position
Assume a seiza position; your posture should be relaxed, your back straight, and the centerlines aligned. Your training partner should grab both of your wrists ryote-dori. Staying completely relaxed, allow his weight to settle on the underside of your arms, keep your mind focused on the one point at the center, and extend

KOKYU-DOSA START POSITION

your ki forward. Keep your arms at an angle greater than 90 degrees. Breathe naturally. Quiet your mind. Establish and maintain me-tsuki and musubi.

Kokyu-Dosa Ryote-Dori Tenshin-Nage
Assume the kokyu-dosa starting position. Push slightly into your training partner's center. Establish te-gatana (hand blades) on the inside of both wrists. Following a vertical circular path, move both of your hands simultaneously as if on the opposite sides of

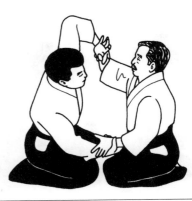

KOKYU-DOSA TENSHIN-NAGE

Kokyu-dosa tenshin-nage

a wheel, with one hand high and the other hand low. Your low hand should rotate over his wrist and pull it into the center. Extend your hand in a circular motion toward the side kuzushi point. Continue until your training partner is completely thrown to the side.

Kokyu-Dosa Ryote-Tori Tenshin-Nage Henka-Waza

Assume the kokyu-dosa starting position. A slight variation to the preceding kokyu-dosa tenshin-nage is to pull your lower hand back rather than into the center. This creates an additional pull to the balance breaking. Continue until your training partner is completely thrown to the side.

Kokyu-Dosa Nikyo

Assume the kokyu-dosa starting position. Push slightly into your training partner's center. As your training partner pushes back slightly, offering some resistance, rotate both of your wrists over your training partner's wrist in a very small outward to inward vertical circular path. Change the path of the circle and rotate your wrists into the center using te-gatana. The edge of your hands should rest on his forearm bones while your training partner's wrists turn completely over and become perpendicular with the floor with his little fingers up. Continue until your training partner acknowledges successful execution of the technique and submission.

Kokyu-dosa nikyo

Kokyu-dosa yonkyo

Kokyu-Dosa Yonkyo

Assume the kokyu-dosa starting position. Push slightly into your training partner's center. As your training partner pushes back to offer some resistance, rotate your hands so that your wrists are aligned with the inside of your training partner's wrists. Following a vertical circular path, bring one hand high and the other hand low, as if connected on a wheel, while applying yonkyo to the pressure or pulse points on both wrists. Continue to rotate your lower hand into the center, while extending your upper hand toward the side kuzushi point. Continue until your training partner is completely thrown to the side.

Kokyu-Dosa Kote-Gaeshi

Assume the kokyu-dosa starting position. Push slightly into your training partner's center. As your training partner pushes back, offering some resistance, redirect the energy slightly to one side by rotating your outside wrist palm up, while moving your other hand to secure his wrist. Holding your training partner's wrist, twisted palm up, continue the outward rotation to free your hand. The direction of the twist is on a vertical circular path toward the outside kuzushi point. Continuing your hand rotation brings his hand back to the top—to the twisted hand. Apply extra pressure toward the outside kuzushi with te-gatana. Continue until your training partner is completely thrown to the side.

KOKYU-DOSA KOTE-GAESHI

KOKYU-DOSA SAYU-UNDO

Kokyu-Dosa Sayu-Undo

Assume the kokyu-dosa starting position. Push slightly into your training partner's center. As your training partner pushes back, offering some resistance, enter and redirect the energy across his body on a vertical circular path. The rotation tends to drop the training partner's shoulder and begin to the break his balance. Extend your arm to the outside of your training partner's jaw line, while rotating your lower hand to the outside of your training partner's wrist. Continue the vertical circular path, with power coming from behind on both the wrist and the jaw line toward the outside kuzushi point. Continue until your training partner is completely thrown to the side.

KOKYU-DOSA SAYU-UNDO (CONTINUED)

SUWARI-WAZA: KNEELING TECHNIQUES

An excellent training application is to have both training partners in the seiza position. Though training in a kneeling position has very little application in today's society, this training does develop strength and mobility in the legs and hips, as well as a solid and fluid center, good ki extension, and kokyu. Eventually, all techniques will be executed from the suwari-waza position.

Sitting on one's knees, kneeling, was the traditional Japanese way of sitting. It was considered an informal and an insult to sit cross-legged. Therefore, the early martial artist advised was to train and fight from the kneeling position. Training this way also provided a means to develop sensitivity and skills in ground fighting or grappling.

Suwari-Waza Starting Position

Assume a seiza position by sitting on your heels with a few inches between your knees; your posture should be relaxed, your back straight, your centerlines aligned. Staying completely relaxed, allow your weight to settle on the underside of your arms, keep your mind focused on the one point at the center, and extend your ki forward. Keep your arms at an angle greater than 90 degrees. Breathe naturally. Quiet your mind. Establish and maintain metsuki and musubi.

SUWARI-WAZA NIKYO

Suwari-Waza Nikyo

Assume the suwari-waza starting position. As your training partner approaches and attacks *shomen-uchi* (downward head strike), enter and initiate contact and intercept, not interrupt, your training partner's attacking hand. Place one hand to the outside and your other hand underneath, palm down, to protect and control. Move slightly off the attack line. Continue the downward momentum and inertia of the attack, but redirect it in an outward circular path. Bring your partner's hand into his shoulder socket to secure it as your other hand slides down the contour of his forearm to his elbow. Twist at the center and rise up on one knee to provide leverage. Moving to the outside prevents any possibility of attack from his other hand. Holding his hand securely, rotate his elbow down and into the center to execute nikyo. Slowly continue pressure until your training partner taps out, signifying successful execution of the technique and submission.

Suwari-Waza Kote-Gaeshi

Assume the suwari-waza starting position. Your training partner should approach and attack *yokomen-uchi* (lateral diagonal strike to the side of the head or neck). Enter and initiate contact and intercept the strike with your opposite hand. Pull your body slightly backward off the attack line. Bring your defensive hand up for added protection. Bring his attacking hand down along a vertical circular path to redirect it, yet using its momentum and inertia, across the front of your bodies. Maintain a cross-block off the top of his arm to control and prevent its rising. Continue the downward circular path across your body, overextending his arm to the outside, dipping his shoulder and creating a loss of balance. Shift your body weight in order to provide full body power in the redirection. Continue the vertical circular path along the circumference of your extended arm and begin to

SUWARI-WAZA KOTE-GAESHI (CONTINUED ON NEXT PAGE)

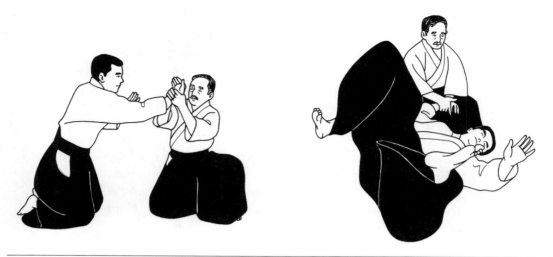

SUWARI-WAZA KOTE-GAESHI (CONTINUED)

bring it up and over. Hold and twist his wrist along the vertical circular path, while shifting the center to provide full body power. Redirect your training partner toward the outside kuzushi point. Continue the momentum until your training partner falls. Holding his hand and pulling it into the center facilitates a safe break fall.

HANMI-HANDACHI-WAZA: ONE STANDS AND ONE KNEELS TECHNIQUES

In another training application, the uke is standing and the tori is kneeling. As in the suwari-waza and seiza, sitting on the knees or kneeling was traditional. Besides the possibility of being attacked by someone else who was kneeling, the possibility exists of being attacked by someone in a standing position. To develop sensitivity and skills for this specific possibility, the hamni-handachi techniques are practiced.

Hanmi-Handachi-Waza Starting Position

Assume a seiza position. Your posture should be relaxed, your back straight, and your centerlines aligned. Staying completely relaxed, allow your weight to settle on the underside of your arms, keep your mind focused on the one point at the center, and extend your ki forward. Breathe naturally. Quiet your mind. Establish and maintain metsuki and musubi.

Hanmi-Handachi Ikkyu

Your training partner approaches and attacks yokomen-uchi (a lateral diagonal strike to the side of the head or neck). Enter by initiating and intercepting, not interrupting, his attack arm. Bring both of your hands straight up the centerline with one hand inside his attacking elbow and your other, defensive, hand atemi to his face. Overextending your training partner's arm on a downward vertical circular path redirects the attack and begins to break his balance. Twisting his body from the center assists the blending and redirecting, and adds full body power and momentum. Continue to follow through in an upward and forward vertical circular path in the opposite direction. Your training partner will have already shifted his weight in order to attempt to regain his balance from the previous overextension. Rotate your hand and elbow over toward the forward kuzushi

HANMI-HANDACHI IKKYO

point. Shikko will assist in shifting your weight behind the techniques and adds full body power and momentum. Pulling his hand outward, while directing his elbow down to the kuzushi point, takes your training partner to the mat. Shifting your weight behind his elbow secures the lock.

Hanmi-Handachi Kote-Gaeshi

Assume the hanmi-handachi-waza starting position. Your training partner should approach and attack with yokomen-uchi. Enter by initiating and intercepting, not interrupting, the attack with the opposite hand, while shifting your weight from the center into the attack. Redirect his attacking hand down on a vertical circular path, overextending, and beginning to break, your training partner's balance. Cross-block his hand from above to control and prevent counterattacks. Continue the downward vertical circular path across your body, and shift your body weight from the center. Begin to turn his wrist out. Continue the forward momentum and inertia on the vertical circular path, while turning his wrist out and shifting your body weight from the center to add full body power behind the technique. Continue as your training partner flips over his own wrist in kote-gaeshi. Holding his hand and pulling it into the center facilitates a safe break fall.

USHIRO-WAZA: TECHNIQUES FROM BEHIND

The advanced aikido practitioner must be able to apply techniques in any context or situation. Previously we covered the standing positions, the kneeling positions, and being attacked while kneeling by an opponent who is standing. Another training application is the attack from the rear, or ushiro-waza.

Ushiro-Waza Sankyo Nage

Assume the aikido ready stance. Your training partner should approach and attack ushiro ryote-dori. Immediately enter and blend with the attack by initiat-

SANKO-NAGE

ing contact and intercepting, not interrupting, the inertia and momentum, by lifting up on and stepping back under your training partner's arm. Reach across with your opposite hand and secure his wrist. The lift and twist of sankyo will begin to control and break your training partner's balance. Securing his hand with his elbow at a 90-degree angle at shoulder level, begin to twist his palm backward. Step in front of your training partner and redirect him on a horizontal circular path to the rear. As your training partner reaches the side, extend his wrist forward toward the kuzushi point, facilitating a throw. Continue to hold his hand, pulling it into the center and assisting your training partner to execute a safe break fall.

Ushiro-Waza Nikyo Kote-Gaeshi

Assume the aikido ready stance. Your training partner should approach and attack ushiro with ryote-dori. Blend with the attack by stepping out to the front with a circular step, rotating your training partner's wrist, and lifting up on his elbow. Your full body spin or pivot will usually break the grip of one hand as your body pulls away. Continue the circular path and momentum to the side, out of range of your training partner's other hand, and rotate your training partner's wrist over until it is perpendicular to the floor with his little finger upward. Redirect the momentum onto a vertical circular path toward the center into

KOTE-GAESHI (CONTINUED ON NEXT PAGE)

KOTE-GAESHI (CONTINUED)

nikyo. Step in, reverse the direction, and execute kote-gaeshi. Hold his hand and pull toward the center to facilitate a safe break fall.

KUBISHIME-WAZA: CHOKES

On a basic level, aikido is practiced most against grabbing approaches and attacks. The advanced aikido practitioner applies more refined techniques against strikes and in a variety of training contexts and situations. Another training application or attack is the use of advanced aikido techniques against chokes.

Kubishime-Waza Ushiro Sankyo Nage

Assume the aikido ready stance. Your training partner should approach and attack ushiro, grabbing one of your wrists and executing a *kubishime* (choke) with his other hand. Enter and blend with the attack by stepping in a circular direction into the choke while raising your grabbed hand up. Your training partner tends to expect a defensive move against the choke rather than the wrist grab, making this strategy easier. Continue the circular step and pull away from your training partner. Stepping under his arm while continuing the circular motion facilitates a release from the choke, while you maintain control of your training

KUBISHIME-WAZA (CONTINUED ON NEXT PAGE)

KUBISHIME-WAZA (CONTINUED)

partner's other hand. Twist the wrist back and up into a sankyo, lifting your training partner on his toes and making him dependent on you for support and balance. Continue to circle your training partner around with sankyo. Step forward, and leading with his wrist toward the front kuzushi point, bring his hand down on a vertical circular path into the center. Complete the throw.

TWO-ON-ONE AND THREE-ON-ONE TECHNIQUES

The basic aikido training scenario is one-on-one. As mentioned previously, an advanced aikido practitioner will refine his or her technical execution and conceptual application through persistent and consistent training and discipline with honest and genuine intent and intensity in a wide variety of situations. One of the application scenarios is to have two or three people hold you simultaneously. The advanced practitioner must maintain mental calm and a relaxed body, and take charge of the situation. This type of training helps to develop great confidence and provides a crowd-pleasing demonstration.

TWO-ON-ONE (CONTINUED ON NEXT PAGE)

TWO-ON-ONE (CONTINUED)

To perform the two-on-one technique, assume the aikido ready stance. Your training partners should approach and attack by each grabbing one of your wrists morote-dori. Step forward, turning or pivoting your body from the center, while raising your hands and bringing both training partners into the center of the technique. Continue to step through, pivoting and stepping back, away from the center. Bring your training partners both into the center so that they collide with each other. Step off to the side, further breaking the balance of both training partners. A step to the back from the center, with your full body weight behind the technique, breaks both training partners' balance and facilitates a fall toward their mutual rear kuzushi (balance) point. Allow your training partners to fall at their own pace.

THREE-ON-ONE TECHNIQUE

To perform the three-on-one technique, assume the aikido ready stance. Three training partners should approach and attack. Two should grab your wrists morote-dori. The third training partner should attack ushiro with kubishime. Slightly turn or twist from the center to initiate contact and establish some iner-

THREE-ON-ONE (CONTINUED ON NEXT PAGE)

THREE-ON-ONE (CONTINUED)

tia and momentum. Bring the two training partners holding your wrists into the
center of the technique to the front. Step out from in between the training partners holding your wrists, using a circular step that uses full momentum and inertia from the center. Continue to spin underneath their arms as all three training
partners begin to collide and interfere with each other's balance. Continue to turn
until all three training partners have the same rear kuzushi point and they cannot
maintain their own balance. Continuing the turn and the collision facilitates a
total loss of balance. A slight push to the rear kuzushi point will send all three
training partners falling on top of each other.

RANDORI: MULTIPLE ATTACKS

Randori is a classical training application. The tori is approached and attacked by several ukes. Often the attacks and responses are predetermined in order to focus on specific techniques. Flowing from one training partner to another makes randori a unique and powerful training experience and application. When practicing randori it is important to stay relaxed and fluid.

To begin assume the aikido ready stance. Three training partners should surround, approach, and attack you.

The first should attack shomen-uchi. Enter and blend by stepping behind the attack, placing one hand atemi to his face to encourage his head to go backward toward the rear kuzushi point. At the same time, grab across his back. Slipping behind your training partner, grab over his shoulder and under his armpit. Simultaneously pull him from behind toward the rear kuzushi point. As your training partner falls, begin to move into the next attack.

The second training partner should approach and attack yokomen-uchi. Enter and blend in the direction of the attack by tenkan stepping to the front with a circular turning motion. Bring both of your hands up the centerline to deflect a strike as well as an atemi (strike or feint) to the face. Follow the forward momentum and inertia of the strike by grabbing his wrist and elbow while pulling back into the center of the technique. Throw your training partner by pulling his arm on a vertical circular path up and into the center. As your training partner falls, look for the next attacker.

The third training partner approaches and attacks with shomen-uchi (an overhead downward strike). Enter and blend with the attack by dropping down in an aiki-drop, emptying the space, and moving into your training partner's legs—intercepting and interrupting his lower body's momentum while encouraging his upper body to continue—and throwing your training partner without touching him.

JIYU-WAZA: FREESTYLE

Usually aikido is practiced in prearranged exercises. The approach and attack is agreed upon, as is the responding technique. While this helps refine the basic fundamental skills to a higher level, it does not teach the body and mind to respond instantaneously and spontaneously. The best way to further refine training and discipline is to begin freestyle, or jiyu-waza, training. In jiyu-waza the student encounters any attack or approach and responds with any waza (technique). Start slowly and relaxed. After a time, increase the pace and the intensity.

RANDORI (CONTINUED ON NEXT PAGE)

RANDORI (CONTINUED)

RANDORI (CONTINUED)

CONCLUSION

The advanced aikido practitioner continually refines the fundamentals of strikes, throws, and locks in a variety of contexts and situations besides the standing position. These additional contextual and situational applications include kokyu-dosa, suwari-waza, hanmi-handachi, ushiro-waza, kubishime-waza, two- or three-on-one, randori, and jiyu-waza. The advanced aikido practitioner will further his or her training by studying combinations, and counters and reversals.

Chapter 10
Combination Techniques

Another way advanced students of aikido learn to improve their technique is by practicing waza against a variety of attacks in order to improve the defense against those attacks. With consistent and persistent training, the student of aikido will be able to convert one technique into another based on the resistance received.

Combination techniques include blending and sequencing. Eventually one should be able to incorporate any approach and attack into any sequence of blending and techniques such as irimi-nage, kaiten-nage, kote-gaeshi, shiho-nage, tenbin-nage, sayu-undo, kokyu-nage, koshi-nage, juji-nage, ikkyo, nikyo, sankyo, or yonkyo.

Learning combination techniques is very important to the advanced aikido practitioner. Aikido often looks a lot like dancing. Aikido is rhythmic and fluid. This type of movement is essential in learning to enter and blend with an opponent. The footwork of aikido facilitates a smooth transition off the attack line, while repositioning the advanced practitioner to redirect and unbalance the opponent effortlessly.

The central concept of nonresistance applies to every aspect of aikido training and technical executions. Training emphasizes the ability to sense resistance and change directions and techniques to make use of the power and force exerted by the defense and resistance offered.

ASHI-SABAKI: FOOTWORK

To provide full body power and force to aikido, footwork is essential. As explained earlier in the chapter on the art of movement, aikido uses three important footwork patterns. They are blending kokyu-ho-ura, irimi-tenkan-ura, and circular tenkan-omote. These footwork patterns move the body by getting it off the line of attack. These movements are very common in aikido applications and should be repeated practiced until the movement is smooth and natural.

The first ashi-sabaki pattern begins just before the hand actually makes contact and grabs the wrist; enter and blend kokyu-ho-ura by sliding your front foot forward into the gyaku-hanmi grab. Allow the forward momentum of the approach and attack to continue by moving slightly off the attack line to the rear, ura. Scoop your hand downward with a slight wrist rotation that ends aligned with the attacker's arm, pointing the direction he is going, with the palm up. Simultaneously, take a circular turning step, tenkan 180 degrees to the rear. You will end up aligned and slightly behind your attacker, looking in the same direction that he is. This same move can be executed to the front, omote.

The second ashi-sabaki pattern begins as your training partner approaches and attacks ai-hanmi; cross-step to his outside slightly off the attack line. Take a natural walking step forward, alongside, to the rear, of attack. With the foot you moved initially, do a circular turning step, tenkan, 180 degrees to the rear. You will end up directly behind and aligned with your attacker, facing the same direction. If the approach and attack is gyaku-hanmi, the initial step is simply to slide forward off the attack line to the rear and then pivot, tenkan, 180 degrees.

The third ashi-sabaki pattern starts as your training partner approaches and attacks; step to the front, omote, slightly off the attack line. Do not interrupt your partner's forward momentum. Take a natural walking step, followed by a 180-degree circular turning step, or tenkan. This puts you behind your attacker.

A great exercise for practicing timing and rhythm is to practice these blending footwork patterns to music. Simply move with each beat. Stay slow, stay relaxed, work on form, and move fluidly. Do not bounce up and down. Keep your head level. With time, pick up the pace. Alternate stepping 180 degrees and 90 degrees.

Another training exercise is to have your training partner approach and attack any way he or she wishes. Your task is to simply enter and blend off the attack line without making any contact or connection that would interrupt or intercept the attack. This can be done randori style with multiple attackers.

Blending Techniques

One of the most characteristic aspects of advanced aikido techniques and training is the ability to enter and blend with an approach or attack. Blending means simply to move with but slightly off the attack line and to lead and redirect the momentum and inertia of the attack. The smoothness of the blending is one way to gauge the level of efficiency and effectiveness of the advanced aikido practitioner. Many advanced practitioners can enter and blend to the extent that there is no longer need for addition technical applications. Their timing is so precise that the attacker loses balance simply because the defender is no longer there.

Awase: Blending Tenkan Ura (Kokyu-ho) Ikkyo

Assume the aikido ready stance. Your training partner approaches and attacks gyaku-hanmi. Immediately enter and blend with your partner's inertia and momentum by sliding your foot forward until it is level with your training partner's front foot. Tenkan ura until alongside your training partner. His wrist remains relatively stationary as the pivot point with your body moving around it. The placement of your training partner's hand palm up facilitates a twisting of his wrist, a bending of his elbow, a structural integration and alignment, and the beginning of a loss of his balance. Step back while swinging your training partner around to the rear. Continue the horizontal circular path, reach across, and secure your training partner's wrist with your other hand. Continue to step behind, following the horizontal circular path, sliding his gripped hand to his elbow. Continue to circle while rotating his elbow over and down toward the kuzushi point. Continue pressure on his wrist and elbow as his body turns from the center, precipitating a fall to the mat. Follow the momentum down, and secure your training partner with an ikkyo.

KOKYU-HO IKKYO-NAGE

Awase: Blending Ura Kokyu-ho Irimi-Nage

Assume the aikido ready stance. Your training partner should approach and attack gyaku-hanmi. Immediately slide your front foot forward until it is aligned with your training partner's front foot. Using your front foot and the wrist as the pivot points, tenkan ura. Twist to a palm-up position to force your training partner to bend his elbow, dip his shoulder, and begin to lose his balance. Step out and continue to swing your training partner on a horizontal circular path to the rear. Continue to turn, step out again, and secure your training partner's wrist

BLENDING URA IRIMI-NAGE

with your opposite hand. Slide your other hand up, following the contour of his arm, to his neck. Continue the circular path with a slight downward dip. Pull your training partner around, using your full body power, and turn from the center. Securing his neck, slide your hand up the contour of his arm until your forearm aligns with his jaw line from the chin to the ear. Push with one hand on his lower back, while guiding his head backward toward the rear kuzushi point. Following through while stepping forward facilitates the irimi-nage.

IRIMI-TENKAN

Awase: Blending Irimi-Tenkan Irimi-Nage

Assume the aikido ready stance. Your training partner should approach and attack ai-hanmi. Immediately enter and blend by simultaneously rotating your wrists upward on a vertical circular path, while cross-stepping and beginning to tenkan ura. Your defensive hand should deliver an atemi to your training partner's rib cage, which creates a further desire to turn into the redirection motion. Continue on a vertical circular motion with your hands and on a horizontal circular motion with your footwork to the rear. Reach up and secure his neck with your defensive hand. Continue to turn, while pulling your training partner's head into the center. As your training partner comes around to the side, cut his upper body's momentum abruptly by moving your forearm, following the contour of his arm up, to align with his jaw line from chin to ear. Lift his chin up and backward toward the rear kuzushi point, while allowing the momentum and inertia of his lower body to continue forward. Rotate his hand downward toward the rear kuzushi point and step forward to add full body power from the center into the execution of the technique. Follow through until your training partner falls safely.

Awase: Circular Yokomen-Uchi Shiho-Nage

Assume the aikido ready stance. Your training partner approaches and attacks yokomen-uchi. Enter and blend with the momentum of the attack by sliding

CIRCULAR YOKOMEN–UCHI SHIHO-NAGE

forward, slightly off the attack line. Initiate contact and intercept, not interrupt, your training partner's attacking hand. Take a large circular tenkan to the front, while redirecting his striking arm on a diagonal circular path. Coordinating your hands and body movement, allow full body movement from the center to be used to redirect and control the attack. The swinging motion of your body will confuse and disrupt your training partner's balance. Grab his wrist with both hands and continue to pull and turn him along the downward diagonal path. Stepping in, begin to lift his arm on a vertical circular path upward. Slide his elbow up to align his forearms and lift his elbow up to encourage your training partner's body to turn. Step under his arm and continue to turn from the center in the direction of the rear kuzushi point. Bring his hands down along the centerline toward the rear kuzushi point. Follow through until your training partner falls safely backward.

Awase: Circular

Assume the aikido ready stance. Your training partner approaches and attacks with morote-dori. Enter and blend with the momentum and inertia of the attack by sliding your front foot forward and stepping slightly off the attack line. Begin to drop your elbow and rotate your hand over the top of his hand. Continue to use your hand as the pivot point and swing your training partner around, redirecting the attack and facilitating a loss of his balance. As your training partner comes around on the horizontal circular path, step underneath, cutting the circle. Bring his hand forward toward the front kuzushi point while dropping to one knee to empty the space and to facilitate the fall. Follow through, letting you training partner roll safely away.

SEQUENTIAL COMBINATION TECHNIQUES

Besides blending, combinations can be sequential. Technically and conceptually, any aikido technique can follow the flow into any other aikido technique. As a training partner approaches and attacks, the defender will enter and blend using footwork and body turning to get off the attack line. The defender will then apply a technique that may be met with resistance. Since aikido is nonresistance, the appropriate response would be to change directions and techniques in accordance with the resistance perceived. Sequential combinations require training and discipline to build a high level of sensitivity in the body and flexibility in the thinking and responding to the changing contextual and situational factors.

Training exercises can purposely be practiced with one technique leading into another, to gain confidence and fluidity.

Nikyo Kokyu-Nage

Assume the aikido ready stance. Your training partner should approach and attack ai-hanmi. Immediately enter and blend by initiating contact and interrupting the momentum and inertia by rotating his wrist over and stepping slightly off the attack line. Redirect the attack toward the front and align with the centerline. Secure his wrist with the defensive hand grab and apply nikyo. Your

training partner may begin to lose his balance. Allow your training partner to rise back up while stepping ura. Redirect your training partner again by swinging him around. As your training partner comes to the side, hold his elbow steady as the pivot point and rotate his forearm and hand over backward toward the rear kuzushi point. Follow through by stepping forward from the center, adding full body power to the throw.

CONCLUSION

The advanced aikido practitioner will consistently and persistently train with honest and genuine intent and intensity in a variety of contexts and situations. The advanced aikido practitioner will continually refine the fundamental strikes, throws and locks, applications, combinations, and counters and reversals.

TIPS FOR REFINING COMBINATIONS

1. Maintain erect posture and structural alignment.
2. Relax and breathe.
3. Calm your mind.
4. Keep movement fluid with footwork and body turning.
5. Develop sensitivity to resistance throughout the technical execution.
6. Practice at a slow pace for the purpose of moving smoothly from one technique to another.
7. Free the mind and be creative.
8. Always follow through and finish the combinations or sequences of techniques.
9. Maintain zanshin.

Chapter 11
Counters and Reversals

Most of aikido training and discipline is achieved through the direct application of a specific technique. As training develops and the basics are further refined, the need to learn how to counter or reverse a technique naturally, sequentially, and developmentally occurs and this becomes part of the training. There are many benefits from learning counters and reversals.

One value of learning advanced aikido counter techniques is the continual refining of basic techniques. Counters and reversals amplify and clarify any weakness in execution or form. If an aikido technique is done correctly, it is very hard to apply a counter or reversal. Therefore, the practice of counters can build sensitivity for where the weaknesses are. The problem with practicing counter techniques is that your training partner will have to practice the initial technique weakly or wrongly in order to provide the opening for practice. This can lead to some bad habits if trained too much.

A value of learning advanced aikido counter techniques is the ability to train in flowing, exchanging, reversing, and countering techniques in a training situation. There is a natural tendency to react to techniques from both the giving and receiving perspectives. Through practice of counter or reversal techniques, one learns to flow differently than one does in the usual practice pattern.

By applying advanced aikido concepts to counter techniques, the advanced student actually learns to defend him- or herself from the application of the basic aikido techniques. All training situations are, by design and definition, artificial. The usual practice pattern is one attack followed by one response. In the real world, every action has a reaction. There is a give and take to reality. Counter technique practice allows spontaneous reactions throughout the technical execution sequence.

Counter techniques make for excellent demonstrations. The flow of one technique into another with the changing of who is the attacker and who is the defender engages the spectators and impresses them with the spontaneity and creativity of the flow of aikido techniques.

Counter techniques are fun to practice and provide variety to training.

KAESHI-WAZA NAGE-WAZA: COUNTER TECHNIQUES TO THROWING TECHNIQUES

Counter techniques or reversals can be applied to any basic aikido technique. Basic aikido techniques are usually throws or locks. Training in counter techniques against throws helps refine the fundamentals.

Kaeshi-Waza Irimi-Nage:
Counter Technique to Entering Throw

Assume the aikido ready stance. Your training partner should approach, attack, and begin to apply irimi-nage. Going with the inertia and momentum of the technique, enter and blend with it by stepping forward. Turn completely to the outside, grabbing your training partner's wrist in sankyo. Rotate your training partner around you on the pivot point on a horizontal circular path. Reverse and redirect him backward, again rotating your training partner around you as the center of the technique. Continue to bring your training partner back. Following through, lead your training partner behind you. Drop down to empty the space,

COUNTER-IRIMI-NAGE (CONTINUED ON NEXT PAGE)

COUNTER-IRIMI-NAGE (CONTINUED)

leading with his wrist toward the front kuzushi point. Continue to follow through, allowing your training partner to roll safely away.

Kaeshi-Waza Shiho-Nage:
Counter Technique 1 to Four-Direction Throw

Assume the aikido ready stance. Your training partner should approach, attack, and initiate shiho-nage omote. Your training partner slides under your arm and

COUNTER-SHIHO-NAGE 1 (CONTINUED ON NEXT PAGE)

COUNTER-SHIHO-NAGE 1 (CONTINUED)

initiates the shiho-nage toward the rear kuzushi point. Spin under his arm, taking the training partner's balance. Continue to pivot, bringing your training partner's arm down with his elbow slightly locked out to further take his balance. Rotate his hand over, while stepping out, and apply nikyo. Continue until your training partner taps out to signify successful execution of the technique and submission.

Kaeshi-Waza Shiho-Nage:
Counter Technique 2 to Four-Direction Throw

Assume the aikido ready stance. Your training partner should approach, attack, and initiate shiho-nage ura. Spin under his arm in the opposite direction and step out, taking control of your training partner's arm. Continue to step out on the circular path, securing your training partner's wrist. Rotate his wrist over until his little finger points up and his wrist is perpendicular to the floor. Apply nikyo. Allow your training partner to rise up. Rotate his wrist in the opposite direction, twisting his wrist outward in kote-gaeshi toward the rear kuzushi point. Continue to rotate his wrist, turning at the center to provide full body power and torque into the technique execution. Continue until your training partner lands safely on the mat.

COUNTER-SHIHO-NAGE 2

Kaeshi-Waza Kote-Gaeshi:
Counter Technique 1 to Wrist-Turnout Throw

Assume the aikido ready stance. Your training partner should approach, attack, and begin to apply kote-gaeshi. Reach up with your defensive hand and secure your training partner's wrist. Step to the rear tenkan. Bring his hand over on a vertical circular path toward his rear kuzushi point. Pivot at the center to provide

COUNTER-KOTE-GAESHI 1

full body power and torque behind the technique. Continue to follow through and bring your training partner's wrist, tucked behind his head, down toward the rear kuzushi point. Continue and secure your training partner to the mat.

Kaeshi-Waza Kote-Gaeshi: Counter Technique 2 to Wrist-Turnout Throw

Assume the aikido ready stance. Your training partner should approach, attack, and initiate kote-gaeshi. As your training partner brings his hand up on a vertical circular path, step in, and continue the circular momentum and inertia while stepping ura tenkan (with a pivoting circular step). Maintaining a hold on his hand, follow the vertical circular path toward your training partner's rear kuzushi point. Step forward from the center to bring full body power and torque into the technique. Continue to bring your training partner's wrist, tucked behind his head, in shiho-nage toward the rear kuzushi point. Lower your center to help drop the weight into the technique for added power. Continue until your training partner falls, and secure him to the mat.

COUNTER-KOTE-GAESHI 2

Kaeshi-Waza Juyi-Nage:
Counter Technique to the Cross-Arm Throw

Assume the aikido ready stance. Your training partner should approach, attack, and initiate juyi-nage. As your training partner steps forward and attempts to grab and separate your arms, rotate his hand to the outside of your arm. Step out and tenkan while securing his wrist and elbow. The swinging motion precipitates a temporary loss of balance for your training partner. Continue a downward cir-

COUNTER-TENBIN-NAGE

cular spiral until your training partner falls face down on the mat. Continue to pivot, following the downward spiral, and secure your training partner.

Kaeshi-Waza Tenbin-Nage: Counter Technique to the Elbow-Lock Throw

Assume the aikido ready stance. Your training partner should approach, attack, and initiate tenbin-nage. As your training partner steps forward, while applying pressure to his elbow, enter and blend by turning your body to the front across the front of his body. Continue to step out and tenkan to the outside. Rotate your wrist up and over your training partner's wrist. Secure his hand with your defensive hand. Pulling forward to break his balance, apply nikyo. Ease up the pressure, stretch out your arm, secure his elbow, and step behind tenkan. Take your training partner face down to the mat on a circular spiral path by applying ikkyo.

COUNTER-KOSHI-NAGE

Kaeshi-Waza Koshi-Nage:
Counter Technique to the Hip Throw

Assume the aikido ready stance. Your training partner should approach, attack, and initiate koshi-nage. As your training partner begins to lower his center of gravity and lift his weight forward, enter and blend by turning at the center and stepping around to the front. Grab the body of your training partner. Step completely around to the front until both of your bodies align at the centerlines. Without losing momentum, allow your center to fall backward, bringing your training partner forward. Pulling into the center, continue to drop and execute uke-waza.

Kaeshi-Waza Juyi-Nage:
Counter Technique 1 to the Cross-Arm Throw

Assume the aikido ready stance. Your training partner should approach, attack, and initiate juyi-nage. As your training partner pushes forward, blend with the momentum but redirect it upward and over his head. Pivot or turn underneath

COUNTER-JUYI-NAGE 1

his arms and bring them down on a vertical circular path. Secure both of his wrists and step out. Continue the vertical circular path of his arms and step in, slightly off the attack line, bringing his hand and arm up for irimi-nage. Continue to follow through toward the rear kuzushi point. Follow through, and throw your training partner safely to the mat.

Kaeshi-Waza Juyi-Nage:
Counter Technique 2 to the Cross-Arm Throw

Assume the aikido ready stance. Your training partner should approach, attack, and initiate juyi-nage. As your training partner pushes forward, blend and utilize his momentum by turning underneath his arms. Continue to spiral and bring his arms forward, leading your training partner toward the front kuzushi point. Bring his arms down, while continuing to pivot. Change or redirect his arms into

an upward vertical circular direction, while stepping off the line. Bring his arms up into irimi-nage. Step forward and redirect your forearm against his jaw line from chin to ear, while trapping his arms against his face. Turning his hand over, aim him toward the rear kuzushi point. Follow through, and throw your training partner to the mat.

KAESHI-WAZA KATAME-WAZA: COUNTER TECHNIQUES TO LOCK TECHNIQUES

To continually progress and evolve in the technical executions and conceptual application of aikido, the training and discipline must offer counters and reversal for locks as well as throws.

Kaeshi-Waza Ikkyo: Counter Technique 1 to the First Teaching or Lock Pinning Technique

Assume the aikido ready stance. Your training partner should approach, attack, and initiate ikkyo from the gyaku-hanmi position. As your training partner grabs your wrist and elbow, enter and blend with the momentum of the technique by stepping into the flow. Begin rotating your wrist on an upward vertical circular path and step around on a horizontal circular path from the center to provide full

body power to the redirection. Step behind your training partner, secure his wrist and elbow, and apply ikkyo. Continue the downward spiral, keeping his hand at the center and applying pressure to his elbow. Continue to follow through until your training partner is secured face down on the mat.

Kaeshi-Waza Ikkyo: Counter Technique 2 to the First Teaching or Lock Pinning Technique

Assume the aikido ready stance. Your training partner should approach, attack, and respond to an ai-hanmi grab by initiating ikkyo by blending back with your grab and beginning to rotate his wrist forward. Your training partner steps forward from the center and rotates your arm forward on a vertical circular path. As your training partner continues on the downward circular path of ikkyo, shift your weight forward rather than let your arm get in front of his body and break your balance. Cross-step around to the front on a horizontal circular path, while dropping your elbow and rotating your wrist on a vertical circular path. Continue the horizontal circular footwork while pivoting from the center, and take control of his wrist and elbow. Stepping to the rear, rotate your arms down and back. Continue the spiral motion, holding his hand at the center and applying downward

COUNTER IKKYO 2 (CONTINUED ON NEXT PAGE)

COUNTER IKKYO 2 (CONTINUED)

pressure to his elbow. Continue to follow through until your training partner is secure, face down, on the mat.

Kaeshi-Waza Nikyo: Counter Technique to the Second Teaching or Lock Pinning Technique

Assume the aikido ready stance. Your training partner should approach, attack, and initiate nikyo from a gyaku-hanmi position. As your training partner steps out while securing your wrist, enter and blend with the technique by stepping in the direction of the momentum while beginning to pivot your center on a horizontal circular path and simultaneously rotating your wrist on a vertical circular path. Bring your defensive hand into the center. Continue your wrist rotation until the te-gatana is on the top of your training partner's wrist, which has now rotated so that it is perpendicular to the mat with the edge of his little finger up. Secure his trapped hand with your defensive hand. Step to the side, bring his trapped hand into his shoulder socket, bend his wrist and elbow to 90 degrees at shoulder level, and align your centers and centerlines. Slide your hand, following the contour of his forearm, to his elbow and apply nikyo by twisting his hand up while pushing his elbow down. Your training partner will react with pain and

COUNTER NIKYO (CONTINUED ON NEXT PAGE)

COUNTER NIKYO (CONTINUED)

compliance. Continue until your training partner taps out, signifying successful completion of the technique and submission.

Kaeshi-Waza Sankyo: Counter Technique 1 to the Third Teaching or Lock Pinning Technique

Assume the aikido ready stance. Your training partner should approach, attack, and initiate sankyo from a gyaku-hanmi position. Your training partner should attempt to secure your wrist and hand and begin the downward circular motion, while twisting your wrist, and step in and under your arm and secure sankyo. As your training partner attempts to travel under your arm, enter and blend with the momentum of the technique by beginning to step forward and around to the front on a horizontal circular path. Continue to step tenkan, with a circular pivot step from the center, to the front and wrap your arms around your training partner's head. Secure and control his elbow with your defensive hand. Step out, securing his wrist and elbow, and begin to apply ikkyo. Step forward into ikkyo, applying downward pressure to his wrist and elbow toward the front kuzushi point. Continue to follow through until your training partner is secured face down on the mat and taps out to signify successful completion and submission.

COUNTER SANKYO 1 (CONTINUED ON NEXT PAGE)

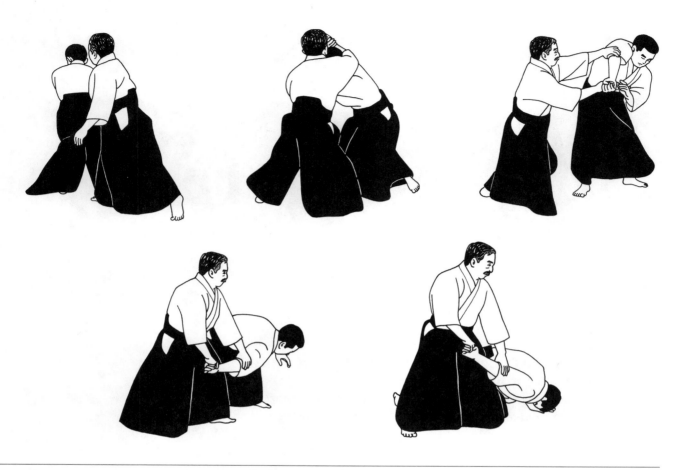

Kaeshi-Waza Sankyo: Counter Technique 2 to the Third Teaching or Lock Pinning Technique

Assume the aikido ready stance. Your training partner should approach, attack, and begin to initiate sankyo. Enter and blend with the technique by immediately redirecting and raising your elbow, stepping forward into the center. Begin to rotate your wrist on an upward circular path. Bring his elbow down as your wrist

COUNTER SANKYO 2 (CONTINUED)

rotates over, secure his elbow with your defensive hand, and step to the rear of the technique so that power will come from behind. Continue to rotate his arm over, while stepping in and aligning with your training partner's contour and posture. Holding his hand at the wrist, continue to rotate his elbow toward the front kuzushi point, and step forward from the center, adding full body power to the technique execution. Continue to follow through until your training partner is face down on the mat, tapping out to signify successful completion of the technique and submission.

Kaeshi-Waza Yonkyo: Counter Technique to the Fourth Teaching or Lock Pinning Technique

Assume the aikido ready stance. Your training partner should approach, attack, and attempt to initiate yonkyo. Enter and blend with the technique before your training partner can switch hands and secure yonkyo from a gyaku-hanmi position after attempting and meeting resistance to sankyo. Redirect the momentum by stepping to the front while dipping and rotating your wrist. Step around to the outside with a tenkan, aligning your centers and centerlines. Continue the

COUNTER YONKYO (CONTINUED ON NEXT PAGE)

COUNTER YONKYO (CONTINUED)

rotation of your wrist on a vertical circular path upward. Your defensive hand should secure your training partner's bottom hand. Keep the pressure on and the momentum in the movement to keep your training partner slightly off-balance. Continue the rotation of both wrists toward the front kuzushi point, while stepping back to place your center and your body behind the technique for full body power in execution. Continue the downward rotation, securing both of his wrists. Execute kote-gaeshi. Maintain control of his hand, pulling it into the center to allow your training partner to execute a safe break fall.

Kaeshi-Waza Ikkyo: Counter Technique to the First Teaching or Lock Pinning Technique

Assume that the aikido ready stance. Your training partner should approach, attack, and attempt to initiate ikkyo from an ai-hanmi position. Enter and blend with the momentum by leaning forward as your training partner attempts to rotate your arm on a vertical circular path. As your arm comes forward and down, redirect the momentum and priority by stepping forward into your training partner's front leg. Place your foot between his legs and behind his lead foot. Bend your elbow to absorb the momentum. Shift your weight into your training partner's center, directed toward the rear kuzushi point. With his foot blocked, lock his knee with your knee, continue to shift your weight into the center toward the rear kuzushi point, and apply backward pressure with your arm to his upper body.

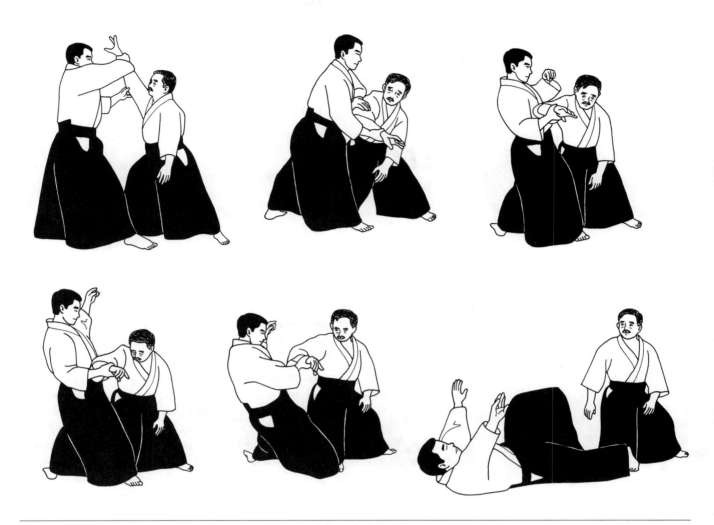

COUNTER IKKYO

Dropping your weight into your leg pushes your training partner's knee from the inside out, while preventing him from repositioning his foot and regaining balance. Continue to apply forward momentum from the center through your legs, and push his inner knee in the direction of the rear kuzushi point. Allow your training partner to fall safely to the mat at his or her own pace.

CONCLUSION

The advanced aikido practitioner continually refines the fundamentals through training and discipline in technical execution and conceptual application to strikes, throws and locks, in various contextual and situational applications, combinations, and counters and reversals. Along with inner development from knowing the history of aikido, developing and implementing a training philosophy, training the mind, and understanding and using ki, the advanced aikido practitioner understands and applies the theories and concepts of body mechanics, movement, and engagement. Most of theses training and disciplinary experiences happen within the walls of the dojo. Taking practice and discipline to the next level often means leaving the dojo.

Chapter 12
Strikes

In aikido the advanced techniques are actually a refining of the basics. The advanced aikido practitioner understands, practices, and continually refines strikes and feints, throws and locks, applications, combinations, counters, and reversals.

Atemi translates to mean preemptive strikes to vital points and parts of the body. Generally, atemi means any strike or feint with the honest intention and intensity to do damage, distract the opponent, or upset the opponent's balance.

Initially, most aikido practice and training involves the use of grabs rather than strikes. These grabs include ai-hanmi (same hand), gyaku-hanmi (opposite hand), ryote-dori (two-handed grab of both wrists), and morote-dori (two-handed grab of one wrist). Grabs are emphasized because they happen in reality, and they make learning the techniques and concepts of aikido easier than strikes do.

TRADITIONAL ATEMI

Atemi, or striking, in the traditional sense, usually follows three paths. The first is the overhead downward strike, shomen-uchi. The second is the diagonal strike, yokomen-uchi. The third is the straight thrust, tsuki. All three atemi resemble and mimic sword strikes.

Shomen-uchi is an overhead downward strike aimed at the top of the head. Start in the ready neutral stance with your hands held in front of your body on the centerline. If the right leg is back, inhale and bring your right hand up overhead. Exhale and step forward with your rear foot at the same time that you bring the edge of the hand directly down the centerline. Continue to follow through on the strike until it reaches your center at waist level.

Yokomen-uchi is a diagonal overhead strike aimed at the side of your head or neck. Start in the neutral ready stance with your hands held in front of your body on the centerline. If your right leg is back, inhale and bring your right hand overhead or to the side of your ear. Exhale and step forward with your rear foot at the same time that you bring the edge of your hand snapping diagonally to the side of your head or neck at approximately a 45-degree angle. Continue to follow through until the strike reaches the centerline of the target.

Tsuki is a direct straight thrust, usually with a fist to the solar plexus, stomach, or heart. Start in the neutral ready stance with your hands held in front of your body on the centerline. If your right leg is back, inhale and pull or chamber your right fist relaxed to the side of your waist with the palm up. Exhale and step forward with your right foot at the same time that you snap or thrust your right fist forward directly on the centerline. At the very end of the snap, thrust or punch turn your fist over palm downward and tighten it.

STRIKES

Other strikes normally associated with boxing are also commonly used. They include the jab, cross, hook, and uppercut. Aikido techniques against these strikes are shown in the self-defense chapter. The back-fist is also a common strike.

The jab is perhaps the most important strike in boxing. While it is not necessarily the most powerful strike, the jab is used to feel out one's opponent and to set up the other strikes. Start in the ready neutral stance with your hands held high, elbows down, looking out between the hands. Inhale as your body rocks backward slightly. As one's body rocks forward, step forward slightly and shoot your forward hand out with a snapping motion.

The cross follows the jab. After executing a jab, as you pull your forward hand back to the side of your head, turn your body at the waist and thrust or snap your rear hand out on the centerline. The term cross describes the path, across the body, as well as across the opponent's lead jab. The cross is a power punch.

The hook is a horizontal strike aimed at the side of the head on the ear or the jaw, the ribs, or the kidneys. After the jab-cross combination, turn your body and front foot, while lifting your elbow, and hook your fist to the side of the target. Follow through to at least the centerline of the target.

The uppercut is a vertically upward strike aimed at the stomach, heart, or the underside of the jaw and chin. Your fist should be turned with the palm facing your body and the elbow held underneath for support and power. Start the strike low, exhale as the strike follows an upward path through the intended target.

The back-fist is thrown using the back of the fist and knuckles to strike the target area.

KICKS

Kicks are not commonly used in aikido. While they are popular in the media and movies, they are often impractical in actual fighting, especially the higher kick. Kicks leave only one foot on the ground and make the stance unstable and easily unbalanced. Nonetheless, it is important to know how to deliver and defend against kicks.

The front kick is snapped or thrust forward on the centerline and can be aimed at the legs, groin, stomach, solar plexus, heart, or head. Start in a ready neutral stance with your hands held relaxed but defensively on the centerline. The rear leg is brought forward on the centerline by first lifting the knee and then following with a thrust or snap of the foot. A snap front kick is often followed by returning the leg to the rear. A thrust kick follows straight through the target and ends with a step forward. The lower kick can be delivered with the top of the foot. Middle kicks are thrust through with the heel of the foot. High kicks usually use the ball of the foot by pulling one's toes back.

The sidekick is also thrust or snapped. Start in a ready neutral stance with your hands held relaxed but defensively on the centerline. As in the front kick, bring your knee up first. As you exhale and thrust your foot out, pivot on your supporting leg and turn your hip over, making the kick come from the side. The side thrust kick can be aimed low at the leg or at a medium level at the stomach, ribs, or kidneys, or high to the head.

The roundhouse kick follows a circular path. Start in a ready neutral stance with your hands held relaxed but defensively on the centerline. Pivot on your front leg, bringing your rear leg around on a circular path. Low kicks can be targeted to the lower leg, inner or outer thigh, usually impacting with the top of the foot. Sometimes, the shins can be used as the contact weapon. At a middle level, the target can be the stomach, solar plexus, ribs, or kidneys impacting with the shin, ball of the foot, or the top of the foot. High kicks target the head, impacting with the ball of the foot or the top of the foot.

The crescent kick gets its name from the fact that the path of the kick is a crescent. Start in a ready neutral stance with your hands held relaxed but defensively on the centerline. Bring your rear leg across in front of your body to the opposite side outside, sweeping it upward and back across your body, impacting with the side of the foot to the ribs or head. An inside crescent kick sweeps upward and inward from the same side of the body, following a circular crescent motion.

Spin kicks require turning the back on the opponent, so should be used with caution. Start with the usual ready neutral stance with your hands relaxed but defensively on the centerline. Slide your front foot forward to create some momentum and spin your body to the rear by moving the back hip. To execute the backspin thrust kick, tuck your rear leg underneath by leading with the knee up and then thrust behind your leg to the front as you pivot on your stabilizing leg. The spin kick can also deliver a crescent kick.

Occasionally, individuals will deliver any of the kicks while jumping. While fancy, there is no stability, they take time to deliver, and are easily avoided and defended against.

OTHER

Besides strikes with the hand and kicks with the feet, strikes can be delivered with the forearms, elbows, shins, knees, and the head.

FEINTS

Feints are important in aikido. An atemi used as a feint or fake draws a reaction from the opponent. The physical movement of that reaction can change the direction of the technique. An example is throwing an atemi or feint toward the head as your opponent pulls away to avoid the strike, follow that path and throw in that direction. A low feint to the stomach area would precipitate your opponent's bending over, which would allow you to use the front kuzushi balance point to your advantage. The mental reaction to a feint often puts the focus in a different place than the actual physical technique does. For example, when meeting resistance to a nikyo lock, a quick feint to the head will cause your opponent to flinch and protect his or her head and release the resistance on your arm, which can immediately be reapplied successfully.

INTERCEPTING AND REDIRECTING ATEMI

Aikido does not utilize blocks. Blocking stops the momentum of the attack and makes the technique static, stationary, and difficult. The aiki approach is to gently and subtly enter and intercept the attack, get off the attack line, and blend with the strike by following and overextending its natural path and direction. The momentum of the attack is the redirected toward a kuzushi balance point until the opponent loses balance.

TRAINING

Solo training in atemi can take several forms. Heavy bag hitting will develop strength and alignment. Speed bag hitting will develop speed. Double-end bag hitting will develop accuracy and movement. Hitting at paper or candles will develop focus and control. Hitting at tennis balls on a string, especially if tied at the head, heart, and groin level, will develop accuracy and movement. Shadow boxing or performing techniques as kata (forms) or free style, will develop flowing, especially if done to rhythm (such as to music).

To develop sensitivity to the use of atemi, slowly practice waza with your training partner. Feel a good opportunity to atemi. Do not forget that you can atemi with a variety of body weapons such as the hands, elbows, feet, knees, and even a head butt. Do not forget to hit to a variety of targets such as the head, heart, stomach, arms, and legs.

Atemi becomes increasingly important during self-defense training. Ideally, all students of aikido should handle even severe threats with compassion and nonviolence.

CONCLUSION

There is some debate about the place and percentage of atemi in aikido. Some feel that because aikido is nonviolent, there is no place for atemi. Some branches of aikido have eliminated them from the curriculum. This raises some question about aikido remaining a martial art. Others feel that we have gotten too far away from the martial art aspects and are calling for a reviving of strong, focused atemi in training and practice.

It is said that O'Sensei Morihei Ueshiba used a high percentage of atemi that were timed so precisely and thrown with such intent that in trying to avoid them one would lose balance and be thrown to the ground. Any exercise of intent or movement toward a vital or balance point is also an atemi. It could also be interpreted that for O'Sensei Morihei Ueshiba, the majority of activity in an encounter was the attacker striking at him, using 70 percent of the time and

---

TIPS FOR REFINING STRIKES

1. Stay relaxed in body and keep your mind calm.

2. Keep your body centered, balanced, and structurally aligned.

3. Keep your elbows down and in.

4. Keep your body behind the strike and kick.

5. Exhale or kiai on impact or full extension.

6. Keep your hands relaxed and defensively on the centerline.

7. Start and return to a ready neutral stance.

8. Practice executing strikes and kicks with honest and genuine intent and intensity so that your training partner actually has to work the technique and gain technical proficiency.

9. Practice receiving strikes and kicks that will make contact and inflict damage if not responded to effectively and efficiently. This builds confidence.

expending 70 percent of the energy, and being thrown all the time by only 30 percent of the energy.

Advanced aikido practitioners continually refine the basics by learning and using strikes and feints. They also understand and apply the advanced techniques of throws and locks.

Part Four

Advanced Applications—
Taking Your Practice to the Next Level

Chapter 13
Self-Defense Techniques

The best way to be able to defend oneself and others against other fighting styles is to do some cross-training in them. Understanding different fighting systems allows the advanced practitioner to explore different distances, tools, and contexts for use in self-defense situations. The ma-ai dictates the attack and the response. One cannot use long-range kicks at close range or grapple at long range. Most styles of martial arts or fighting contain most of these tools and ranges. The difference between styles mostly lies in emphasis.

It is important to remember that training is not sparring, sparring is not fighting, and fighting is not combat. Each has its own unique rules of engagement and intent. Training is very methodical and predictable with intent to learn. Sparring is less predictable but has rules of engagement and intent to win by the criteria set by the contest. Fighting in the street has few, if any, rules, and the intent is to beat the other person, causing some bodily harm. Combat is without any rules of engagement and the sole intent is to kill the enemy before he kills you and the people next to you.

A basic discussion and description of the strikes and kicks used in self-defense training and discipline were included previously in the chapter on strikes.

A SELF-DEFENSE MINDSET
The development of a self-defense mindset is essential in aikido. Aikido is a martial art, but its intention is to provide a means to protect oneself and others.

Essential to the self-defense mindset are two intentions. First, you must believe that uke, or in this case your attacker, will really follow through with the intention to do you great bodily harm or even death. Second, you must intend to follow through and stop them. There must be no hesitation in execution within a self-defense context. That is why the self-defense mindset must be chosen, developed, and trained before having any encounter.

The way you train will be the way you fight. It is false confidence cultivated through unrealistic training that leads to many injuries or deaths in self-defense. When training for self-defense purposes have the mindset of intention.

ATTACK AWARENESS AND PREVENTION
The best way to defend yourself is not to be in a situation where you have to. A little environmental awareness beforehand can prevent many situations. One can prevent, manage, or resolve confrontations best with good manners, a sense of

humor, and humility. There will be a few, hopefully very few, situations in which you will not be able to prevent, manage, or resolve conflict verbally. First, always try to walk and talk your way out of confrontations.

Be aware that this can be a dangerous world and that simply because you are tolerant and compassionate toward your fellow man does not mean that the rest of the world feels that way. Some people, due to poor self-esteem and coping skills, feel entitled to take whatever they want by whatever means they have to. You are fair game to them whether you think you are or should be.

No one can prevent confrontations that are outside one's awareness. There is no need to live with fear and paranoia. Very few people are criminals, much less dangerous. Nonetheless, criminals do exist, and you must be ready for them because they are ready for you.

TRAINING FOR SELF-DEFENSE APPLICATION

Training is very context and scenario driven. That means that the environment you train in will be the one in which you fight best. The dojo is an artificial context. In the dojo, there are rules of etiquette and engagement, which are very different from the ones you may face in the street. In the street, surprise, rather than a prearranged attack and defense response, will greet you. You will be caught off-guard. Your senses are sharpened and then dulled by the adrenaline pump, rush, and eventual dump.

Most of the approaches and attacks shown and demonstrated here come from formal styles of martial arts. The street fighter may or may not know any of these. They will have seen movies and honed skills on previous victims. They will not fight within one system. Therefore, after you feel comfortable with the different attacks, have your training partner mix them up. Have an attack launched while in the middle of a conversation. There are stories of O'Sensei Morihei Ueshiba telling his students to attack him at anytime, in and out of the dojo. None were able to find a weakness. He was always ready.

Train in street clothes. Train in a park, parking lot, or alley. Train in the dark or blindfolded. Train standing, seated, and lying on your back. Train coming out of or going into a doorway or your car. Train turning corners. By training in a number of unconventional and unexpected contexts and scenarios, you will develop greater abilities and confidence in your skills.

STRIKES AND PUNCHES

The boxer is one of today's most effective fighters. The boxer fights in a very specific distance, in between the kicker and the grappler. At a kicking range, the boxer uses footwork to cut off the right and maneuver or manipulate the situation. The boxer will move to bring his or her training partner into their power range to use their most powerful tools, the hands. The offensive arsenal of the boxer includes the lead jab, cross, hook, and uppercut.

The boxer throws the jab by pushing or snapping the lead hand forward in a straight line. The boxer usually holds the rear hand close to the head to protect it. The jab, usually considered a power punch, is the tool that feels out the training partner, establishes the distance and tempo, counters an offense, and sets up combinations.

The boxer throws the straight cross from the rear hand, usually preceded by the jab. Thrown hard, pushing off the rear leg, the cross is a power punch capable of knocking the boxer's training partner out.

The boxer delivers the hook, unlike the jab or cross, as a horizontal punch on a tight circular path toward the side of the head or body. Twisting his hip adds additional power by putting the body into it.

The uppercut is the least used tool of the boxer and requires much closer range. The uppercut, as the name implies, comes up from underneath, almost like an upward hook. The boxer delivers, and usually targets, the uppercut to the chin or solar plexus.

JAB

Establish the aikido ready stance by remaining centered and balanced. Your training partner should approach and attack with a lead jab. Enter and blend with the jab by pulling back slightly out of range and off the attack line. Slightly slap block or guide his hand off the attack line. Your defensive hand should be on the centerline. Slide your blocking hand along the contour of his arm, to control his elbow and deliver atemi to his ribcage. Slide your blocking hand up the contour of the arm to his neck, and slide your striking arm down the contour of his arm to his elbow. Immediately step behind your training partner, staying safely out of range of his other hand. Use a tenkan backward to redirect and bring your train-

ing partner around. The abrupt swinging motion will further undermine your training partner's balance. Begin to slide your hand from his elbow to his jaw line, following the contour of his arm. Continue to bring your training partner around until he runs into your arm at the empty space created at your side. Redirect and reverse the direction of his head with your forearm along his jaw line from chin to ear, while encouraging his lower body to continue on the circular path by placing and pushing with your other hand on his lower back. Step forward, turn your upper hand and your training partner's head over and down, directing them toward the rear kuzushi point. Follow through with irimi-nage until your training partner falls safely on the mat. Stay close to prevent and respond to any attempt to attack again.

Jab-Cross

Establish the aikido ready stance by remaining centered and balanced. Your training partner should approach and attack with a typical jab-cross combination. Enter and blend with the jab by leaning back slightly off the line and guiding the jab off the attack line. Your training partner should continue to attack with the

JAB-CROSS

cross. Blend with the attack by turning your body from the center, while deflecting and redirecting the cross off the attack line and away from your body. Following or blending with the attack's momentum, step to the front, bringing the attack arm along, while locking your training partner's other elbow with your defensive hand. Lock your training partner's cross arm at the elbow, while guiding his other hand toward the rear kuzushi point. Turning your body from the center makes for a small pivot and more full body power behind the execution of the technique. Continue to bring his locked arm in, and rotate his upper arm toward the kuzushi point while stepping forward to add full body power from behind the technique. Continue to follow through until your training partner submits or fall safely to the mat. Stay close to prevent and respond to any additional attempts to attack.

Jab-Cross-Hook

Establish the aikido ready stance by remaining centered and balanced. Your training partner should approach and attack with a lead jab. Enter and blend with the jab by sliding back slightly off the attack line and gently slapping or guiding the jab away. Your training partner should follow up with the cross. Blend with the cross by turning from the center in the direction of the cross, while gently slap-

ping or guiding it off the attack line. Your training partner will then attempt to deliver the lead hook. While redirecting the previous cross hand, enter and blend with the hook by stepping into it and bringing up your defensive hand on the centerline. Turning from the center, intercept the hook with both of your hands, controlling his elbow. Continue the momentum and inertia of the hook, while redirecting him downward and pulling the center back or letting the strike pass. Follow up with irimi-nage, sayu-undo, kote-gaeshi, or shiho-nage.

Uppercut

A typical boxing combination is the jab-cross-hook. An additional uppercut is often thrown in. Following the upper circular momentum and path of the attack would suggest that the shiho-nage would be an appropriate and effective response.

KICKS

Using kicks to approach and attack requires a much longer range or ma-ai than that of a boxer who uses his hands as a primary attack tool. All striking martial arts have variations on similar kicks.

Basic Front Kick

To execute a front kick, use either the front or the rear leg. Assume a neutral ready stance with your hand held relaxed but defensively on the centerline in front of your body. Maintain your balance and raise your knee in front of your body. Snap or thrust your leg out forward. The impact can be taken with either the top or ball of your foot. The front kick targets the groin, solar plexus, stomach, or head.

Front Kick Exercise

Establish the aikido ready stance by remaining centered and balanced. Your training partner should approach and attack by imitating a front kick. Stay mobile to detect and position the center for the attack. As your training partner executes the front kick, enter and blend with the technique by stepping into it slightly off the attack line and bringing both hands defensively up the centerline to redirect his kicking leg and to guard the center. Wrap your blocking arm around his leg, locking

FRONT KICK (CONTINUED ON NEXT PAGE)

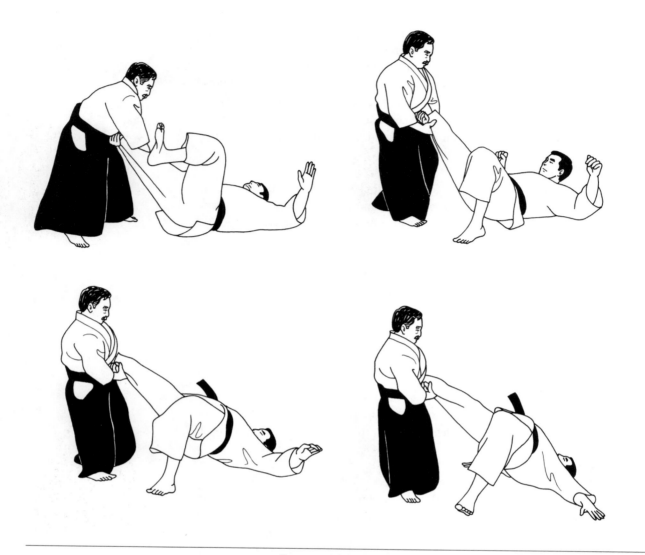

FRONT KICK (CONTINUED)

his knee while sliding your defensive hand down along the contour of his body and leg to his knee. Apply outward pressure to the inside of his knee toward the outside kuzushi point. Shift your weight from the center to provide full body power behind the technique. Continue until your training partner has landed on his back. Maintain the hook under his ankle and over his knee. Slide your hand, following the contour of his leg, up to his ankle, and trap his foot with your body. Lean his body backward and lift his legs to apply a submission leg lock. Continue until your training partner taps out, signifying successful completion and execution of the technique.

Basic Side Kick

To execute a side kick, either use your front or rear leg. Raise your knee, and then snap, push, or thrust your foot out horizontally as your hips pivot, putting extra power into the kick.

Side Kick Exercise 1

Establish the aikido ready stance by remaining centered and balanced. Your training partner approaches and attacks with a rear side kick. Enter and blend with

SIDE KICKS 1 (CONTINUED ON NEXT PAGE)

SIDE KICKS 1 (CONTINUED)

the side kick by sliding slightly backward and off the attack line while executing a double-hand cross-block to the leg. Secure a solid grip on his leg and pull slightly forward beyond your training partner's intended location to facilitate the loss of balance. Let his leg go, redirecting it away from the attack line, and begin immediately to enter toward the rear of your training partner. If your training partner provides a lead arm, follow the contour of his arm up to his head. Place your defensive hand in the small of his back. Turn your body from the center toward the rear kuzushi point. Continue to step through and turn from the center, placing your weight behind the technique and adding full body power and torque. Follow through with irimi-nage. Stay close to prevent and respond to any additional attempts to attack.

Side Kick Exercise 2

Establish the aikido ready stance by remaining centered and balanced. Your training partner should approach and attack with a lead side kick. Enter and blend with the side kick by pulling his center back slightly, while trapping his leg in a double-hand cross-block and guiding the side kick off the attack line. Step out to the side, off the attack line, while rotating your hand underneath his attacking foot. Secure and bend your knee, aiming it toward the front kuzushi point. Pivot step totally behind your training partner, causing him to turn and lose balance.

SIDE KICKS 2 (CONTINUED ON NEXT PAGE)

Continue to secure his leg. Follow through by stepping forward and pulling upward on his leg, driving your training partner to the mat. Follow the fall of your training partner to the mat. Continue the momentum, close the ma-ai, and execute a leg lock. Continue pressure until your training partner taps out, signifying successful completion and execution of the technique and submission.

Basic Roundhouse Kick

The roundhouse kick is a circular kick usually executed off the rear leg. This kick follows a circular path upward until it hits its target and then comes back down. Your body pivots and throws maximum weight and momentum into the kick. One of the unseen tricks or body mechanics of the roundhouse kick is to

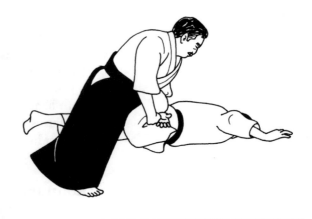

SIDE KICKS 2 (CONTINUED)

pivot on the toes of the supporting leg. This allows full body weight to be placed behind the kick. The hip comes up and rotates over. The body aligns with the foot, knee, hip, and shoulders all directly on the same line. Aim your roundhouse kick low to the legs, to the front or back of the thighs, to the ribs, or to the head.

Roundhouse Kick Exercise 1

Establish the aikido ready stance by remaining centered and balanced. Your training partner should approach and first attack with a lead jab. Your training partner should follow up with a rear roundhouse kick. Immediately enter and blend

ROUNDHOUSE KICK 1

with the technique by cutting directly into the center of the technique, and block the circular path of the kick. Keep one hand low to block the kick while your other hand rises defensively toward his head for atemi or to block any further hand attack. Bring your low block arm up underneath his kicking leg while pushing your other hand into his face. Step forward from the center, coordinating both hands, as if your hands were on a wheel, in a vertical circular path toward the kuzushi point. Step out of the way and allow your training partner to roll away at his own pace. Stay close to prevent or respond to any additional attempts to attack.

Roundhouse Kick Exercise 2

Establish the aikido ready stance by remaining centered and balanced. Your training partner should approaches and attack with a lead jab and follow up with a rear roundhouse kick. Immediately enter and blend with the technique by stepping directly in, closing the ma-ai into the center of his technique. This action cuts off and intercepts the path of the roundhouse kick. Hold one hand low to block his leg, while raising your defensive hand along the centerline into his face. Lift his leg and push into his chest. Without stepping forward, turn your hand, like a wheel, toward the kuzushi point directly beneath your training partner.

Allow him to drop to the mat at your feet. Stay close to prevent and respond to any additional attempts to attack.

Basic Crescent Kick

To execute the crescent kick, use your front or back leg and follow a vertical circular path. Throw the crescent kick to and from the inside or outside.

Basic Spinning Kick

The spinning kick can deliver a variety of kicks. The body can spin into a side or crescent kick easily. The execution is usually a quick spinning of the body to add momentum and surprise to the delivery. While spin kicks are very dramatic, they are not very wise and are seldom used in an actual fight, since your have to turn your back to spin on an attacker. The spin telegraphs your intention and takes valuable time. It is better to use that that time in more direct and faster measures.

GRAPPLING

Many people think that most fights end up on the ground. Therefore, a fighting art emerged that places great emphasis on the ground or grappling game. The process of going from a standing to a ground game consists of closing the distance, grabbing, and taking your training partner down.

The common takedown in a grappler's arsenal is simply to charge forward, duck down, and grab both legs. The grappler will then pick up your legs, causing you to lose balance and be thrown or fall down with great force. The grappler will then attempt to land on top. From this position, your training partner will mount and pummel you severely in a ground-and-pound. The grappler may also attempt to get an arm or leg in a submission hold. Grapplers are excellent fighters even if they are the one on the bottom.

The grappler will tend to become tied up with only one training partner and can become the target for friends of the person he or she has taken down. This is one of the few weaknesses of a grappling art.

BASIC TAKEDOWN

Establish the aikido ready stance by remaining centered and balanced. Your training partner should approach, faking high, and attack with a low-line double-leg takedown. He should then wrap both of his arms around the outside of your

GRAPPLER (CONTINUED ON NEXT PAGE)

GRAPPLER (CONTINUED)

knees and step in between your legs for maximum leverage. Lean forward onto his back, while stretching your legs out away from the center. Force your training partner's head toward the forward kuzushi point to aid in shifting the focus and priority of the technique. Reach around and grab his head and neck in a choke or neck crank. As your training partner attempts to pull away from the neck crank and the forward kuzushi point, trying to regain control and balance, blend with and follow the resistance toward his rear kuzushi point. Never let go of the neck crank. Reach out to provide some support for the landing and to prevent serious injury. Follow the momentum of the fall and roll onto your training partner. Mount him while maintaining the neck crank. Keep your weight forward. Lift up on his neck until your training partner taps out, signifying successful completion of the technique and submission.

CONCLUSION

Aikido is an effective and efficient martial art that applies to self-defense applications. Self-defense is more than just the practice of techniques in a fight. Self-defense includes developing a mindset, attack awareness and prevention, and training against various nontraditional strikes, kicks, and takedowns.

Chapter 14
Demonstrations, Competition, and Seminars

Eventually, the advanced aikido practitioner will venture off the home dojo mat and attend or participate in demonstrations, competition, and seminars. These are all avenues for helping take the practice of aikido to the next level.

DEMONSTRATIONS

It is always most important in any demonstration or presentation of aikido to be able to stay conscious of who the people are that you are presenting or demonstrating for and what the purpose is of the presentation or demonstration.

People at different levels of awareness and sophistication in aikido will require different levels of presentations and demonstrations. The public knows very little about aikido and needs more education to help explain what it is they are seeing. The public will appreciate the big circle of aikido, whereas the more sophisticated and advanced practitioners of aikido will appreciate the small and subtle applications of concepts. Some people feel drawn only to the martial arts or self-defense aspects of aikido. The spiritual or philosophical perspectives of the art will only draw others. Children will have shorter attention spans than adults will. You may also want to decide if you are presenting to the children or to the parents.

The purpose of a presentation and demonstration will dictate and direct much of its content and its duration. If the purpose is to educate the public, as stated, the content should be larger circle techniques. These may be flashy and may focus on self-defense applications, since that is what draws many people to the martial arts in general. If the purpose is to educate and enlighten, the slower blending techniques may be more appropriate and effective. If you are teaching a seminar, the presentation and demonstration may begin with a general technique and then progress into several variations, combinations, and counters.

Always keep in mind what audience you are presenting and demonstrating to and what the purpose is. Good marketing and effectiveness implies good gathering of information and advance planning.

COMPETITION

O'Sensei Morihei Ueshiba specifically did not want aikido to develop into a sport. For that reason, he discouraged competition. He felt that competition imposed an artificial context and rules, which diminished aikido's application as a legitimately applied martial art. He also believed that competition and the striving for championship status would only further encourage, develop, and inflate the self-centered ego. The learned identity ego, in Eastern thought, is one of the major barriers to spirituality.

> *Sports are widely practiced nowadays, and they are good for physical exercise. Warriors, too, train the body, but they also use the body as a vehicle to train the mind, calm the spirit, and find goodness and beauty, dimensions that sports lack.* (UESHIBA, M. 1991, P. 32)

O'Sensei Morihei Ueshiba, as the founder of aikido, discouraged competition. He felt that the techniques of aikido were too dangerous to apply in an artificial competitive context and that competition would create ego blocks to spirituality. *"Aikido is for the spiritual development of the entire human being,"* states Doshu Moriteru Ueshiba (UESHIBA, M. 2002, P. 14). Aikido discourages the use of trickery, deception, excessive force, or even the concept of winning and losing. Through competition, the focus of sports, contestants consider winning as everything. The mental discipline of aikido is to overcome our own ego for spiritual development, as opposed to employing aikido in the service of the learned ego identity, to overcome someone else, thus strengthening what aikido is trying to minimize.

Nonetheless, some have felt that competition would be good and necessary for the art of aikido and its practitioners. Shodokan or Tomiki branches of aikido have developed aikido as a sport competition in an attempt to formalize training, artificially test effectiveness, and spread aikido to the general public. Many find this very congruent and appropriate for the best interest of aikido as they see its evolution. Others see competition as divergent from the expressed vision of O'Sensei Morihei Ueshiba. He believed that competition supports the psychological ego through the goal of winning over others. This goal subtracts from the training and practice of aikido as the application of deep spiritual truths.

Aikido kyogi, or competition aikido, is unique to Shodokan aikido, developed by Kenji Tomiki, who also taught Judo at Waseda University. Many often refer to Shodokan aikido by its founder's name, Tomiki aikido. He felt that to adapt to a new era and context that real fights should become competitions in the same way as other martial arts, such as kendo and judo. Tomiki Sensei wanted to show aikido, in the context of traditional Japanese budo, as a significant training system of physical education to be seen on an international level. For those reasons, he created competitive aikido.

Shodokan, or Tomiki, aikido, bases competition on the principles of *shizen-hontai* (natural posture), *yawara* (defense), and *kuzushi* (balance breaking). All principles and concepts are important in all aspects of aikido but are not judged or scored for the purpose of winning. Techniques include both *atemi-waza* (striking) and *kansetsu-waza* (joint techniques to throw or pin).

There are three main types of competition, randori, embu, and kata, plus mixed teams. Randori pits two players against each other, using allowed techniques and following specific rules. Randori may be hand to hand or hand to tanto (knife). Embu or kata is where pairs of players perform specific techniques and are scored and judged against other pairs. There are compulsory pre-decided-on techniques and free embu. Mixed team competition combines randori and kata scored and judged against other teams.

There are strict rules of etiquette in competition for the players and referees. Competition scores are based on the effectiveness and legality of the technique, *kaeshi-waza* (reversal techniques), number of penalties for illegal techniques or injuries, posture, aggressiveness, and sportsmanship.

ATTENDING SEMINARS

In the beginning, students usually spend most of their time, appropriately, learning the basics from one instructor. This is wise. Too much information, too soon, is very confusing. Each style and instructor will have subtle differences that the beginning student will not be able to integrate or appreciate.

Most sensei expect and encourage the advanced aikido student to attend seminars. O'Sensei Morihei Ueshiba himself studied many different styles of martial arts before developing aikido. Even his aikido evolved as he worked with it. Experiencing different instructors and styles can broaden an aikido student's perspective. Seeing and feeling aikido from different perspectives allows an advanced student to appreciate and integrate the common denominators. They learn what makes the technique work technically as well as conceptually. They also see and learn from the idiosyncrasies of the individual instructors' styles and personalities.

While there is some separation and political organizing in aikido, its foundation is blending and harmony. The advanced aikido student must overcome the philosophical differences in perspective and application. Seminars are an excellent way to meet and train with other aikido practitioners who are traveling on the same journey but on a slightly different path toward the same goal and objective. Appreciating the differences and similarities in various styles of aikido allows aikido to be an expressive art of harmony and unification for all practitioners. This is as O'Sensei Morihei Ueshiba meant it to be.

CONCLUSION

Eventually, advanced aikido practitioners will venture outside their home dojo and attend demonstrations, competitions, and seminars. This helps them take their practice to the next level. Next, advanced aikido practitioners will share their knowledge with their kohai, junior students, and begin to teach or even start their own school.

Chapter 15
Teaching Aikido

To truly learn aikido, teach. Aikido is very personal. All teachers are different in their understanding and application of aikido. The aikido teacher cannot teach a student everything he or she needs to know about aikido. Traditional Japanese teachers would suggest that the instructor demonstrate with minimal, or no, explanation. Imitation or practice follows this. The student must "steal" the knowledge, meaning learn from his or her own practice and experience. This process of stealing made the knowledge and the experience the property of the student. True knowing is taken, not given. When questioned about a technique, O'Sensei Morihei Ueshiba would simply throw the questioner. Because there are subtle changes based on the approach and attack of the uke, no verbal explanation can clarify better than the physical execution of the technique.

Eventually, with consistent and persistent training, the student must find his or her own understanding, truth, and expression of aikido. Therefore, from a Zen type of standpoint, the teacher can only point the way. The student must travel and train alone.

STARTING YOUR OWN SCHOOL

There are many things one can do with advanced training and rank in aikido. Many people simply stop training because they have reached their goal. Some will continue to train because they have been caught up in the process of training and practice and realize that there is always so much more to learn. Others will want, and be encouraged to, start their own school.

Most businesses fail. They fail for many reasons, but the most common ones are lack of knowledge, lack of planning, and lack of follow-through.

Very few martial artists are also educated businesspeople. If your journey takes you toward teaching classes or opening a school, it would be wise to get educated about business practices and common errors. Talk with your current sensei about his or her teaching and business practices. The library is always an excellent place to improve your knowledge and education for free. There are often one-day seminars at local community colleges on small business practices. Get educated. You do not have to figure it all out yourself. Many people have already learned the hard way and have written and lectured about it. Learn from them.

Having a good business plan is important. Complete and comprehensive business plans can make the difference between success and failure. A business plan should have clear goals and objectives that can be accomplished and an overall mission statement and philosophy that ties it all together. There should be a realistic assessment of the current situation and resources. It should be easy to describe the steps to get from where you are now to where you want to go. All business plans include a section on the marketplace, who your customer is, who your competition is, and what makes your services and benefits unique and different within your smaller market niche. Where within that market niche will you locate your school? It must be visible and available to attract new students. It is important to know how to reach prospective new students through advertising, promotion, and a good marketing plan. There are many ways to get free advertising and exposure through press releases, special events, articles, and getting involved with the community. Business is business and this implies that you must have a financial plan for income, expenses, and accountability.

To follow through on a good business idea, and a comprehensive business plan, one must be willing to do the tasks required. This means making a realistic assessment of one's ability to work alone as an entrepreneur. In addition, many people face their own issues with money. Since aikido is considered a spiritual art, the issue of payment and worth can be confusing and contradictory. One must be able to acknowledge the worth in a financial sense of what one offers and feel worthy of letting that abundance into one's life.

CHARACTERISTICS OF INSTRUCTORS

Instructors in aikido need to have many qualities. These qualities bring in new students, maintain students' interest and participation, and stimulate advanced practitioners.

The instructor needs to have good business sense to be able to maintain a dojo or class. Without business sense, there is no class.

The instructor needs to have and model a high level of ethics and morals. Since aikido is a spiritual as well as a martial art, it is very important that instructors have a code of conduct for themselves in and out of the dojo. The instructor represents aikido to the students, their families, and the community.

The instructor must possess a high level of proficiency in technical execution and conceptual application of the aikido techniques. Students will imitate the preciseness of the instructor's demonstrations. Therefore, the cleaner the instructor's ability to demonstrate and illustrate the techniques, the more likely it is that the student will imitate and progress to advanced stages.

The instructor must be able not only to demonstrate but also to communicate the essence and the details of aikido. There may be some language barriers and difficulties, but the instructor should be able to get his or her point across clearly. The instructor should encourage and understand the questions students ask and be able to provide clear and relevant answers.

The instructor should have credibility and legitimacy. It is easy to fool the public into thinking that someone has a strong background in martial arts. Having a direct lineage and respect for one's teachers models the correct attitude to training, discipline, accountability, and responsibility. Therefore, the instructor should be willing to produce documentation for every rank obtained. He or she should also continually honor past teachers and maintain the appropriate and responsible affiliation if they stay an active member or advertise the former teacher's name, style, or federation.

The instructor, being human, will have his or her own character and personality. Being human, no one is perfect. Therefore, an instructor should act with humility and take measures to protect the students from their shortcomings. The instructor also needs to demonstrate and model a high level of integrity, modesty, confidence, honesty, patience, and consistency.

The instructor should have a uniform consistency in curriculum and grading criteria. The instructor needs to avoid playing favorites or being arbitrary in his or her promotional policies.

The instructor needs to continually train, progressing and refining his or her own aikido.

CONCLUSION

The teacher of aikido must teach the basic rolls, falls, grabs, strikes, and locks.

The teacher of the advanced aikido practitioner has a much tougher job. He or she must teach and model a high level of proficiency in technical execution and conceptual application. The advanced aikido practitioner will work on his or her inner development through understanding the influence of Omoto on O'Sensei Morihei Ueshiba and aikido, have a training philosophy, train his or her mind, and understand and use ki. The theories and concepts for the advanced aikido practitioner include the art of body mechanics, movement, and engagement. The advanced aikido practitioner will continually refine the fundamentals of strikes, throws and locks, applications, combinations, counters, and reversals. Taking his or her practice to the next level, the advanced aikido practitioner learns self-defense techniques, and participates in demonstrations, competitions, seminars, and teaching. The advanced aikido practitioner continually refines his or her fundamentals through consistent and persistent training and discipline with honest and genuine intent and intensity in a variety of contexts and situations.

Ultimately, there is no basic or advanced aikido. There is only the training. Train wisely and train well.

Appendix A
Interviews with Sensei Phong Thong Dang

Two very important interviews show the depth of courage and knowledge of Sensei Phong Thong Dang. The first appeared in *Aikido Journal* in 1994, and the second in *Aikido Today Magazine* in 2001. These two interviews appear here in their entirety with the expressed permission of the editors of those magazines.

AIKIDO JOURNAL #101 (1994) INTERVIEW WITH SENSEI DANG THONG PHONG
By Stanley Pranin (AJ/SP: *Aikido Journal*/Stanley Pranin)

(Dang Thong Phong: Born February 10, 1935 in Thua Thien Province, Central Vietnam. After graduating from high school, he was drafted into the Thu Duc Military Officer Training School. Served as director of the Thu Duc Military Martial Arts and Gymnastic School Association of the Republic of Vietnam Armed Forces. In 1968, founded the Tenshinkai Aikido Federation and serves as its president. Has extensive experience in Han Bai Duong Shaolin Kung-fu, is 5th dan in aikido, 6th dan in taekwondo, and 5th dan in judo. Relocated to California in 1986, where he currently operates his Tenshinkai Dojo.)

AJ/SP: *I want to thank you very much for inviting me to come today. I became very interested in learning more about your background when I read the newsletter you sent me describing your beginnings in aikido. To begin with, I want to ask you how you came to establish this dojo here in Orange County.*

Sensei Phong: It seems to be my karma. After more than forty years of learning, practicing, and teaching various martial arts, their spirit has permeated my blood and my bones. After so many years, it's like I'm addicted to the arts. During the last thirty years, I have tried to establish dojos whenever and wherever possible. Four months after we resettled in California, we moved to the city of Garden Grove in Orange County, and when I noticed that there was no aikido dojo, I decided to open one.

AJ/SP: *Where were you living in Vietnam?*

Sensei Phong: Saigon.

AJ/SP: *I believe that you began training in aikido very early, perhaps in the late 1950s...?*

Sensei Phong: I started training in judo and shaolin kung-fu in the early fifties. However, in 1958 my brother Tri Thong Dang Sensei returned to Vietnam from France and started teaching aikido. I have practiced this wonderful art since then. But at that time, I was not able to fully devote myself to aikido due to my family responsibilities. My father passed away when I was very young. My mother had to work hard to raise the three children who were left at home. Therefore, besides going to school, I had to spend my extra time working to help out my mother. I also assisted teaching shaolin kung-fu and judo at the Han Bai Duong School of Martial Arts, one of the most famous martial arts schools in Saigon, founded by the late Dr. Nguyen Anh Tai. The chief instructor was my own teacher, Vu Ba Oai Sensei.

It wasn't until 1961 or 1962, when a representative from the Hombu Dojo, Mutsuro Nakazono Sensei, came to Vietnam to begin laying the foundations of aikido there, that I was able to spend more time practicing the art. Because of my ten years of judo training, I was able to absorb the essence of aikido without much difficulty, and I progressed quickly. Nakazono Sensei taught both aikido and judo at the Association for Judo and Aikido, founded by Tri Thong Dang. Since I was often able to accompany Nakazono Sensei to his many seminars at training centers for paratroopers and police officers, I was able to learn many of his special techniques.

AJ/SP: *Nakazono Sensei is a very interesting person. I met him once in Paris in 1970. I believe he had a strong judo foundation and that he had began learning aikido in Manchuria.*

Sensei Phong: It is true that he was very good at both judo and aikido, but he also held high ranks in other martial arts as well, including kendo. He had a total of twenty-seven dan ranks.

AJ/SP: *When did Nakazono Sensei study aikido?*

Sensei Phong: I'm not sure, but my brother probably knows.

AJ/SP: *How long did Nakazono Sensei remain in Vietnam?*

Sensei Phong: About two years.

AJ/SP: *I believe your brother left Vietnam in the 1960s?*

Sensei Phong: Yes, he left in 1964.

AJ/SP: *So you were left in charge of the dojo when your brother left for America?*

Sensei Phong: When Tri Thong Dang Sensei left in 1964, I was responsible for looking after the local aikido and judo school. At that time there was no federation. Later, I started to establish a number of dojos, both civilian and military, throughout the country. Since I hoped to form an aikido federation, I worked very hard for two years to save enough money to make a trip to the Hombu Dojo to further my aikido training. There I took the exam for sandan, a rank high enough for me to lead the new federation. I then returned to Vietnam and started the official process of establishing the aikido federation at the beginning of 1968.

AJ/SP: *Those who train in aikido in the United States or even in Japan are accustomed to a basic training pattern including warm-ups, basic techniques, and so on. Were there any differences in the way aikido was taught in Vietnam or was it more or less like it is taught in dojos throughout the world?*

Sensei Phong: Because of my extensive judo background, I place a lot of emphasis on warm-ups, including aiki taiso, working the joints, and practicing rolling and falling techniques. These are very important. Traditionally my classes have always lasted an hour and a half, with about thirty minutes of that time devoted to warming up.

AJ/SP: *That's very important. I personally feel that the training we get in simply conditioning the body and keeping it flexible is as important as the training in techniques.*

Sensei Phong: That is true. A person who does a good job of warming up will achieve good results during the rest of their training as well.

AJ/SP: *I've been in aikido for thirty-one years now. Teachers who were in their forties when I began are in their seventies now, and I've observed that while some have maintained very good physical condition, others have not. They would teach, but seldom train themselves, and I don't think they did stretching exercises. Now that they are older it is difficult for them to perform aikido vigorously.*

Sensei Phong: Your observation is quite correct. Daily training is necessary. When teaching a technique, a good teacher has to demonstrate not only the details of the movement and their essence, but also the intrinsic power of those techniques. Practicing daily will help develop and maintain that ki, I believe, well into old age.

AJ/SP: *When you were running the dojo in Vietnam, I imagine the political conditions were quite severe. Did the government place restrictions on aikido practice at that time?*

Sensei Phong: In Vietnam, most styles have a strong presence because the Vietnamese people love the martial arts. Anyone who wants to operate a dojo must first prove that they are proficient in their specialty. After consideration by the Ministry of Youth and Sports, an application is sent to the Ministry of the Interior where the applicant's political and civic backgrounds are investigated. Anyone who has a prior conviction will not be granted permission to teach.

In 1975, after the Communists took over the South, all forms of martial arts practice were prohibited. The Communist government didn't allow martial arts activities until 1979. All styles of martial arts are under the direction, at the lowest administrative level, of the State's Agency of Sports and Games. Currently, privately owned dojos are not permitted. I believe, however, that in the near future, the government will be more tolerant towards the opening of private dojos.

AJ/SP: *It sounds as though there was a very rich background of martial arts in Vietnam, including the Chinese and Japanese styles, as well as indigenous styles. I know that even today in much of Southeast Asia there remains strong resentment against the Japanese because of what happened during World War II. Are there still strong feelings, and did you ever encounter feelings of resistance to Japanese things among your students?*

Sensei Phong: There hasn't really been so much resentment towards the Japanese, or against Japanese martial arts particularly, under either the former South Vietnamese government or the current government. In fact, Japanese martial arts were preferred over Korean martial arts. Many different styles of Japanese martial arts were popular among the Vietnamese.

AJ/SP: *What was the reason for that?*

Sensei Phong: It was because of an influx of Japanese movies depicting the high level of Japanese nationalism. That was the reason for the preference. A student would obey his martial arts teacher perhaps more than he would his school teacher. If his martial arts teacher told him to die, then he would die. On the other hand, Korean movies were rarely shown in Vietnam and not many people were aware of the Korean patriotic spirit, which is no less than that of the Japanese.

AJ/SP: *Did you have some kind of link with Japan when you were allowed to begin teaching again in the 1980s? Did any Japanese shihan visit or were any of your students able to travel?*

Sensei Phong: At that time it was forbidden for ordinary citizens to contact foreigners, so I couldn't contact any of the teachers in Japan. It was only after I successfully escaped to America, on my eighteenth attempt, that I was able to contact those people again.

AJ/SP: *I gather from reading the interview in your newsletter that you have had some very memorable and dangerous experiences. Also, you have a background in other martial arts besides aikido and judo, including some more combat-oriented arts. In situations where your life has been in danger, what techniques or training did you find were the most important to you for survival?*

Sensei Phong: Since 1975 I've faced many dangerous situations, but what has helped the most has been my ability to remain calm. This has helped me out of a lot of dangerous situations.

AJ/SP: *That's very interesting. People who begin learning a martial art—especially young people—often are interested in very quickly acquiring techniques that they can use on the street.*

Sensei Phong: I've been practicing martial arts for a total of about forty-three years, but I've never had to apply techniques on anybody. In most cases, when people have tried to start a fight with me, I have responded with calmness to avoid an embarrassing situation.

AJ/SP: *That's amazing to hear, especially in light of your background in a wartime situation. I think it is a credit both to your own training and to the ability of the martial arts to develop a sense of calm in a person.*

Sensei Phong: In 1967, the International Taekwondo Federation invited me to South Korea to visit and learn more about the Federation's organization. At the end of my two-week visit, I expressed my desire to visit Japan and Hong Kong. Some Korean instructors advised me against a trip to Hong Kong, saying that the place was not safe, mostly because I was a foreigner, and an easy target for robbery. But I decided to make the trip, not because I am a risk-taker, but because I truly had confidence in my ability to remain calm and in control of myself.

AJ/SP: *Recently, I had the opportunity to interview an Okinawan karate teacher. He is not particularly famous but is highly regarded nonetheless. He described what it was like to grow up in Okinawa amidst dangerous conditions. His brother was a very accomplished Goju-ryu karate practitioner and was often called upon to settle disputes or fights. I asked him what techniques or approaches his brother used to settle such disputes. He replied that his brother was so strong and so skilled that he had only to show up and everyone would calm down and there would be no more fighting.*

I know that it was very difficult for you to leave Vietnam under the present government and that you made many attempts to escape. Could you relate the story of your successful escape when you were finally able to leave Vietnam for the United States?

Sensei Phong: Fifteen of my eighteen attempts to escape were made by sea, while the other three were by land. During five of those attempts I was chased by Communist patrols or policemen. I was arrested twice and imprisoned for eight months the first time and for thirty-seven months the second time. During those thirty-seven months I was alternately held in prison and then taken out to the fields to do hard labor, a cycle that was repeated over and over.

Before my eighteenth attempt, one of my students who had successfully left Vietnam had written back to his mother that the trip had been very well-orchestrated. His mother contacted me and told me to use a similar method. I didn't want to go then because the last time I had been arrested my family had no news of me for over a year. So I was very reluctant. At that time people were beginning to be able to leave legally, so I hoped to go the legal way. However, it would have been impossible for me because of my previous escapes from prison.

Because of my status as an officer in the South Vietnam Armed Forces teaching aikido to some of the American Embassy personnel, I had been able to have my family evacuated at the very last minute by the American Embassy. I, however, had to wait for another evacuation flight that never materialized, and was forced to remain behind.

My escape was accomplished by sea. We spent about two months journeying from one island to another, passing through about five in all, before arriving at Galang Island in Indonesia, where one of the United Nations High Commissioner for Refugee's camps was located. Finally, I arrived at the San Francisco International Airport on February 25th, 1986, and was greeted by my wife and two sons, after more than eleven years of separation.

We first settled in Sacramento, but it was difficult for me to find work there. I stayed there for four months and then was invited to visit Orange County by some of my former students. I went down to have a look at the area and decided to return to San Francisco to get my family. After moving to Orange County I didn't have enough money to open a dojo right away, so I got a job working for five dollars an hour, ten to twelve hours a day. I did that for about a year-and-a-half and then borrowed some money to open the dojo. After a month and a half in that first dojo, which was on Brookhurst Way in Garden Grove, the landlord took the place back to bulldoze it and sell the land, so I lost everything. I immediately started to look for another place, and two months later signed a five-year lease for my current 3,000 square foot dojo.

Initially, I ran into serious financial problems because the dojo was so new, and nobody knew about it. For the first year and a half I worked for nothing and had to put a lot of money into the dojo. Eventually the number of students increased to the point where I could cover expenses.

AJ/SP: *I have been in hundreds of dojos over the years and I can always tell when someone has a good sense of professionalism. For example, I see the cleanliness of this dojo and the displays here. I know you are very sincere in your teaching and I also think you have a very good understanding of how to present your art to the public in a very attractive way.*

Sensei Phong: Thank you very much.

AJ/SP: *You haven't had a great deal of experience with American culture or with doing business here, but it makes me think that some of the most important principles of running a dojo are common sense and would work anywhere.*

Sensei Phong: I have had extensive experience in organizing and teaching over the last thirty years. Prior to 1975, I was the head of a federation in South Vietnam consisting of more than thirty dojos and ten thousand members. I was also General Secretary of both the judo and taekwondo federations. I began teaching more than thirty years ago. I have learned through my experience that one has to sacrifice in the present, at the beginning, if one wants to reach a goal later, in the future. I discovered that in America, skill is not enough—knowledge and experience in organizations are sometimes more important to achieve success.

Currently, in addition to my teaching responsibilities and the daily operation of our federation, I am preparing to write a book, and if possible, to produce a videotape on aikido techniques for those who want to learn more about Tenshinkai Aikido. It will also be my gift to future generations.

AJ/SP: *If an American looks in the phone book, for example, and finds an American teaching some martial art, I don't think he would have any problem in training with that teacher. But an American in the United States might consider it unusual to learn a Japanese martial art from a Vietnamese teacher. Have you had to deal with that sort of situation and if so how have you responded?*

Sensei Phong: What you say is very true. An American who comes to this dojo to learn a Japanese martial art from a Vietnamese person—especially from a very small Vietnamese person—must have quite a few doubts. However, many people who have visited a number of other dojos before coming here like the way I teach aikido because my style is much softer than some others, with many light movements.

AJ/SP: *I believe many of the members in your dojo come from the Vietnamese community here in Orange County. What language do you use when you teach?*

Sensei Phong: For general sessions I speak in Vietnamese, except when interacting on an individual basis, when I use English. Sometimes an interpreter is needed to clarify a complicated point. Currently about seventy percent of my adult students are Americans or Westerners, while ninety percent of the students in the children's classes are Vietnamese.

AJ/SP: *I've noticed through reading your newsletter and conversations with Eric Womack on the way over here that you have made efforts to reach out and have exchanges with teachers from other dojos, for example Kim Peuser and Hoa Newen from the Oakland Aikido Institute, and with Frank McGouirk. I think that such exchanges are very positive in that they help make your dojo and your activities known, as well as expose your students to other approaches to the art.*

Sensei Phong: I would like my students to expand their experience by having chances to train with other teachers.

AJ/SP: *Given the very violent culture in which we live, I imagine that many prospective aikido students are interested in learning self-defense. Aikido techniques, or let's say some of the softer approaches to aikido, are often criticized by other martial artists as not being effective in real situations. How do you respond to doubts prospective students may have about the technical effectiveness of aikido?*

Sensei Phong: When the Steven Seagal movies came out we got a lot of new students, but many of them ended up dropping out because they expected that they could perform as well as Steven Seagal after just a few months of training. I often emphasize to beginners that expecting to be able to apply aikido techniques effectively after only a short period of training is unrealistic. Only after at least two years of hard work can one appreciate the effectiveness and beauty of this art. And that is only the beginning—the path of aikido is such a long one that sometimes we have to spend an entire lifetime traveling it. The more we practice, the more we discover its hidden beauties. This is because aikido is more than a system of self-defense; it is also an art that promotes the humanistic aspect of the martial arts.

AJ/SP: *Aikido, in O'Sensei's view, is a very spiritual martial art and the ideals of aikido place a great deal of emphasis on ethics, learning how to get along with other people, avoiding fights whenever possible, and so on.*

Sensei Phong: When I teach, I emphasize not creating dangerous situations and not hurting one's opponent or one's fellow students. I don't want to mention any names or schools, but there are several martial arts teachers who show off by striking their students very hard, sometimes injuring them. I don't approve of that sort of thing.

AJ/SP: *I've touched upon that subject many times over the years in* Aiki News/Aikido Journal, *but despite O'Sensei's philosophy, even among aikido teachers there are more than a few high-ranking individuals who regularly injure people dur-*

ing aikido training. This sort of thing disturbs me because it's not an isolated occurrence, and it's not being done by outsiders but by some of the high-ranking teachers.

Sensei Phong: Yes, I agree.

AJ/SP: *It seems a very fine line that we walk between learning a martial art that is effective and being able to apply this in a humane way, always exercising full control. Sensei, in conclusion, is there any area you would like to talk about or emphasize?*

Sensei Phong: As a Vietnamese expatriate my mind is always on Vietnam and my goal is one day to return there to teach the other students. Some of them have not learned anything new for the past eighteen years and they are waiting for me. That is my most cherished dream. My students are currently running all the dojos in Vietnam, and they are waiting expectantly for me to come back. The aikido system in Vietnam belongs to the Tenshinkai Aikido Federation and when I return I will distribute diplomas under the Tenshinkai Aikido Federation.

AJ/SP: *Do you have any plans for a trip to Japan in the future?*

Sensei Phong: If I have the opportunity I would like to go back to Japan to learn more and expand my experience, in order to be a better teacher.

   Although I still face financial difficulties most of the time, I always emphasize technique and I never give out diplomas or rank to those who have not attained a certain level.

   Finally, I would like to express my sincere gratitude to you for accepting my invitation to visit, despite the long distance. On behalf of the Tenshinkai Aikido Federation, I wish you excellent health and success in continuing to edit one of the most professional martial arts magazines in the world today.

The following interview was originally published in *Aikido Today Magazine*. The interview is reproduced here with the expressed permission of Editors Susan Perry and Ronald Rubin.

AIKIDO TODAY MAGAZINE #75, VOL. 15, NO. 3; MAY/JUNE 2001, PAGES 11–15.
Interview—Dang Thong Phong Sensei
By Lynn Seiser and John Tran

Dang Thong Phong Sensei, founder and president of the International Tenshinkai Aikido Federation, holds a 6th dan in aikido, a 6th degree black belt in taekwondo, a 5th dan in judo and 8th degree black belt in han bai duong (Vietnamese Shaolin kung fu). After fifty years of dedication to the martial arts, he continues to teach daily at his dojo in the City of Westminster, Orange County, California.

   The second of three sons of a revolutionary father, Phong Sensei was born February 10, 1935 in Phu Le, a former Imperial City in central Vietnam. He grew up during the Vietnamese revolt against the French occupation.

ATM: *Sensei, what is your background in aikido?*

Sensei Phong: I began training in the martial arts in 1950 when I was fifteen years old. My brother-in-law, a medical doctor, had a martial arts school in Saigon, where he taught judo and Vietnamese Shaolin kung fu. In 1958, my brother, Dang Thong Tri, returned from France and introduced aikido to the martial arts school. From the first, I was impressed by the fluidity of the technique.

When Tri Sensei introduced me to aikido, I could see that it fit my stature very well. (I am five feet tall and light.) The philosophy of aikido also fit my way of living.

Later, when I went to Japan to train with O'Sensei, I noticed that, despite his size, his techniques were very strong and effective, and I was deeply impressed with his philosophy.

ATM: *Where and when did you begin to study aikido?*

Sensei Phong: Near the end of 1959, Tri Sensei established his first aikido dojo.

The next year, Aikikai Headquarters (Hombu Dojo) sent Mutsuro Nakazono Sensei—who had been an aikido instructor in France—to help Tri Sensei teach and to spread aikido in Vietnam.

Nakazono Sensei and Tri Sensei instructed at Tri's martial art school at armed-forces installations, and at law-enforcement institutions. The techniques that they taught to the government armed forces were very combative, while those they taught to the police stressed restraining.

My background in judo made me a good *uke*. I could take the throws and falls very well. In judo competition, if your shoulder did not touch the ground, there was no point. So, I tended to roll rather than take a flat fall. Because of this, Nakazono Sensei asked me to be the *uke* for instructional demonstrations.

Receiving technique directly from Nakazono Sensei helped me to improve my own technique, because I could feel how the techniques were supposed to go. I was able to learn new techniques—different applications than I had learned from my brother, Tri Sensei. I really began to understand the aikido's versatility, and that drew my interest even more into the practice of aikido.

I was very fortunate to be able to follow Master Nakazono. From the moment I started, I began to envision a career in the martial arts.

In October of 1964, when Tri Sensei came to the United States, I took over his school in Vietnam. That is how my career in martial arts started, and I have done nothing else since.

ATM: *What was life like for you in Vietnam as you grew up?*

Sensei Phong: My father joined the revolutionary war against the French colonization of Vietnam. He was rarely at home because he was out fighting the French and had to move around. Since we were watched closely by collaborators, we also were on the move.

Being young, I stayed home to help my mother make a living and to help raise our family. My early life was not very pleasant—but that built my character. My struggle in early life taught me much.

ATM: *How has aikido changed your life?*

Sensei Phong: Yes. The practice of martial arts, including aikido, has taught me courage and responsibility. It has given me the idea of giving myself completely to something and of showing leadership. Also, I have been influenced by aikido's idea of harmony—by its ideal of working with people without harming them.

ATM: *How does aikido differ now from when you began?*

Sensei Phong: The basic aikido techniques themselves haven't changed much since I first learned them. But, over the years, I have come up with new techniques that are more appropriate for a man of my size.

In the past, I have taught a lot of very dynamic techniques—especially techniques like *kote-gaeshi* and *koshi-nage* that require big break falls. These techniques are better for the younger bodies that can take it, but they are not always appropriate for older students. Now, I often emphasize techniques like *kokyu-nage*, which don't require the harder falls. I especially like to teach *kokyu-nage* techniques; I like to teach the dynamic movements of changing directions. When you practice the dynamics of *kokyu-nage*, you train your ki.

ATM: *Which teachers have most influenced your aikido?*

Sensei Phong: O'Sensei and the Doshu Kisshomaru Ueshiba are two of my most important influences.

I met Doshu Kisshomaru in 1967, when I first went to Japan to study aikido. The first week I was there, Doshu took me around and showed me the office, the training halls, and the place where O'Sensei worked. The warmth of his reception and hospitality left a lasting impression.

I had brought with me a picture of my 200 aikido students to present to O'Sensei. He held it up to show the class and talked at some length about it. Although I didn't understand a word he said, I was moved to tears on that day. So, my first impression of O'Sensei was very fond.

From the first time I saw O'Sensei teach and perform, I was very impressed. Watching him strengthened my love and respect for aikido as a martial art.

In 1993, Doshu Kisshomaru invited me to the celebration of aikido's 50th anniversary. I think that he invited me because he was aware of my work to keep the Tenshinkai aikido Federation going after I moved to the U.S. in 1986. aikido masters from all over the world attended the ceremony. About ten were invited onto the stage and introduced. I was honored to be the only non-Japanese teacher invited to stand on stage. I was also personally invited to a private reception dinner. The two students I had brought with me—one from America and another from Canada—were also invited to attend the dinner. Again, the treatment and reception we received left a lasting impression.

ATM: *When you left Vietnam, did your organization, Tenshinkai Aikido Federation, continue?*

Sensei Phong: Hombu Dojo had recognized the Federation on the organization's world map but removed it when I came to the U.S. Later, I went back and organized a trip for Masatake Fujita Sensei so that he could see the organization and watch its members demonstrate. He reported back to Japan on Vietnamese aikido and was able to get Tenshinkai aikido put back on the map. For the last five years, they have had their own Board of Management. Hombu Dojo sends instructors every year to teach there.

In 2001, I will join Vietnamese Tenshinkai aikido to invite Doshu Moriteru Ueshiba and Fujita Sensei to visit Vietnam. That will be a very great honor. We hope our Asian, American, French, and Canadian members can join us in Vietnam.

ATM: *On a different topic—Do you have a family? If so, how do you involve them in aikido? Do you think it is important to involve the families of your students in the dojo?*

Sensei Phong: I arrived in Sacramento, California, from Vietnam, in 1986. There I was reunited with my family. My wife and two sons had been living in the U.S. for ten years.

I initially taught my sons Shaolin kung fu and taekwondo, because there were no mats for us to work out on. When we moved to Orange County, California, and started a dojo, we had mats. So I trained them both in aikido. My oldest son got his black belt. My youngest son reached brown belt when he was in high school. Now they are 25 and 26. I still have a picture of them on my dojo wall throwing each other.

About two-thirds of my students are children. I believe that having parents involved in activities at the school helps with student retention. I try to keep parents informed about their children's activities and progress, and I try to have a lot of community activities at the dojo.

When parents decide to send their children to me, I talk with them and explain the philosophy of aikido. Often, because aikido is a nonviolent form of martial art, its fits well with their desires. Understanding the philosophy, they bring their children here and encourage them to stay and practice. They know their children are not going to go out and get into fights in the streets.

Helping family members understand aikido is also important for adult students. Two of my students were so heavily involved in their training that their partners accused them of spending more time with me than with them. They both had to drop out after they got their black belts because family support was not there. So, I sometimes meet with family members to explain the benefits and advantages of aikido training and to get their support.

ATM: *In your opinion, what are those benefits?*

Sensei Phong: From aikido, people learn the philosophy of living harmoniously and forgiving. I have applied these lessons to my own life.

About fourteen months after marrying, I was separated from my family. I was an officer in my home country of Vietnam and, when the war there ended, I was imprisoned for seven and a half years. My wife and two small boys came to the U.S. We were separated for about ten years.

At first, because of the long separation, there were differences of expectations and problems with communication. I had been in re-education prison camps with Communists so long and endured so many hardships that my life had changed, as had my way of thinking. Meanwhile my wife and sons had been living in a free society. So, our expectations were very different. There was a lot to overcome and it was hard to get together.

Training in aikido had taught me to work hard and keep my family together.

Drawing on my aikido training, I was able to resolve the family conflicts. Now, my wife always attends and supports our dojo activities—always helping out.

Aikido is now my way of life. I come to the school to teach and then I go home to take care of my family. There is nothing else. That is my life, the dojo and my family.

ATM: *In 1999 you were inducted into the Martial Arts Hall of Fame for the second time. What did that mean to you?*

Sensei Phong: The World Martial Arts Hall of Fame recognized my achievements. I am personally very honored to have been recognized by so many masters and teachers. I am happy it has been a real achievement in my life.

ATM: *You were invited to demonstrate at the 1999 All Japan aikido Demonstration in Tokyo. What was the experience like?*

Sensei Phong: I don't understand how we got invited. There were a very few invitations and an even more limited number of demonstrations. Perhaps we were invited because Fujita Sensei visited our school and saw our students' skills. I felt very honored to be there.

There was only one other American school: the American Aikido Association under Toyoda Sensei also demonstrated.

On the day of the demonstration, the announcer spoke only Japanese. By the time we figured out when we would be called, we only had four to five minutes to get ready. It really took some concentration. I don't feel I did my best but the demonstration wasn't too bad. It only lasted one and a half minutes.

ATM: *In 2000, you celebrated your fiftieth anniversary in the martial arts. What have those fifty years meant to you?*

Sensei Phong: I am very thankful to the Tenshinkai Aikido Foundation and all the students who helped to make that day special for me. I was very proud that so many government officials and local dignitaries celebrated with us. It was an important day.

One of the greatest achievements I have had in the last 50 years is the opportunity to share my experience. A long time ago, many good instructors only taught their secrets to family and relatives. But that way, over time, the art gets lost. Now things are changing. Experience should be shared freely so the art can proliferate. I teach what I know to every student I have. I am very happy that I have been able to establish an organization to proliferate aikido.

When I teach a class there is no set technique for the day. I do not operate that way. The training is based on the technique that comes to mind. Sometimes I just remember one or invent one. I always hope some student will notice and pick up on it. That way the art will not be lost. My philosophy is to show as much as I can so that the art won't get lost.

ATM: *You have high degree black belts in several other arts. How has training in those other arts affected your aikido?*

Sensei Phong: The other arts have enriched my aikido, making it fuller. In the Shaolin arts, for example, there is an emphasis on stance. So, I tend to keep my back straight and my center low to maintain balance.

Even O'Sensei adapted what he learned from other martial arts into aikido. That is what I want to do.

ATM: *How does training in the U.S. differ from training in Vietnam or Japan?*

Sensei Phong: In the U.S., people are larger. So, my techniques have to be more dynamic. I have to be more aware of resistance so that I can change directions. As I grow older, I notice that my technique gets stronger. Earlier the power wasn't there, but with age my technique continues to get smoother and stronger. I think I have developed more ki.

ATM: *What advice would you give students?*

Sensei Phong: I would remind beginning students that aikido is a noncompetitive form of martial arts.

In the beginning, there is a lot of training in the basic movements. It is necessary to train in the basics to get a firm foundation for the more advanced techniques. Beginners need to have realistic expectations for themselves and the art of aikido.

Every time Steven Seagal releases a new movie, the number of beginning students increases. Within a few months, most of them have dropped out because the art is not what they expected. It takes understanding to train in aikido movements. The types of movement we use in aikido are very different from those used in other martial arts, such as karate or taekwondo. Beginners need to understand the meaning and philosophy of training.

My advice to intermediate students is to go back to basics. The basics are the foundation for the more advanced techniques. The basics have to be strong. It does not help to know too many techniques. Always go back to basics. The good thing about training in basics for a long time is that it builds ups automatic reflexes. Nothing else builds these reflexes. But, without them, the students will not be able to execute counters effectively.

I would say the same thing to the advanced students. Go back to basics to build natural, automatic reflexes. By going back to basics, students learn to make the transition from one technique to another more fluidly. Also, the basics help with body movement; even higher belts need to be reminded to keep their backs straight and to keep their center of gravity close and in balance.

I advise the higher belts, from *shodan* up, to help train the lower ranked students. That is the best way to retrain yourself in the basic techniques. In fact, because of the practice of helping others, all the instructors here have a very good understanding of the fundamental techniques.

ATM: *What personality characteristics or beliefs indicate that someone will be a good student or, perhaps a future instructor of Tenshinkai aikido?*

Sensei Phong: It is not enough that people practice aikido to improve their health or as an exercise or to relieve stress. They also need the drive and enthusiasm to train. It is also very helpful to have the support and understanding from their family. This allows them to keep their attention on their training.

Another factor that helps students become good instructors is to be truthful with themselves. Good instructors are truthful and sincere.

Also, good instructors are very patient. Patience is very important because there are many challenges to face. The majority of students here are children, for instance. Often they lack focus, they have short attention spans, and they even talk back. Instructors need to be patient to deal with these behaviors. Instructors need to know how to deal with children of different ages and different backgrounds. They need to be able to work with them all.

Instructors have to teach basic techniques over and over again. Here again, it helps if they have patience.

Instructors who can maintain these characteristics will be very good. As they train and teach, they will change. Even past black belt level, they continue to grow. When they are asked about certain techniques, they have to think and review to teach. The teaching helps them become even better. Teaching is a great way to improve your own technique.

ATM: *You recently started the Tenshinkai Aikido Foundation, a nonprofit, public-benefit corporation. What do you hope to see it accomplish?*

Sensei Phong: Until a few years ago, Tenshinkai aikido was organized and taught by me. The Tenshinkai Aikido Foundation was formed to expand aikido. The federation will train instructors to have their own schools or teach in different locations such as colleges or universities. In the past we have had students who wanted to teach but budget was a big issue. The foundation can support the proliferation of the art. That is the purpose of the foundation, to help spread the art of aikido.

The Tenshinkai Aikido Foundation is a public organization. It is open to all people who want to join and help run it. Currently, I am the president. Due to the workload of International Aikido Federation, I hope to find someone to help run the foundation. The idea is that the federation will be in charge of the technical aspects of the art and the foundation will be in charge of the expansion of the art.

Suppose, for example, that a student moves to another state and wants to open a new school. That can be very hard without an established reputation. The foundation can help with advice, contacts, and—we hope—finances.

ATM: *What do you see as the future of aikido?*

Sensei Phong: Aikido originated with O'Sensei. No matter how many branches or styles aikido develops, there always will be a tie to the original aikikai. No matter what names people choose for their organizations and styles, we are all affiliated with the original aikido Hombu Dojo of O'Sensei.

Many times, I have been invited to teach at schools that are not formally affiliated with Aikikai Headquarters. I want us all to be united. We all practice aikido and our arts have the same origin. Ai means harmony.

Aikido will continue to develop slowly because it is not a competitive art. One way to assure that it will spread faster is to hold more demonstrations so that more people see the art.

The atmosphere in the aikido dojo is friendly and noncompetitive; we come together to help each other. That is what visitors observe and that is what will help the art to last a long time.

Aikido needs more dedicated instructors. It is hard to find teachers who really love teaching, dedicated teachers. A black belt is not necessarily ready to open up a school. People need to train in aikido regularly for at least ten years to get enough experience to open up a dojo. Also, people should already have some teaching experience. That is one of the advantages at my dojo. I can help people by observing them teach and offering advice. I started teaching after only two years of study. It was difficult, because it was too soon. My students do not have to go through that. I can help them to become good instructors.

Also, dedicated teachers must be able to accept students from different backgrounds. They have to have open arms—to be loving and caring. Aikido is not just learning technique. It is learning to become a better person and to live harmoniously with everyone.

ATM: What is the future of Tenshinkai aikido?

Sensei Phong: I recognize that Tenshinkai is not very widespread or well known. Most of its members are in Southern California, because that is where I am. What we need is to establish communication with other dojos. I should go to other dojos, and other people need a chance to come here. That would help Tenshinkai become more popular.

Many schools open, are active for a while, and then close. I think that, often, they close because the instructors don't have enough training. They need excellent skills in the teaching and execution of techniques as well as the ability to organize and manage the business of the dojo. I think the federation can help by offering training and aiding in building up new dojos. We will be holding more seminars here, too. It is important continually to upgrade techniques.

I look forward to making training videos and producing books, too. These will provide more avenues for spreading and preserving Tenshinkai aikido.

ATM: *Any last thoughts?*

Sensei Phong: Tenshinkai, meaning from the heart of heaven, is the name that O'Sensei himself gave to this aikido. I want to keep Tenshinkai as it was originally intended to be—free of political bias or side-taking. I want to keep it open to everyone who wants to train and move toward a better life.

I wish everyone could train to live harmoniously with love and understanding.

POSTSCRIPT

In September 2001, a fire destroyed the headquarters and dojo of the International Tenshinkai Aikido Federation located in Westminster, California. Within a week, the dedication of Sensei Phong and his students, and strong community support and compassion found them training again in the back warehouse room of a local medical center. The generosity of the center and the community were deeply appreciated by Sensei Phong and his students.

The dojo and headquarters relocated again to their current location in June 2002. Phong Sensei went right back to teaching daily classes and his students went right back to training as usual.

Appendix B
Questions and Answers from Aikido Instructors

To give different perspectives and insights, the authors invited several highly ranked and highly regarded aikido instructors to contribute their valuable thoughts to this book. These instructors responded to four questions. Their responses are unedited. The instructors were:

Shihan Francis Takahashi, 6th dan, Chief Instructor at the Aikido Academy in Temple City, California, and Aikido Associate, West Coast.

Stan Pranin, 5th dan, Editor of *Aiki News/Aikido Journal*, producer of the Aiki Expo, and aikido historian.

Shihan Bill Witt, direct student of Saito Morihiro Shihan (Iwama, Japan), 7th dan, Chief Instructor of Aikido of Silicon Valley, California. "You pose some interesting questions. I am not sure how long you would like the answers. Personally, I have adopted a saying: 'Brevity is the soul of wit (Witt).'"

Shihan Hiroshi Ikeda, 7th dan through Mitsugi Saotome Shihan and the Aikido World Federation (Hombu Dojo). Ikeda Shihan is the founder and Chief Instructor at the Boulder Aikikai in Colorado, the owner/entrepreneur of Bu Jin Design (a high quality martial arts supply manufacturing and mail-order company), a calligrapher, and an well sought-after and highly regarded guest instructor at seminars around the country and abroad. The translators for his contribution were Jane Nason and Jun Akiyama, and the editor was Ginger Ikeda.

Sensei Frank McGouirk, 6th dan, Chief Instructor at Aikido-Ai in Whittier, California, Abbot of Dharma Kai Zen School, and certified Qi Gong, Tai Chi, and Dharma teacher.

Sensei Daniel Mizukami, 6th dan, Chief Instructor Los Angeles Aikikai.

What would you want to say to advanced students of aikido?
Shihan Francis Takahashi relates, "What I would want to share with the advanced student of aikido, or any art form for that matter, is to *never be isolated* from the *basic truths and fundamental values* that attracted that student in the first place. It appears to me that 'being advanced' is simply being able to better appreciate and apply the lessons, personal growth and new understandings that result from *daily training*, and to enjoy an ever-increasing hunger for even more of the *essentials* that the basics promise us. All of this knowledge and experience needs to come

about from surviving, growing, and thriving over the untold years of training that it takes."

Stan Pranin relates, "I think that advanced students should train with a sufficient level of concentration and severity to insure that they undergo a change in their general perception and awareness of his or her surroundings.

Shihan Bill Witt relates, "When I was given 4th dan by Saito Sensei, he told me that I was not a member of his dojo anymore, and I should go out and find my own aikido. He considered this level to be a demarcation between basic and advanced levels of the art. He also told me that up to 4th dan the students trained their bodies. After this point they trained their minds. Aikido is a very personal art, since it involves using one's own body with skill. The changes in one's movements are built over time, and while there is no sudden enlightenment or quantum jump in personal awareness or development, the 4th dan level is a good self-test of personal maturity in aikido."

Shihan Hiroshi Ikeda relates, "O'Sensei's genius was to create a martial art of peace—an art that could tame martial strength and inspire and enliven people through love. Much as the master swordsman could transform his 'killing sword' to the 'life giving sword,' so it is within our power as aikidoists to choose how we will use our art and how we will use our lives. Becoming skilled in aikido techniques is undeniably an integral and important goal of training (shugyo). However, shugyo is also very much about becoming an accomplished technician who is equally accomplished in his humanity and spirituality in forging meaningful relationships with others. In striving to rise to the next grade or rank, a practitioner may become caught up in only the *waza* aspect of aikido and may lose sight of other aspects of spiritual growth that O'Sensei intended. I believe that the essence of aikido is not only waza, but also the communication and interaction that transpires between people, based upon *aiki*—love, compassion, respect, and kindness. I would hope that practitioners would train diligently while keeping in mind that aikido is, to the last, a martial art that embraces not only the practice of technique, but also compassionate communication among people."

What do you consider the basic and advanced concepts of aikido?

Shihan Francis Takahashi offers, "I personally do not see a real difference between 'basic' and 'advanced' *concepts* of aikido. Rather, I do see a wide range of interpretations of aiki principles, further resulting in the myriad of styles and appearances of aikido technique and explanations. The *real essence of Ueshiba Sensei's aikido remains unchanged as concepts*, merely requiring that we pay the price to understand and embrace them."

Stan Pranin offers, "For me, the basic concept consists of identifying an attack and learning how to create a physical/energy blend with the attacking movement. On the advanced level, this basic skill is refined to operate at increasing levels of sophistication and subtlety. The ability to perceive grows to the point that it extends beyond the training environment and permeates all aspects of the practitioner's life."

Shihan Bill Witt offers, "O'Sensei felt there were four levels to aikido: basic, flexible, ki-flow, and takemusu aiki. My teacher told me once that the basic techniques we learn in the dojo are not aikido. I was shocked. He went on to explain that students needed structure. In the beginning, to build up their bodies and to develop a core repertoire of movement. This was the function of basic technique, and flexible technique too, I might add. As one's training progresses through these first two stages, the foundation is set for ki-flow and takemusu aiki. There is a clarity of mind that is required for one to morph into the third and fourth stages. Takemusu aiki is truly an extemporaneous form of aikido. While it may contain recognizable basic techniques, it allows the practitioner to forget conscious form and technique to deliver movements genuinely in tune with what O'Sensei described as universal principles."

Shihan Hiroshi Ikeda offers, "Aikido encompasses training in technique and training the spirit, and the two go hand-in-hand. With this in mind, 'basic' aikido is what we learn when we imitate the movements of our instructor in a safe and friendly environment. As we memorize and perform the basic techniques (*kihon waza* and *ukemi waza*), we rely upon the cognitive portion of our brain telling our body what to do. With continued physical training, we eventually internalize the movements. At some point, we happily discover that we have begun to move and respond automatically, without conscious thought. I feel that this is the point that constitutes the beginning of true study at a technically advanced level. From the platform of solid, internalized *kihon waza*, we then enter the realm of advanced study, exploring the technical complexities of energy, balance, ma-ai, perception, and a host of other phenomena. As we deepen our understanding of these things, the more rapid and finely tuned our reflexes become, and the greater our control. Basic training of the spirit begins with our first class, where we encounter dojo etiquette and interaction with fellow training partners. It continues as we become aware of glimpses into our own psyche, observing, examining, and learning from our personal reactions to the challenges that training presents. As with physical training, spiritual training must also be mindful. How does one determine what constitutes an advanced level of spiritual development? I believe, in part, it is the same as for physical training—the more advanced we become, the shorter our reaction time and the better our control. Do we practice kindness as an instinctive reaction? Are we the first to offer our subway seat to the frail elder, or do we hesitate? Interestingly, being technically advanced is not necessarily commensurate with being spiritually advanced, and vice versa. We each arrive at the dojo with unique skill sets and understandings, ready to learn. The beauty of the path of aikido is that we all can gain something from each other, basic and advanced."

What do you see in the execution of aikido techniques that lets you know that this is an advanced student who knows, understands, and applies the concepts of aikido?

Shihan Francis Takahashi states, "There is a notion that, by studying the behavior of any student at any level on the mat for a reasonable period of time, would allow the trained observer to *discover much about the character, development, and agenda of that person,* regardless of the skill that he or she may portray at that moment in time. I am afraid that much is open to differing interpretations, even among the various high ranking and acknowledged leaders and teachers of aikido, as to what is ultimately important. For me, I prefer to study the person directly, and then assess skill level."

Stan Pranin states, "You can tell the level of an advanced student by how they interact with the attacker. When a student begins to move simultaneously with the attack or even to anticipate the attack, this will be an indication they have progressed to another higher level."

Shihan Bill Witt states, "There seems to be an extra presence with an advanced student—an aura, if you will. I first noticed this while judging dan examinations. After awhile it became easy to tell how well a student would do on the examination simply by the way they walked onto the mat and bowed in. Even allowing for differences in body style and personality, it was character that started to shine. It would be wrong, however, to say that this trait appeared with everyone at the shodan examination. People learn at different rates, and there are so many factors involved in learning aikido that some people rise to the occasion later than others. If aikido is to be a lifelong study, however, whether one's character comes out sooner or later is a mere moment in time."

Shihan Hiroshi Ikeda states, "When in the dojo and practicing a prescribed technique, an advanced student first of all would demonstrate respect for his or her partner's ability level. S/he would be focused and would perform a smooth, precise technique, adjusting instinctively to accommodate the size and speed of the partner. Throughout the technique, the advanced student would allow no openings or opportunities in which the partner could gain an advantage. The follow-through would be complete. Further, in a randori or a street situation, where nothing is prescribed or choreographed, an advanced aikido practitioner would accept the randomness of the situation and would be unperturbed at the unexpected turn of events. S/he would field the attacks with spontaneous, accurate responses, maintaining control of the situation as the dynamics of the event evolved. It is possible that occasionally the advanced student will experience 'flow.' Like the relationship between a musician and his instrument, one can tell if the music is simply coming out of the instrument as it is being played, or if the performer is producing the music with his body and soul, at one with the instrument. In aikido, this state of 'flow' would translate into maintaining perfect control of one's opponent and one's self in any given situation."

What would you ask of advanced students regarding the future of aikido?

Shihan Francis Takahashi says, "The future of aikido will always remain in the hands of those who are willing to *persevere with integrity*, commit to the *fundamentals*, and always *refine his or her enlightened vision* of how to adapt aiki principles to an ever-changing society. Both skilled and unskilled *stewards of Ueshiba aiki* will be needed over time. We will need technicians, historians, benefactors, and the ever-fresh *influx of talent.*"

Stan Pranin says, "I would ask of advanced students that they constantly refer back to the original concepts of the Founder Morihei Ueshiba to thoroughly understand the core ideas of the art that consist of peaceful reconciliation and preparedness."

Shihan Bill Witt says, "Over the years, the best students I have seen are the ones who committed themselves to one sensei. They learned not only a particular style of technique but the philosophy of the sensei as well. When two students of different senseis meet, it is sometimes difficult to agree with one another on the details of teaching or training, but it is not difficult to respect one another. The 4th dans of today will be the aikido leaders of tomorrow. In the last thirty years, aikido has undergone a huge expansion throughout the world. I can't help but believe that the expansion is almost geometrical. Practically speaking that will mean someone who commits to teaching may someday be dealing with a more difficult business climate. All other things being equal, the only thing that will make one person stand out from the others will be character. Aikido needs two types of advanced students—those who wish to become teachers and those who practice *tashinamu*, the willingness to do something simply for the sake of doing it well and without regard to recognition. Aikido needs the type of person who wants to teach and open a dojo. Aikido needs more the second type of person, who provides the quiet example of a personal relationship through training and generates enthusiasm with the newer students."

Shihan Hiroshi Ikeda says, "Aikido is a living art, and as such it naturally, inevitably evolves. As O'Sensei created it, aikido is a *budo*. I believe we should draw from his illustrious example, seeking and embracing knowledge as he did, ever evolving as if our own lives depended upon it. In this way, we may discover at least a fraction of what he knew, and our training will be true and real and honest. In *budo* knowledge equals power equals survival. A broad knowledge base is essential, so I urge advanced students to go in search of knowledge and never deny yourselves the opportunity to learn something new. Be curious, be creative! Keep your mind open. Look inside your dojo, but don't stop there—look to all the aikido dojos of the world and look to other arts. Filter, test, experiment, then store and apply the information you find useful. Constantly refresh your perspective. Your aikido will change; you will grow; aikido will grow."

Sensei Frank McGouirk offered the following insights: "My last teacher in kung fu, Zen Master Ji Bong Sa Nim, emphasized that there were nine levels of martial art mastery. (1) The first level is developing the energy to go to the dojo day after day, month after month, year after year and making a commitment to the path. (2) The second is developing intention or in Chinese, "I." The student's body begins to respond and coordination is improved. (3) The third level is that of jing (essence or power). Here the student develops such aspects of the art as weapons training and the skills in sparring and self-defense. For many individuals this is the last stage of their development and many teachers at even high ranks emphasize only these aspects of their arts. (4) Yondan level in aikido is Sensei designation. At this stage the 'internal system' becomes important. Most students will lose interest as the training becomes more internally focused and less athletic. The focus now is on elementary 'nei kung' practice and the student will develop internal strength and feel the ki move in the body. (5) Above level four begins the area of 'hsin' or mind and spirit training. Level five means to use the martial arts training to develop a mind that becomes perfectly still. This is the serious practice of Taoist and Buddhist meditation techniques. Highly skilled masters of nei kung are able to control their attackers without actually touching them or lightly striking them, causing a delayed reaction of internal damage or sickness. (6) This ability to project the chi is the core of level six. (7) Now the student must study the entire 'tien hsueh' system of healing and self-healing. Knowledge of herbs, massage, acupuncture, and qi gong is the essence of the seventh level. (8) This is the level of attaining everyday mind. Turning a key in a door is the same as an aikido spiral, rotating the wheel of one's auto for a left turn is the same as a breath throw, etc. (9) My teacher called this 'moment world.' It is the realm of the enlightened mind, perceiving one's constantly changing condition and situation in order to act with courage and intuition in each passing moment. Attaining this level means the student will develop a compassionate mind that is always concerned with saving all sentient beings from suffering. This is the ultimate goal of martial arts training and the condition of a true warrior, the warrior who has attained wisdom." McGouirk Sensei asked, in typical Zen Koan fashion, "Beginning students, advanced students, masters . . . Same or different? . . . KWATZ!" The response was, "As you know, there is no beginning, advanced, or masters. There is no same or different. There is only the training."

Sensei Daniel Mizukami, 6th dan, Chief Instructor of Los Angeles Aikikai initially declined the invitation to contribute to this book. He was finally persuaded to allow his letter to be included because the authors believed it expresses personal humility and valuable experienced insight. "Thank you very much for your generous invitation to contribute to the next *Aikido Basics* book. It was an honor to be considered for this by Sensei Phong. However, I must respectfully decline this opportunity. While I have been practicing aikido for many years, I personally feel that I am still a 'beginner' in this art. I also feel that aikido, possibly more so than any other martial art, is a personal endeavor. While all martial arts have a spiritual connection to something, the way O'Sensei envisioned aikido makes the personal connection even stronger, in my considered opinion. I feel that each student who practices aikido needs to find their own spiritual connections to themselves, to others, and to the world at large. We as teachers can offer guidance, but your questions address concepts, which I feel each student should come to on their own. Thank you for your consideration. Good luck in your endeavors."

"Domo Arigato Onegaishimasu Sensei."

Appendix C
Technique Chart

APPLICATION/ SITUATION:	STANCES:	APPROACH/ ATTACK:	AWASE (BLEND):	WAZA (TECHNIQUE):	FINISH:
Tachi-waza (standing)	Ai-hanmi (same side)	Ai-hanmi (same-side grab)	Irimi-tenkan: (entering)	Irimi-nage (entering throw)	Nage (throw)
Hanmi-handachi (one standing and one sitting)	Gyaku-hanmi (opposite side)	Gyaku-hanmi (opposite-side grab)	Kokyu-ho: Dynamic blend tenkan ura (rear)	Kaiten-nage (rotary throw)	Mawashi (pin to ground)
Suwari-waza (sitting)		Morote-dori (two-handed grab one)	Dynamic blend tenkan omote (front)	Kote-gaeshi (wrist turnedout throw)	
Two-on-one		Ryote-dori (two-handed grab two)	Tenshin (sweeping body turn)	Shiho-nage (four-direction throw)	
Three-on-one		Shomen-uchi (overhead downward strike)	Dynamic no blend	Tenbin-nage (elbow lock throw)	
Randori (multiple-person attack)		Yokomen-uchi (oblique strike)	Static/standing	Kokyu-nage (breath/timing throw)	
Kokyu-dosa (seiza ryote-dori ki exercise)		Tsuki (punch)	Double blend	Ikkyo (1st arm lock)	
Nage-waza (throwing techniques)		Sode-dori (sleeve grab)	Atemi (strike/feint)	Nikyo (2nd wrist turned in lock)	
Katame-waza (locking techniques)		Eri-dori (collar grab)	Footwork	Sankyo (3rd wrist twist)	
		Hiji-dori (elbow grab)		Yonkyo (4th inside wrist lock)	
		Kata-dori (shoulder grab)		Gokyo (5th ground wrist pin)	
		Muna-dori (lapel grab)		Hiji-gime (arm bar)	
		Ryo-kata-dori (both shoulders grab)		Juji-nage (propeller throw)	
		Ushiro-waza (from behind)		Koshi-nage (hip throw)	
		Kubishime (choke)		Aiki-nage (drop throw)	
		Tanto (knife) (five angles)		Otoshi-nage (leg pickup)	
		Gun (take away)		Uke-waza (lateral dash sacrifice throw)	
		Jo (sword)		Ude-garami (arm hook takedown)	
		Boken (staff)		Henka-waza (variations)	
		Geri (kicks: front, side, roundhouse, crescent, back, and spinning)		Nagashi-waza (combinations)	
		Boxer (jab, cross, hook, and uppercut)		Kaeshi-waza (counters)	
		Grappler (takedown, mount, and submission)		Shiei-waza (self-defense)	
		All Waza/techniques will be learned with the right and the left hand.		All waza will be executed omote (entering to the front) and ura (turning to the rear)	

Appendix D
Concept Chart

BASIC	ADVANCED
Physical technical/tactical execution	Conceptual application
Kamae: stances	Rei: etiquette
Physical technique/tactical execution	Sangen: triangle, circle, square
Tachi-waza: standing techniques	Conceptual/strategy application:
Nage-waza: throwing techniques	Tachi-waza: standing
Katame-waza: pin/lock techniques	Suwari-waza: seated or kneeling
Ashi-sabaki: footwork	Hanmi-handachi: one standing/one seated
Sabaki: body movement	Ushiro-waza: from behind
	Randori/jiyu-waza: multiple and freestyle
Ukemi: break falls and rolls	Kokyu-dosa: seiza ryote-dori ki exercise
Sequential step by step	
Conscious selection of approach/attack and	One fluid movement
response/defense	Natural selection in response
Resistance: force/muscle	Sophisticated and subtle technique flow
Mental/thinking	
Belts and promotional matters	Sequential process:
	Enter and blend
	Redirect and unbalance
	Throw or control
	Let go and move on
	Conceptual:
	Shoshin: beginner's mind
	Mushin: calm and empty mind
	Shizen-tai: natural relaxed state of being
	Me-tsuke: soft eye focus
	Ma-ai: distance
	Irimi: enter
	Musubi: connection
	Awase: blending
	Kuzushi: balance breaking
	Kiai: yell
	Atemi: strike

	ADVANCED (CONTINUED)

	Kokyu: breath
	    Ki: energy
	        Keep one point center
	        Relax completely
	        Weight on underside
	        Extend ki
	    Zanshin: lingering mind
	    Shugyo: rigorous daily training
	    Misogi: purification techniques
	    Takemusu-aiki: spontaneous execution
	    Sumikiri: total clarity of body and mind
	    Tashinamu: to train for its own sake
	        without recognition or promotion
	
	Miscellaneous concepts:
	    Nonresistance
	    Good posture and relaxed body
	    Lines of attack and centerlines
	    Timing and rhythm (not speed)
	    Center (maintain it, move from it, and become it)
	    Contact (initiate, intercept, intent)
	    Structural alignment
	    Contour (follow it)
	    Power from behind and underneath
	    Circular motion and force (centrifugal and centripetal)
	    Movement, momentum, and inertia
	    Minimize
	    Leverage and pivot points
	    Wave motion
	    Dropping weight
	    Humble confidence
	    Respect and loving protection of others
	
	Responsibility:
	    Personal responsibility: honor and ethics
	    Social responsibility: compassion
	    Spiritual expression: faith
	
	Budo/bushido: way of the warrior
	
	Weapons:
	    Aiki-ken: wooden sword
	    Aiki-jo: wooden staff
	    Aiki-tanto: wooden knife

	ADVANCED (CONTINUED)

	Dojo (training hall or school) relationships and responsibilities:
	    Uke/tori: fellow students and training partners
	    Kohai: junior
	    Tohai: equal
	    Sempai: senior
	    Sensei: teacher
	    Shihan: master instructor
	
	Cross-training:
	    Other martial art styles
	    Strength
	    Flexibility
	    Cardiovascular
	    Skill
	
	Self-defense:
	
	Now, get back to training. KWATZ!

GLOSSARY

Ai: Harmony

Aiki: United, blending or harmonizing with spirit

Aikido: The way of harmonizing energy or spirit

Aiki-drop: A no-touch throw performed by dropping down, emptying space

Aiki-jo: The 5-foot or less stick/staff used in aikido, usually associated with Saito Sensei

Aiki-jujitsu/jutsu: Styles of martial arts with emphasis on aiki and fighting

Aiki-ken: The wooden sword used in aikido, usually associated with Saito Sensei

Aiki-otoshi-nage: A throw performed by picking up the training partner's legs

Arigato: Thank you. (informal)

Ashi-sabaki: Footwork

Atemi: Strike to a vital point

Ato: Move back

Awase: Blend

Bo: Wooden staff over 5 feet in length

Bo-jutsu: Wooden staff fighting

Boken: Wooden sword, commonly referred to as a ken

Budo: Martial way

Bugei: Early word for combative martial art

Buki-waza: Weapons technique

Bushi: Early term for samurai

Bushido: Way and code of the warrior

Chinkon: A calming tranquility of the soul

Chudan: Middle, weapon held horizontally

Chudan-zuki: Punch to abdomen

Daito-ryu: Martial art that influenced aikido

Dan: Black belt ranks

Do: Way

Dogi: Training uniform

Dojo: Training hall or school, the way (do) place

Dojo-cho: Leader or head of dojo

Domo: Thanks. (informal)

Domo arigato: Thank you. (formal)

Domo arigato gozaimashita: Thank you very much. (very formal, for something that just ended)

Domo arigato gozaimasu: Thank you very much. (very formal, for something that is happening)

Doshu: Head or keeper of the way

Dozo: Please, go ahead.

Gedan: Low, weapon held point downward

Gedan-zuki: Downward punch

Geikikan-jutsu: Ball and chain fighting

Geri: Kick

Gi: Short for dogi, training uniform

Giri: Duty

Godan: Fifth-degree black belt

Gokyo: Fifth pinning technique

Gomen-nasai: Excuse me, I'm sorry.

Gono-sen: Initiating immediate response, counterattack

Gyaku: Reverse, opposite, inverted

Gyaku-hanmi: Reverse posture

Gyaku-uchi: Reverse strike

Gyaku-zuki: Punching with rear hand, cross

Hachidan: Eighth-degree black belt

Hai: Stage of learning breaking from form or variation

Hai: Yes.

Hajime: Start.

Hakama: Traditional pleated split-legged skirt or pants

Hanmi: Half-forward stance, oblique stance

Hanmi-handachi: Attacker standing and defender kneeling or seated

Happo-baraki: To be totally aware of one's surroundings

Hara: Abdomen, stomach, center

Hayaku: Quickly

Henka-waza: Variation techniques

Hidari: Left

Hiji: Elbow

Hiji-dori: Elbow grab

Hiji-gime: Elbow/arm bar

Hitoemi: Equal stance with feet parallel

Hombu: Home or headquarter school

Iaido: Sword drawing

Iai-goshi: Hips lowered in stable position

Iaijutsu: Defensive-sword-drawing fighting style

Iie: No.

Ikkyo: First pinning technique

Irimi: Entering

Irimi-nage: Entering throw

Irimi-tenkan: Entering and turning

Iwama-ryu: The school in Iwama, Japan, under Saito Sensei with an emphasis on weapon training

Jiyu-waza: Freestyle techniques

Jo: Short stick or staff

Jodan: Upper, weapon held pointing upward or above the head

Jodan-zuki: Upper strike

Jo-jutsu: Short stick/staff fighting

Judan: Tenth-degree black belt

Juken-jutsu: Bayonet fighting

Junbi-taiso: Warm-up exercises

Juji-nage: Cross-arm throw

Juken: Baronet and rifle

Jutsu: Combative fighting system

Jutte-jutsu: Metal truncheon fighting

Kaeshi: Counter, reversal

Kaeshi-waza: Counter techniques

Kaeshi-zuki: Counterthrust

Kaiten: Rotation

Kaiten-nage: Rotary throw

Kamae: Posture, stance

Kami/kamisama: Spirits

Kan: Intuition

Kashima Shinto-ryu kenjutsu: Offshoot of Katori Shinto-ryu, influential on aiki-ken

Kata: A prearranged practice form or pattern

Kata-dori: Shoulder hold

Katate-dori: Held by one hand

Katate-uchi: One-handed strike

Katori Shinto-ryu kenjutsu: Early sword-fighting school

Keiko: Training/practice

Kendo: Sword sport

Kenjutsu: Offensive sword fighting

Ki: Vital energy

Kihon: Fundamental

Kiyotsukete: Be careful.

Kiza: Kneeling on the toes

Kohai: Junior student

Kokoichi: Offense and defense becomes same

Kokyu: Animated breathing

Kokyu-dosa: Breath power movement, exercise technique from kneeling position

Kokyu-ho: Turning step with breathing and ki extension

Kokyu-nage: Breath or timing throw

Kosa-dori: Hand grab

Koshi: Hip

Koshi-nage: Hip throw

Koshiita: Back plate on hakama

Koshukai: Lecture classes

Kote: Wrist

Kote-gaeshi-nage: Wrist turned out throw

Koutai: Change

Kubi: Neck

Kubishime: Chokes

Kudan: Ninth-degree black belt

Kuzushi: Balance breaking

KWATZ!: The shout (kiai) of a Zen master to startle a student out of internal mental obsessing and into external present awareness

Kyu: Ranks before black belt

Kyu-jutsu: Bow and arrow fighting

Ma-ai: Distance

Mae: Forward

Mate: Wait.

Mawashi: Ground pinning arm bar, to turn, a rotation

Mawatte: Turn around.

Men: Head

Me-tsuki: Soft eye focus

Men-uchi: Strike to head

Migi: Right

Misogi: Purification rituals or practices

Mokuso: Closed-eye meditation

Morote: Both hands

Morote-dori: Two hands grabbing one hand

Mudansha: Kyu ranks, lower than black belts
Mune: Chest
Mune-dori: One or two hand lapel hold
Mune-tsuki: Abdominal strike to belt knot
Mushin: Empty (mu) mind (shin)
Musubi: Connection
Nagashi: Flow
Nagashi-waza: Flowing or combination techniques
Nage: Throw
Nage: Refers to the person doing the throwing technique
Nage-waza: Throwing technique
Nanadan: Seventh-degree black belt
Nidan: Second-degree back belt
Nikyo: Second pinning technique
Obi: Belt
Oi-zuki: A step punch
Omote: Entering to the front
Omoto: Shinto religious cult that influenced O'Sensei
Onegaishimasu: Please. (asking for something)
O'Sensei: Great teacher, referring to Morihei Ueshiba
Otagai-ni-rei: Bow to each other
Otoshi: Drop
Randori: Multiple fellow student and training partner training
Rei: Bowing
Reigi: Etiquette
Renshu: Hard work on basics
Ri: Stage of training
Rokkyo: Sixth pinning or control technique, hiji-kime-osae
Rokudan: Sixth-degree black belt
Ronin: Samurai without a master
Ryote-dori: Both hands grasp both hands
Ryokata-dori: Grabbing both shoulders
Sabaki: Body motion
Samurai: To service, Japanese feudal warrior in service to a master
Sandan: Third-degree black belt
Sankyo: Third pinning technique
Sasumata-jutsu: Forked-staff fighting
Seidan: Weapon held pointing toward the eyes
Seiza: Sitting posture, kneeling on both calves
Sempai: Senior student, higher rank
Sen: Initiating response after analysis
Sen-no-sen: Initiating response or intent
Sensei: Teacher/instructor
Sensei-ni-rei: Bow to teacher/instructor
Shihan: Master teacher
Shiho-nage: Four-direction throw
Shinai: Split bamboo sword
Shikko: Knee walking, on one's knees
Shinshin: Mind and body
Shinto: Religion that believes in spirits, nature, and ancestor worship, very influential on O'Sensei Morihei Ueshiba

Shinzen-ni-re: Bow to shrine
Shodan: First-degree black belt
Shomen: Face/head, straight ahead
Shomen-uchi: Frontal downward head strike
Shoshin: Beginner's mind
Shu: Stage of learning that preserves form, kata
Shugyo: Rigorous daily training, pursuit of knowledge
Shuriken-jutsu: Blade-throwing fighting
Shuto: Edge of hand
Sode: Sleeve
Sode-dori: Sleeve grab
Sodegarami-jutsu: Barbed-pole fighting
So-jutsu: Spear fighting
Soke: Head of a family system or style
Soto: Outside
Sumimasen: Excuse me. (to attract attention)
Suwari-waza: Seated technique
Suwatte: Sit down.
Tachi: Standing
Tachi-waza: Standing technique
Taisabaki: Body turning
Takemusu-aiki: The spontaneous execution of an aikido technique
Tanden: Abdomen, stomach, center, hara
Tatami: Tradition mat
Tatte: Raise
Te-gatana: Hand blade
Tenbin-nage: Elbow lock throw
Tenkan: Circular pivoting footwork
Tenkai: Step and pivot, sweeping body turn
Tenshin: Heaven and Earth
Tenshinkai: Organization of heaven on Earth
Tenshin-nage: Heaven and Earth throw
Tenugui: Small hand cloth
Tessen-jutsu: Iron-fan fighting
Tetsubo-jutsu: Iron-bar fighting
Tohai: Of same rank
Tori: The person defending
Tsugi-ashi: Lunge or shuffle footwork
Tsuki: Punch
Uchi: Strike, inside
Uchi-deshi: Live-in student
Uke: Training partner who receives the technique, the attacker
Ukemi: Falling ways, receiving with the body
Ura: Turning to the rear, back
Ushiro: From the rear, behind
Ushiro-eri-dori: Neck/collar grab from the rear
Ushiro-kubi-shime: Rear choke
Ushiro-ryote-dori: Grabbing both wrists from the rear
Ushiro-ryote kata-dori: Grabbing both shoulders from the rear
Ushiro-tekubi-dori: Wrist grab from the rear
Ushiro-udoroshi: Pulled down from behind

Wakarimasu: I understand.

Waza: Technique

Yame: Stop.

Yodan: Fourth-degree black belt

Yoi: Ready

Yoko: Horizontal, to the side

Yoko-uchi: Sideward strike

Yokomen-uchi: Diagonal strike to head or neck

Yonkyo: Fourth pinning technique

Yudansha: Members of dan black belt rank

Yukuri: Slow

Yuru-yaka ni: Smooth

Zanshin: Lingering mind, spirit, or connection

Zenpo: Front

Zori: Japanese sandals worn outside dojo

REFERENCES AND RESOURCES

BOOKS

Csikszentimihalyi, M. *Flow: The Psychology of Optimal Experience*. New York: Harper & Row, 1990.

Dang, Thong Phong and Seiser, Lynn. *Aikido Basics*. Boston: Tuttle Publishing, 2003.

Dang, Tri Thong. *Beyond the Known: The Ultimate Goal of the Martial Arts*. Boston: Charles E. Tuttle Publishing Company, Inc., 1993.

Dang, Tri Thong. *Towards the Unknown: Martial Artist, What Shall You Become?* Boston: Charles E. Tuttle Publishing Company, Inc., 1993.

Deguchi, Hidemaru. *The Creation of Meaning*. Kameoko, Japan: The Omoto Foundation.

Deguchi, Onisaburo. *The Divine Signpost*. Kameoka, Japan: The Omoto Foundation, 1904.

Dobson, Terry and Miller, Victor. *Aikido in Everyday Life: Giving in to Get Your Way*. Berkeley: North Atlantic Books, 1993.

Fujita, Masatake. *Aikido Keiki Ho: Aikido Training Method*. The Hague, Holland: Stitching Promotie Aikido Nederland, 1997.

Jackson, S. and M. Csikszentmihalyi. *Flow in Sports: The Key to Optimal Experiences and Performance*. Champaign, Illinois: Human Kinetics.

Leonard, G. *Mastery: The Keys to Success and Long-Term Fulfillment*. New York: Plume Books, 1992.

Murphy, M. and R. A. White. *The Psychic Side of Sports*. Menlo Park, CA: Addison-Wesley Publishing, 1978.

———. *In The Zone: Transcend Experiences in Sports*. New York: Penguin Books, 1995.

O'Conner, Greg. *The Aikido Student Handbook*. Berkeley, CA: Frog Ltd., 1993.

Pranin, Stanley A. *The Aiki News Encyclopedia of Aikido*. Tokyo: Aiki News, 1991.

Tohei, Koichi. *Aikido: The Co-ordination of Mind and Body for Self-Defense*. London: Souvenir Press, 1961.

———. *Ki Development Methods: Coordination of Mind and Body*. Tokyo: Ki No Kenkyukai Headquarters, 1973.

———. *Book of Ki: Coordinating Mind and Body in Daily Life*. Tokyo: Japan Publications, 1976.

———. *Ki in Daily Life*. Tokyo: Ki No Kenkyukai Headquarters, 1978.

Ueshiba, Kisshomaru. *The Spirit of Aikido*. New York: Kodansha America, 1984.

———. *Aikido*. Tokyo: Hozansha Publications, 1985.

———. *The Art of Aikido: Principles and Essential Techniques*. New York: Kodansha America, 2004.

Ueshiba, Kisshomaru and Moriteru Ueshiba. *Best Aikido: The Fundamentals*. New York: Kodansha America, 2002.

Ueshiba, Morihei. *Budo: Teachings of the Founder of Aikido*. New York: Kodansha International, 1991.

———. *Budo Training in Aikido*. New York: Kodansha America, 1997.

Ueshiba, Moriteru. *The Aikido Master Course: Best Aikido 2*. New York: Kodansha America, 2003.

Westbrook, A. and O. Ratti. *Aikido and the Dynamic Sphere.* Rutland, Vermont: Charles E. Tuttle Company, Inc., 1970.

VIDEOS/DVD

Aikido Journal. Aiki Expo 2002—Friendship Demonstration Part One and Two, 2002.

Aikido Journal. Aiki Expo 2003—Friendship Demonstration Part One and Two, 2003.

Aikikai Hombu Dojo. *Aikido; Vol. 1–7.* Tokyo: World Aikikai Foundation.

INTERNET

www.AikiWeb.com
www.AikidoJournal.com

MAGAZINES

Aikido Today Magazine by Arete Press, 1420 N. Claremont Blvd. #204C-D, Claremont, CA 91711. Telephone: 909-624-7770, Fax: 909-398-1840, www.aiki.com, Editor Sensei Susan Perry.

INDEX

ABOUT THE AUTHORS

Sensei Phong Thong Dang holds a Ryokuba (sixth-degree black belt) in aikido, a 6th dan in taekwondo, a 5th dan in judo, and an 8th dan in Vietnamese Shaolin kung fu. The World Martial Arts Hall of Fame inducted Phong Sensei twice, once for his expertise in aikido and again for his lifelong dedication to the martial arts for over fifty years. Phong Sensei received his third-degree black belt/Sandan directly from the Aikikai Hombu Dojo and aikido founder, O'Sensei Morihei Ueshiba, and his son Doshu Kisshomaru Ueshiba. O'Sensei Morihei Ueshiba gave the name Tenshinkai, meaning from the association of heavenly hearts or heaven on Earth, to the unique flowing and powerful style of aikido from Vietnam. O'Sensei Morihei Ueshiba personally gave the honor and responsibility of spreading tenshinkai aikido directly to Phong Sensei. Phong Sensei has been featured in *Aikido Today Magazine, Aikido Journal, Karate Illustrated, Martial Arts and Combat Sports, Arts Martiaux: Traditionnels D'asie,* and *Black Belt Magazine.* Phong Sensei teaches daily at the headquarters and home school/dojo of the International Tenshinkai Aikido Federation in Westminster, California.

Lynn Seiser, Ph.D., MFT, is a perpetual student of the martial arts. He has trained for over thirty years in various forms of martial arts and fighting. Currently, he studies and holds Sandan (third-degree black belt) rank in Tenshinkai aikido under Phong Sensei at the Westminster Aikikai Dojo in Westminster, California. Dr. Seiser has educational degrees in psychology, philosophy, and marriage, family, and child counseling. Dr. Seiser is an internationally respected psychotherapist, marriage, family, and child counselor with over twenty-five years direct clinical experience in the treatment of offenders and victims of violence trauma and abuse. Dr. Seiser has coauthored several books in the martial arts, clinical psychotherapy interventions and techniques, and a chapter on visualization in sport psychology. He has regular Southern California columns in a local newspaper and magazine. His work has appeared in *Black Belt Magazine, Martial Arts and Combat Sports,* and *Aikido Today Magazine.* Dr. Seiser founded AikiSolutions to provide consultation and training in sport and performance psychology and conflict prevention, management, and resolution. He maintains his counseling and consultation practice in Long Beach and Tustin, California. He lives with his wife in Irvine, California.